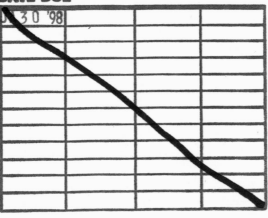

CONTEXTS OF CONGRESSIONAL DECISION BEHAVIOR

David C. Kozak
The National War College

**UNIVERSITY
PRESS OF
AMERICA**

LANHAM • NEW YORK • LONDON

Library of Congress Cataloging in Publication Data

Kozak, David C.
    Contexts of congressional decision behavior.

    Includes bibliographical references.
    1. United States. Congress—Voting. 2. United States.
Congress—Communication systems. I. Title.
JK1067.K68   1984   328.73'0775   84-7500
ISBN 0-8191-3999-8 (alk. paper)
ISBN 0-8191-4000-7 (pbk. : alk. paper)

The views and opinions expressed or implied in this book, written by an Air Force officer while in the Department of Political Science at the United States Air Force Academy, are those of the author and do not necessarily reflect the views of The National War College, the United States Air Force, or the Department of Defense.

All University Press of America books are produced on acid-free paper which exceeds the minimum standards set by the National Historical Publications and Records Commission.

ACKNOWLEDGEMENTS

This effort, which began as a doctoral dissertation, owes an enormous debt of gratitude to many people who were most generous with their time. Without their help, this research never would have been completed. Many professors at the University of Pittsburgh provided invaluable help and counsel. Those particularly generous with their time were Professors P. Beck, Carroll, Hammond, James, Jones, Margolis, Ogul, Owen, Rockman, and Thayer. Also of immense help in plotting research strategy were several prominent legislative process scholars at other institutions: Professors Kingdon, Mann, Polsby, and Stimson. Curtis Cook of the Political Science Department at the United States Air Force Academy (USAFA) provided both substantive suggestions and administrative assistance so that an Air Force officer could conduct research on Capitol Hill. The Air Force Institute of Technology (AFIT) sponsored the author's doctoral program and provided the opportunity for Washington-based research. Colonel Ralph Hoffman and his staff at the National War College, Ft. McNair, D.C., provided an additional base of operations during the research period plus genuine encouragement and hospitality. Colonel Erv Rokke, Head USAFA Department of Political Science, contributed by fostering an atmosphere of collegiality and scholarship that encourages the completion of dissertations. Professor William Keefe, dissertation committee chairman, contributed throughout with his constant exhortation "say it in direct English." My hope is that subsequent work by this author will reflect his high sandards. Helen Lynch, Tricha Prediger, and Sue O'Keefe, all professional typists, provided gifted typing skills and a most pleasant working relationship.

Additionally, the author would like to express gratitude to the following for their help along the way: to my parents—Cliff and Grace—for steering me toward an academic career; to several professors at Gannon College—Richard Beyer, Martin Gildea, and Joseph P. Scottino—who set examples with their professionalism; to two brilliant professors at Kent State who inspired with their sophisticated political analyses—James G. Coke and Robert S. Getz; to three motivating professors at Wichita State—Ken Ciboski, Jim McKinney, and Neil Snortland—who taught the love of professional literature; to Bard O'Neill, formerly

iii

of the USAFA Department of Political Science and now a tenured professor at The National War College, who provided both friendship and intellectual invigoration to an unparalleled degree; to Colonel Mal Wakin, Associate Dean USAFA, who gave me the opportunity to undertake the Pittsburgh program; and to Professor Roger Davidson who thoroughly reviewed the manuscript and helped more than he'll ever know.

This research would not have been possible without the support of Congressman and Mrs. Jim Lloyd and the Lloyd staff--all of to whom this work is dedicated. Throughout the duration of the research they made appointments with members and staff; provided a base of operations; secured necessary congressional documents; and constantly offered friendly smiles and the caring question: "How did it go today?" These wonderful people accepted me as one of their own and, for that, I will be eternally grateful.

The American Political Science Association's Congressional Fellowship program gave me the unique opportunity to revisit the Congress in 1981-82 and to retest the findings while serving on the staffs of Congressman Andy Jacobs (D., Ind.), and Senator James Exon (D., Neb.).

I am inadequate in expressing thanks to my family. My wife and best friend Maryanne--a college English professor--typed all of the draft chapters and edited the final copy. Jeffrey and Timothy provided numerous, pleasant distractions along the way and a sense of pride with their question "Daddy--when is your book on Congress going to be done?" Jacqueline Kozak, namesake for Jackie Lloyd, enriched us all by being born during the process of revision and editing of the completed dissertation that finally has led to this book.

This work is dedicated to the Honorable Jim Lloyd (formerly, D., Calif.), Jackie Lloyd, and the Lloyd staff (Brigid, Don, Ginger, Lisa, Lola, Jerry, Marsaleete, and Theresa). Without their help, interest, concern, and, most important, friendship, this research could not have been accomplished. Thanks folks, for everything--especially my chair.

TABLE OF CONTENTS

ix

FORWARD

by Congressman Andy Jacobs (D, Ind.)*

If you believe that the Federal Government should be "of the people, by the people and for the people," then you probably also believe that the people ought to know more about the Federal Government than can be learned from a few paragraphs of newsprint now and then or blips on network news.

Such information, like a bookstore outline purchased for a shortcut through a literature course, is the essence of brevity which is said to be the soul of wit. But Aldous Huxley tells us that "the soul of wit may become the body of untruth."

To know what one must know to be an effective citizen, an effective stockholder in this vast public corporation, one must read and listen a lot. The effort is both a public and, if you value your well-being, a private duty; Fred Friendly said, "What you don't know can kill you." And Ben Franklin, when asked what sort of government had been brought forth for the fledgling nation, replied, "A republic, if you can keep it."

With this volume Dr. David Kozak contributes mightily to keeping the congressional part of our government working and working properly. His infor-mation is extensive and comprehensive, a solid body of truth.

Dave Kozak is not only thorough in this work. He is also skilled in it. The following pages are power-ful stuff gently said by a premier scholar of the political process we call self-government. The stock-holders can find out here in vivid detail how their money is spent and how their lives are regulated, protected and even threatened.

If you are a student and you are reading this as a scholastic requirement, you might not recognize as readily as the rest that these chapters are super-chargers for what the founders called our pursuit of happiness. But they are.

*Congressman Jacobs was first elected to the U.S. House in 1964. He is Chairman of the Ways and Means Health Subcommittee.

CHAPTER I

THE CONTEXTUAL APPROACH TO LEGISLATIVE BEHAVIOR: INTRODUCTION, PROSPECTS, PROBLEMS

The Congressman as a decision-making actor with regard to recorded, roll-call floor votes has persistently been a topic of interest among congressional scholars. A steady effort has been made to identify the various forces, factors, actors, and decision rules that influence congressional decision-making.

Students of Congress recently have engaged in developing what might best be called contextual or conditional perspectives on legislative decision-making. This research constitutes a new emphasis and direction in the study of Congress. In contrast to the conventional practice of formulating general propositions with which to explain legislative decision-making, the newer vein of research has sought to identify different contextual patterns of the legislative process.

This book has two purposes: 1) to better explicate the conditional theory of micro (individual level) legislative behavior that seems to underlie this recent work and 2) to test it among 361 interview protocals gathered from members of the U.S. House of Representatives during a four-month period (March-July, 1977) of the first session of the 95th Congress. This chapter will review literature that is distinctive in its conditional approach, identifying both the benefits and problems of the approach.

Introduction: The New Contextual Emphasis in the Study of Congressional Decision-Making

The study of legislative behavior seems to have evolved in the fashion of intellectual advancement described by Thomas S. Kuhn in The Structure of Scientific Revolution.[1] Kuhn contends that knowledge of a particular topic advances through the development and refinement of paradigms. With regard to the post-World War II empirical study of legislative decision-making, three major stages of advancement can be detected: (1) the legislator as "participant," (2) the legislator as a "determined actor," and (3) the legislator as a "contextual

1

decision-maker."[2] Each stage offers a distinctive
construct for viewing the legislator as a
decision-making actor. Each succeeding stage aspires
to a higher level of generalization and attempts to
overcome the perceived shortcomings of the preceding
stage.

Before proceeding, two points of clarification
should be made. First, common to any classification
scheme, the problem here is that not all works on
congressional decision-making neatly fit into one or
the other of the three categories. In classifying
decision-making literature, however, an attempt will
be made to do so on the basis of a work's major
thrust. In other words, major works concerning
congressional decision-making can be categorized on
the basis of the main constructs they seem to offer.
Second, there is no neat chronological separation of
the stages. Although each succeeding stage in many
ways was developed from reactions to the preceding
one, the contemporary period finds examples of all
three.

The first, and most rudimentary, stage views the
legislator as a participant in political combat. It
is the approach notably developed in Bertram Gross's
The Legislative Struggle[3] and in case studies such
as Steven Bailey's Congress Makes a Law[4] and Daniel
Berman's A Bill Becomes a Law.[5] The crux of this
model is a focus on the legislator as one of several
competitors in the legislative process. It focuses
attention on the role of external actors--President,
bureaucrats, interest groups, constituents,
courts--in legislative decision-making. Although a
number of important contributions have been made by
this view--most notably the notions that the
legislative process is a complex labyrinth and that
all competitors engage in various strategies and
tactics--the case-study approach was strongly
criticized for its limited generality and
applicability. Scholars became aware that the
findings of a case study do not necessarily transcend
the specifics of the case at hand.

In reaction to the criticism of limited
generality, coupled with a desire to become more
scientific, legislative process scholars began to
intensely study roll-call data and to collect
attitudinal data from legislators themselves. This
work constitutes the second major stage of

development where the legislator is depicted as a determined actor.

This second approach has two major characteristics. The first is the notion that the legislative decision-maker is predisposed to vote in a given way because of either certain characteristics of demography, party, constituency, and region or a common, universal decision process. The second characteristic of the determined actor stage is an attempt to construct a general model with which to analyze legislative decision-making. Almost all of the major research efforts of the last two decades seem to posit this kind of general, determined actor model in that they seem to be searching for the primary determinant of typical legislative behavior. In this category are Julius Turner's Party and Constituency,[6] David Truman's The Congressional Party,[7] Roger Davidson's The Role of the Congressman,[8] John Kingdon's Congressmen's Voting Decisions,[9] Donald Matthews and James Stimson's Yeas and Nays,[10] Cleo Cherryholmes and Michael Shapiro's Representatives and Roll Calls,[11] John Jackson's Constituencies and Leaders in Congress,[12] and David Mayhew's Congress: The Electoral Connection.[13] Each employs congressional decision-making as a dependent variable and then seeks to discover various independent variables that best explain the dependent variable of decision-making. More significantly, each provides an overall model--implicitly, perhaps, a "single factor theory"--with which to explain congressional decisionmaking. For the roll-call studies of Turner and Truman, the mode is one of party loyalty with deviations based on constituency. For Davidson, it is persistent role orientations. Kingdon offers two models; (1) a consensus decision mode whereby Congressmen follow the path of least resistance and (2) a rank ordering of the relative influence of various internal and external actors on congressional decision-making. For Matthews and Stimson, the norm of congressional decision-making is "cue-taking"--i.e., an expertise-based shortcut by which a member follows the lead of another Congressman, usually a member of the decision-maker's state delegation who serves on the relevant committee. For Cherryholmes and Shapiro, ideological predisposition and communications best explain congressional voting. Jackson offers a weighted, multiple actor input model. Mayhew presents an

3

"economic incentives" model that stresses the member's drive for reelection.

To reiterate, literature classified at this stage of development (a) views the Congressman as a determined actor and thus (b) attempts to provide a general construct which best explains that determination. Throughout, there is an emphasis on general propositions. Major findings are expressed in the following general form:

o "It does not appear that they [senators] are influenced by one person or one set of influences on one bill and an entirely different person or set on the next. This routine is largely invariant with the type of legislation."[14]

o A Congressman hears from few actors when making a decision, "most often from those who agree with him."[15]

o "Fellow Congressmen appear to be the most important influence on voting decisions, followed by constituency."[16]

o "Other members are the major source of a Congressman's information."[17]

o "Congressmen confine their searches for information only to the most routine and easily available sources."[18]

o Congressmen generally are not well-informed when making a decision.[19]

o Party affiliation is the factor most strongly related to congressional voting.[20]

o Members base most votes on ideology.[21]

o Most members have a "politico" style of representation and a district focus.[22]

The third level of development holds the legislative decision-maker to be a contextual actor. This stage is a reaction to the plethora of competing models and generalizations. It rejects the notion that any one model of the legislative decision process can have a monopoly on truth. It emphasizes different decision tracks within the Congress.

The distinguishing characteristics of the third level of contextual decisions are (1) the identification of different contexts of legislative decision-making, (2) the formulation of classification schemes or typologies that attempt to capture the essence of issue-based behavioral variations within the Congress, and (3) the utilization of contextually-qualified generalizations.

The contextual approach has gained prominence in the works of Theodore Lowi.[23] Lowi provides a framework within which various case studies can be integrated. His basic premise is that the U.S. policy process unfolds in various policy arenas. Different areas of governmental activity constitute different arenas of power. In his words, "Each arena tends to develop its own characteristic political structure, political process, elites, and group relations."[24] He then distinguishes among "distributive," "regulatory," and "redistributive" policy arenas. Table 1.1 is Lowi's summary of the major patterns found in these different arenas.

Other works that can be classified at the contextual level include Aage Clausen's How Congressmen Decide: A Policy Focus,[25] Roger Cobb and Charles Elder's Participation in American Politics,[26] Lewis Froman and Randall Ripley's "Conditions for Party Leadership,"[27] Charles O. Jones' "Speculative Augmentation in Federal Air Pollution PolicyMaking"[28] Warren Miller and Donald Stokes' "Constituency Influence in Congress,"[29] David Price's "Policy-Making in Congressional Committees: The Impact of Environmental Factors,"[30] Randall Ripley's Congress: Process and Policy,[31] and "Congressional Party Leaders and Standing Committees,"[32] Ripley and Grace Franklin's Congress, the Bureaucracy and Public Policy,[33] James O. Wilson's Political Organizations,[34] and David Vogler's The Politics of Congress.[35] Like Lowi, each stresses conditional patterns of influence and decision-making in Congress.

Some contextual studies merely call attention to legislative process variations and patterns. Miller and Stokes identify "several distinct patterns of representation" that "vary according to the type of

Table 1.1

Arenas and Political Relationships: A Diagrammatic Survey*

Arena	Primary Political Unit	Relation Among Units	Power Structure	Stability of Structure	Primary Decisional Locus	Implementation
Distribution	Individual, firm, corporation	Log-rolling, mutual-non-interference, uncommon interests	Non-conflict-ual elite with support groups	Stable	Congressional committee and/or agency	Agency centralized to primary functional unit ("bureau")
Regulation	Group	"The coalition," shared subject-matter interest, bargaining	Pluralistic, multi-centered, "theory of balance"	Unstable	Congress, in classic role	Agency decentralized from center by "delegation," mixed control
Redistribution	Association	The "peak association," class elite, i.e., elite and counterelite	Conflictual ideology	Stable	Executive and peak associations	Agency centralized toward top (above "bureau"), elaborate standards

*Source: Theodore J. Lowi, "Distribution, Regulation, and Redistribution: the Functions of Government," Public Policies and their Politics, ed. by Randall B. Ripley (N.Y.: Norton, 1966), p. 39.

policy at hand": civil rights, government regulation, and foreign affairs. In their words, no single tradition of representation fully accords with the reality of American legislative politics."[36] Similarly, Clausen searches for differential influence in certain "policy domains." In his investigation of five such domains or issue areas--government management, social welfare, international involvement, civil liberties, and agricultural assistance--he discovers various "patterns of influence." For government management, he finds a party influence. For social welfare and agricultural assistance, he identifies a party-constituency influence. A constituency influence dominates legislation involving civil liberties, while both constituency and presidential influences are salient for international involvement.[37] Froman and Ripley emphasize the variability of party leadership influence. According to them, "the extent of party leadership. . . is itself variable."[38] Specifically, they contend that party leadership is most likely to influence legislative outcomes when the following conditions are present: (a) low visibility, (b) procedural question, and (c) the absence of counter pressure from constituencies and state delegations.[39] Ripley also emphasizes the conditional nature of the influence exerted by various actors. The visibility of an issue, he finds, will determine the relative influence of outside actors (constituency, interest groups, bureaucrats, and the President) on congressional decisions.[40] Concerning inside actors, he stipulates varying conditions under which party leaders will be influential vis-a-vis committee leaders.[41] Price makes the distinction between "clientele-centered" issues and those that are "publicly salient." He suggests that legislative decisionmaking varies according to the degree of conflict, public salience, and presidential involvement on a given issue.[42]

Other conditional studies make use of the Lowi typology to highlight variations in the legislative process and legislative behavior. Vogler uses the Lowi scheme to illustrate the variable influence of lobbyists, the President, and public opinion in the Congress. In Vogler's words,

On some types of issues pressure groups do
seem to be able to influence the votes of
legislators and the eventual policy outcome;
on others, special interests, pressure
groups, and lobbyists are relatively
ineffective. The same sort of discrepancies
that we find in the literature on lobbies
exist in studies of the influence of the
President and the executive branch, and
other outside actors on legislative
policymaking. Consideration of the
different types of policies is useful for
some understanding of the role of the
President in legislative policymaking.[43]

Ripley and Franklin focus on policy relationships.
Utilizing the Lowi typology, they argue that
"different relationships have varying degrees of
importance in determining final policy actions."[44]
Table 1.2 is their summary of the different policy
relationships and influence patterns that appear to
follow different "policy types."

Finally, some conditional studies posit
distinctive typologies for classifying various
contexts of legislative decision-making. In a
variation of Braybrooke and Lindblom, Jones
identifies "four quadrants of decision-making," each
involving a different kind of decision process,
decision style, and analytical methods, and each
varying from the others in terms of both the degree
of understanding and the degree of changes involved
in the decision.[45] Wilson notes the variable
nature of interest group involvement in the
legislative process. He argues that "the substance
of a policy influences the role of organizations in
its adoption.[46] To him, "The extent and nature of
organizational activity in an issue area will also
depend on the incidence of costs and benefits."[47]
He then identifies four mixes of costs and benefits
that affect group involvement: distributed benefits
and distributed costs (majoritarian politics),
concentrated benefits and concentrated costs
(interest group politics), concentrated benefits and
distributed costs (clientele politics), and distributed benefits and concentrated costs (entrepreneurial
politics). Cobb and Elder argue that the scope of
political conflict varies according to a host of
certain issue characteristics. They suggest that
variations in legislative behavior will follow

8

Table 1.2

Characteristics of Different Policy Types*

Policy Type	Main Feature	Primary Actors	Relationship among Actors	Stability or Relationship	Main Decision-Maker	Visibility of Decisions	Influence of			
							Lobbies	Congressional Committee	Congress Committee	President
Distributive, domestic	Short-run, disaggregated decisions, no losers	Congressional subcommittees and committees; executive bureaus; small interest groups	Logrolling	Stable	Congressional subcommittee or committee	Very low	High	Determinative	Supports Committee	None
Regulatory, domestic	Application of a general rule; some win, some lose	Full House and Senate; executive agencies; trade associations	Competition; bargaining	Unstable	Congress	Moderate	High	Creative	Determinative	Moderate
Redistributive, domestic	Long run reallocation of resources among classes; winners and losers clearly defined	President and his appointees; committees and/or Congress; peak associations; "liberals and conservatives"	Ideological and class conflict	Stable	Executive	High	Moderate	Low or important in compromises	Obstructive until winning coalition present	Leadership; lobbying; legislative

*Source: Randall B. Ripley and Grace A. Franklin, Congress, The Bureaucracy, and Public Policy (Homewood, Ill.: Dorsey Press, 1976), p. 17.

variations in the following issue characteristics:
(a) the degree of specificity, (b) the scope of
social significance, (c) the extent of temporal
relevance, (d) the degree of complexity, and (e) the
degree of categorical precedence.[48]

Although there is variation in jargon, focus, and
the level of conceptualization of different works
that can be classified at this third level of
development, each work makes the same basic
assumption: <u>the legislative process is highly
conditional</u>. Each calls attention to patterned,
issue-based variability in Congress. In fact, the
major difference between third and second level
analysis is best captured with the distinction
between dynamic and static designs. As noted above,
those works which can be classified at the second
level offer parsimonious theories concerning what are
perceived to be the dominant characteristics or modes
of legislative behavior. Literature at the third
level of analysis, on the other hand, assumes that
the legislative process is highly variable, highly
contextual, conditional, and differentiated. It
emphasizes multiple-patterned dynamics of
decision-making.

According to the newer approach, research that
attempts to generalize about the legislative process
or to identify its most typical characteristics,
although making a contribution, overlooks and
oversimplifies contextual variations in congressional
decision-making. To the proponents of this new
emphasis in the study of the Congress, congressional
decision-making is best understood, not with a series
of static propositions that purport to summarize a
process in general, but, rather, through the
identification of recurring variations and the
construction of typologies which acquaint us with the
nuances of a complex, multifaceted phenomenon. Third
level constructs alert us to the notion of conditional regularity--i.e., that there are different
decision contexts in Congress and that Congressmen
behave differently in different contexts.
Congressional decisionmaking is best understood with
a number of different models rather than with one
model, with the appropriateness of each of the models
depending on the presence of certain conditions.

By way of summary, Table 1.3 contrasts the three
levels of intellectual development of congressional

Table 1.3

A Comparison of Three Levels of
Congressional Decision-Making Theory

Contrasts	Level		
	I	II	III
Decision-maker seen as:	Participant	Determined actor	Contextual decision-maker
Data sources:	Case studies	Roll calls/ attitudinal	Case studies (to date)
Examples:	Bailey, Gross	Truman, Kingdon	Lowi
Emphasis:	Legislative process as "political struggle"	General Propositions/ general model of "typicalness"	Variable Contextual patterns
Generalize to:	Process	Actors	Issues

11

decision-making theory. As has been noted throughout this chapter (and shown in the figure), contextual work is distinctive in that it presupposes a construct that emphasizes variable, dynamic patterns of legislative behavior. Although some second level literature implies variations in legislative behavior at the "actor" level (for example, it is assumed that meaningful differences occur between Republicans and Democrats or between "junior" and "senior" legislators), third level literature presumes that a meaningful differential exists primarily at the issue level (that is, distinctive patterns are based on the kind of policy issue and type of decision at hand). In contextual literature, there is a strong assumption that legislative decision-making is best understood in terms of issue variations, not actor variations, though to be sure actor differences are acknowledged as important.

Not only those works we have classified at the third stage take an issue-based contextual approach. Truman, for example, acknowledges the conditional nature of the legislative process with his intro-ductory statement that "no study that is limited to a single two-year period and is focused upon one set of primary data can produce unqualified conclu-sions.[49] Turner, as revised by Schneier, employs a contextual approach of sorts by noting that different substantive issues produce variable patterns of partisan voting in Congress.[50] Both Kingdon, and Matthews and Stimson employ a loose contextual scheme. Kingdon examines the variable influence of constituency and interest groups under different conditions of issue salience.[51] Matthews and Stimson stipulate the conditions under which members are likely to engage in "cue-taking" and contend that cue taking applies mainly to "normal decisions."[52] But as noted above, these works, as well as the others in level two, attempt in the main to provide a general model at the actor level. When they deal with "issue contexts," they do so in an off-handed fashion. What is unique about the most recent body of literature (and why it must be considered a new emphasis in the study of legislative behavior) is the explicitness, formality, sophistication, primacy of purpose, and research orientation with which it attempts to discern different contextual patterns and to utilize them as the basis for formulating conditional theory of the legislative process. In the remainder of this chapter, we will seek to

12

identify the advantages such a theory offers
legislative process scholars and the limitations of
contextual literature given the state of its
development.

The Advantages of a Developed Contextual Theory

The development of a contextual theory of the
legislative process offers congressional scholars two
distinct pay-offs. First, contextual theory affords
the opportunity for the integration of contending
models of the legislative process. Second, it
provides the basis for constructing an analytical
theory of the legislative process.

1. The Integration of Contending Models of the Legislative Process

Presently, legislative process studies are
plagued by numerous competing models. On both the
macro or organizational and the micro or individual
level, there are various contending perspectives or
explanations. Each offers a generalized view of the
legislative process and legislative behavior, that,
as most students of Congress would be quick to note,
is neither totally right nor totally wrong. In
Kingdon's words, "If we were to be able somehow to
arrive at a way to fit important aspects of these
models together, our theoretical thinking about
legislative behavior might be advanced
considerably."[53]

At the macro level, one finds three very
prominent perspectives on how Congress processes
issues: (1) the "traditional" model, (2) the
"subgovernment" (whirlpool/triangle/subsystem)
approach, and (3) the "Mayhew thesis."

The traditional perspective, which is best
elucidated in Nelson Polsby's Congress and the
Presidency, argues that Congress functions as the
"forge" or "anvil" of democracy--i.e., it is the
place where accommodations are fashioned and hammered
out, bargains are struck and interests are
brokered.[54]

The subgovernment approach has been made popular
by Ernest Griffith's Congress: Its Contemporary
Role,[55] Douglas Cater's Power in Washington,[56]
and James Freeman's The Political Process.[57] The

essence of this perspective, as Edward Schneier notes, is that "the legislative, executive and private institutions that are immediately concerned with a given policy-set make policy in this arena."[58] In other words, most congressional policy decisions are thrashed out among "proximate policy-makers": relevant congressional subcommittees, the bureau with assigned administrative responsibility, and an "affected public."

The Mayhew thesis, expressed in his Congress: The Electoral Connection, argues that congressional policy-making, as the result of the desires of members for reelection, reflects "assembly coherence"--delay, particularism, servicing of the organized, and symbolism.[59]

At the micro level there is no dearth of alternative schemes for explaining the behavior of individual legislators. Jackson[60] and Matthews and Stimson[61] attempt to summarize the major micro theories of legislative behavior. Combining the efforts of both works results in a list of four different theories purporting to explain why Congressmen vote as they do. They are: (a) a "trustee" or "public-interest-statesman" model, (b) an "instructed delegate" or "representational" model, (c) an "ideologist" or "policy-predispositions" theory, and (d) a "cue-taking" or "organizational" explanation.

An obvious advantage of the contextual theory is that it acknowledges the conditional appropriateness of various models. For example, the Lowi scheme, although having significant shortcomings, as we shall argue, integrates several models of legislative decision-making: distributive issues are "subgovernment" decisions; regulatory issues are decided on the basis of "policy coalitions" and reflect Congress in its "traditional" sense; redistributive issues invoke "ideological" responses. Thus, there is every reason to expect that developed contextual theory would afford students of Congress the opportunity to specify the conditions under which each major macro and micro perspective is likely to be valid. The contextual line of reasoning alerts us to the probability that there is no one best explanation of legislative outcomes; there are several.

2. The Construction of an "Analytical Theory" of the Legislative Process

A consistent theme of those works that attempt to inventory the legislative process field is the need for a theoretical framework with which various studies and research efforts can be synthesized.[62] For example, Norman Meller notes that:

> Like raindrops on a dirty windowpane, legislative behavior studies afford brief glimpses at a broader vision of the legislative process, but have failed to furnish a framework enabling its full comprehension. Studies are yet too diverse and lack replication; conflicting findings have not always served as stimuli for subsequent clarificatory research. Also, there has been too ready a subsuming of the basic unity of the legislative process and too little attention given to the generation of an inclusive theory.[63]

Heinz Eulau and Katherine Hinckley argue that "legislative research, despite much progress in recent years, remains in infancy." They call for "accelerated theoretical advance" through a strengthening of the "converging tendencies in theory construction."[64] Herbert Weisberg emphasizes that,

> The 15 percent of the votes which cannot be predicted by a single model still have not been predicted. And, more importantly, the field lacks the organizing theory by which to assemble all the separate elements which have been studied.[65]

Finally, Wayne Shannon argues that

> if social research is conceived as an individual exercise of competence and an occasional thrust of brilliant imagination, there is some of each to be found here. If, on the other hand, it is conceived as a quest for highly reliable generalizations and causal explanations that culminate in nicely integrated theoretical structures, this literature, collectively, leaves much to be desired. If the latter is to be the

15

goal that we seek, we had better get our
heads together.[66]

A developed contextual approach to the
legislative process would be a step toward the
all-inclusive kind of theory called for by these
authors. Specifically, a contextual scheme would
advance theory in two ways. First, as noted above,
by providing the basis for the integration of
contending theories, the contextual model would offer
the opportunity for an inclusive theory of
"converging tendencies." Second, and more important,
through the use of typologies, a contextual scheme
would provide the basis for developing abstract
proportions that Stuart Nagel refers to as
"nomothetic" propositions. These propositions are
general in form, and contain few if any references to
specific objects, places, and times.[67] They are
general statements in which the proper names of
countries, personalities, and institutions are
replaced by references to abstract variables.[68]
The goal of all social science endeavors should be
formulation of abstract statements. Such statements
provide the basis for analytical theories of social
phenomena.

For students of Congress, the typologies of the
contextual approach offer the opportunity for
providing abstract propositions. Such propositions
can lead to the analytical theory of the legislative
process for which these epistemological works on
congressional research are calling. Such schemes as
those of Lowi, Wilson, and Jones provide the basis
for examining contextual variations in the
legislative process in terms of general variables
such as policy types, policy arenas, and issue
characteristics, rather than in terms of substantive,
proper names such as "civil rights," "law
enforcement," and "foreign policy."

In sum, a sophisticated contextual perspective
would be a major advancement of theory--i.e., theory
in the sense of Nagel--of the legislative process.

Problem: The Undeveloped State of Contextual Schemes

Contextual schemes can contribute much to
sophisticated notions of the legislative process,
legislative behavior, and democratic process. They
offer the potential for abstract propositions

16

concerning legislative behavior. It is very disappointing, therefore, to discover that, with few exceptions, those writings that are considered to be the crux of contextual literature fail to conform to the requisites of social science theorizing and research. Most disheartening, however, is the primative state of theorizing. Specifically, as a body of literature, all of the major works that employ a contextual approach suffer from three major deficiencies: (1) the lack of developed and explicit conceptualization, (2) the lack of additive, systematic research, and (3) the absence of truly abstract concepts.

1. The Lack of Developed and Explicit Conceptualization

Contextual schemes suffer from three specific problems of conceptualization. First, no standard language has developed. Each of the contextual works offers its own unique typology. The result of this multiplicity of jargon and typologies is, of course, the lack of a standard scheme, for the only tie that binds is adherence to an implied contextual model.

Second, contextual literature lacks an explicit rationale for explaining the identified relationships. None of the authors who use this approach spell out the causal schemes implied in their writings. They fail to explain the theoretical basis of relationships between independent and dependent variables. For example, Lowi in his pioneering work suggests broad patterns of legislative decision-making, but he does not provide a succinct explanation of suspected relationships. He does not directly tell us why different types of bills are related to differences in legislative behavior. Subsequent studies, which might be classified as spinoffs or derivatives of Lowi because they are predicated on his distributive-regulatory-redistributive typology, do no better. For example, although Ripley and Franklin do much to identify and differentiate variables and to clarify causal schemes, they do not provide a sharp explanation that suggests why different policy types are associated with different kinds of decision processes. These criticisms also apply to those contextual approaches that do not build on Lowi's typology.

Third, contextual literature fails to distinguish between macro and micro levels of analysis or to specify how they are linked together. Although certain patterns are discerned at the macro level, there has been no attempt to specify precisely how these macro variations translate to the micro level. Authors utilizing a contextual approach fail to provide us with a standard, operationable set of benchmarks at which we can observe predicted patterns of legislative behavior. What is different about the decision environment of distributive, regulatory, and redistributive issues that leads legislators to employ different kinds of decision processes? What happens with regard to a member's decision-making behavior on distributive issues that is different from redistributive issues? These concerns are simply not addressed in current research.

There has been some progress in the conceptual development of conditional schemes, especially the works of Jones, Cobb and Elder, and Price. In these they argued that "issue characteristics" and not policy types are related to legislative process patterns. Generally speaking, however, contextual approaches because of the lack of standardization, the lack of explicitness concerning causal schemes and independent and dependent variables, the absence of a compelling rationale, and the failure to link macro and micro phenomena, must be considered at best conceptually primitive.

2. The Lack of Direct, Additive, Systematic Research

Contextual literature also suffers from the absence of rigorous empirical scrutiny. As Hofferbert notes, "to date, little empirical work has been fruitfully conducted with any of these typologies. . . . The evidence is not yet in concerning the typologies . . . but it is disturbing that . . . the bait has not been taken by the researchers."[69] No doubt this state of affairs is the result of the general conceptual fuzziness of conceptual schemes noted previously. Indeed, Cobb and Elder[70] argued that, at least with regard to the Lowi scheme, a contextual approach is unoperational because the policy types are not mutually exclusive--that is, all policies have some distributive, regulatory, and redistributive aspects. Therefore, it is most difficult to establish an objective classification of policies.

To decide whether a policy is mainly distributive, regulatory, or redistributive would require enormous study of policy impacts, that in itself would involve highly "subjective" types of assessments on the part of the researcher.[71]

Lowi[72] tries to empirically "test" for some of his expected patterns. Ripley and Franklin attempt a test of the Lowi scheme with a series of disparate case studies. Yet, Lowi has not been examined in the fashion legislative process scholars traditionally test their schemes: in a single session of Congress where various factors internal to the legislature (e.g., leadership, member composition, party control of the presidency, party alignment) can be held constant. Contextual schemes other than Lowi also generally lack broad-based research. Jones verifies his scheme with only case studies of congressional responses to the environmental movement. Both Cobb and Elder, and Wilson, are limited to anecdotal examples in support of their schemes. Price relies on impressionistic views of commerce policy-making over a period of several Congresses. As a body of literature, contextual approaches to the study of Congress have not been examined nor researched in keeping with the high standards and precepts of scientific method and the demands of generality.

3. The Absence of Truly Abstract (Nomothetic) Concepts

There have been several attempts to uncover conditions and variations in the legislative process through empirical research. The most noteworthy are Miller and Stokes's "Constituency Influence in Congress,"[73] Clausen's How Congressmen Decide,[74] and Clausen and Cheney's "A Comparative Analysis of Senate-House Voting on Economic and Welfare Policy, 1953-1964."[75] The third and final criticism that can be made of contextual literature is that even those few works that have employed rigorous methodologies have not utilized truly abstract concepts. Although the Miller and Stokes and Clausen works empiricaly demonstrate a contextual working of Congress, their models do not utilize general variables, relying instead on substantive policy categories or issue domains. Miller and Stokes use "civil rights," "foreign policy" and "social welfare," Clausen focuses on "government management," "social welfare,' "international involvement," "civil

19

liberties," and "agricultural assistance;" and
Clausen and Cheney use "economic policy" and "welfare
policy."

To summarize, those works that can be considered
"contextual" are either conceptually fuzzy or
unsystematic, on the one hand, or lack the true
abstract quality necessary for useful and
sophisticated theorizing, on the other hand. These
deficiencies may be a reflection of the relative
infancy of literature that stresses a contextual
working of the Congress. Nevertheless, given the
potential advantages to be gained from the study of
legislative contexts, there can be no doubt that
attempts to improve on the contextual model are
worthwhile and significant. This is especially so
because numerous textbook approaches and spinoff
studies have been stimulated by the various
contextual schemes, especially Lowi.[76] In fact, so
great is contemporary interest in contextual schemes
that they may very well have become the new fad of
legislative process scholars, succeeding such topics
as legislative process, case studies, roll-call
analysis, legislative behavior, small-group
decision-making, and comparative legislative
policies. Yet, we have yet to demonstrate the
validity of a contextual effect in a thorough fashion.

Summary and Conclusions

Floor voting in the U.S. Congress generally has
been considered an important act of legitimation in
the American political system. Political scientists
have devoted much time and energy to explaining the
decision behavior of Congressmen. Their works have
addressed major questions such as how do Congressmen
decide? Who influences Congressmen? How do they
define their job? Who do they hear from when making
a decision? How do they inform themselves? What
kind of representation is afforded by Congress? How
does Congress, as an institution, function and how
does it process issues? And, what contributions does
Congress make to national policy?

Traditionally, students of Congress have employed
static research designs to answer these questions.
Static studies use general propositions to understand
legislative behavior, such as "Congressmen hear from
few actors when making a decision" or "fellow members
are the most consistently consulted information

20

source." Static models generalize about legislative decision-making. Others emphasize cue-taking, policy positions, constituency, or consensus decision-making. The result has been a plethora of competing models.

A review of legislative process literature has allowed us to differentiate a new line of contextual research from the more traditional, static models of legislative behavior. The newer perspective calls attention to different decision settings within the legislature, such as the distinction between distributive, regulatory, and redistributive arenas. The essence of this newer thrust is a firm emphasis on contextual patterns in legislative behavior. It employs issue-based qualifications when discussing how Congressmen decide. While static theories implicitly stress patterns of decision-making based on differences in party, constituency, and background characteristics such as length of service, the contextual model emphasizes issue-based variations.

Static designs imply that the legislative actor goes through the same intellectual process and steps and exhibits the same behavior when making each and every decision. Although the premises on which decisions are based may vary, the process remains the same. Thus, according to those who utilize this type of construct, legislative decision-making is best explained by a parsimonious theory based on general propositions. Conversely, contextual constructs depict the legislator as one who utilizes various processes and exhibits different behaviors depending on the kind of issue at hand. Authors who utilize a contextual perspective emphasize the applicability of multiple models. According to contextual literature, if one desires a sophisticated perspective on legislative decision-making, he is better served by an approach that acknowledges various decision contexts of the legislative process than by a static, all-inclusive model that stresses typicalness, generality, normality, or universality.

Although the notion of contextually dynamic decision-making offers a promising line of investigation, it is not well developed. It has not been formulated, operationalized, nor researched in keeping with the standards of the discipline.

It is the goal of this book to coherently explicate propositions concerning the individual level of legislative behavior underlying, or at least implied by, contextual schemes and to offer a design that operationalizes the theory with abstract concepts, provides an acceptable empirical test of propositions logically deduced from said theory, and attempts to link the findings of the research to literature concerning the democratic process in America.

[1]Thomas S. Kuhn, The Structure of Scientific Revolution, 2nd ed. (Chicago: University of Chicago Press, 1970).

[2]See the following for historical and analytical reviews of legislative behavior research: Heinz Eulau and Katherine Hinckley, "Legislative Institutions and Processes," in Political Science Annual 1966, ed. J.A. Robinson (Indianapolis: Bobbs-Merrill, 1966), pp. 85-181; Norman Meller, "Legislative Behavior Research," Western Political Quarterly 13 (1960): 131-53; Norman Meller, "Legislative Behavior Research Revisited: A Review of Five Years' Publications," Western Political Quarterly, 18 (1965): 776-93; Norman Meller, "Legislative Behavior Research," in Approaches to the Study of Political Science, ed. M. Haas and H.S. Kariel (Scranton: Chandler, 1970), pp. 239-66; Robert L. Peabody, "Research on Congress: A Coming of Age," in Congress: Two Decades of Analysis, ed. R.K. Huitt and R.L. Peabody (New York: Harper & Row, 1969), pp. 3-73; and John C. Wahlke, "Behavioral Analyses of Representative Bodies," in Essays on the Behavioral Study of Politics, ed. A. Ranney (Urbana, Ill.: University of Illinois Press, 1962), pp. 173-90.

[3]Bertram M. Gross, The Legislative Struggle: A Study in Social Combat (New York: McGraw-Hill, 1953).

[4]Stephen K. Bailey, Congress Makes a Law (New York: Columbia University Press, 1950) and Daniel M. Berman, A Bill Becomes a Law (New York: Macmillan, 1962). Other good examples of the case study approach are: Robert Bendiner, Obstacle Course on Capitol Hill (New York: McGraw-Hill Book Company, 1964); Eugene Eidenberg and R.D. Morey, An Act of Congress (New York: Norton, 1969); Robert L. Peabody et al., To Enact a Law (New York: Praeger, 1972); and Eric Redman, The Dance of Legislation (New York: Simon and Schuster, 1973).

[5]This characteristic of legislative behavior research is emphasized by Mayhew in his description of the "Sociological Approach." See David R. Mayhew, Congress: The Electoral Connection (New Haven: Yale University Press, 1974), pp. 1-3.

[6]Julius Turner, Party and Constituency, rev. ed. by Edward V. Schneier (Baltimore: Johns Hopkins Press, 1970).

[7]David B. Truman, The Congressional Party (New York: Wiley, 1959).

[8]Roger H. Davidson, The Role of the Congressman (New York: Pegasus, 1969).

[9]John W. Kingdon, Congressmen's Voting Decisions (New York: Harper & Row, 1973).

[10]Donald R. Matthews and James A. Stimson, Yeas and Nays (New York: Wiley, 1975).

[11]Cleo H. Cherryholmes and Michael J. Shapiro, Representatives and Roll Calls (Indianapolis: Bobbs-Merrill, 1969).

[12]John E. Jackson, Constituencies and Leaders in Congress (Cambridge, Mass.: Harvard University Press, 1974).

[13]Mayhew, Congress.

[14]John E. Jackson, "Statistical Models of Senate Roll Call Voting," American Political Science Review 65 (1971): 468.

[15]Lewis, Dexter, The Sociology and Politics of Congress (Chicago: Rand McNally, 1969), p. 159. Also see: Lewis Anthony Dexter, "The Job of the Congressman," Readings on Congress, ed. R.E. Wolfinger (Englewood Cliffs, N.J.: Prentice-Hall, 1971), p. 81.

[16]Kingdon, Congressman's Voting, p. 22.

[17]Kovenock discovered that information inputs coming directly from members of the House were three times as great as from other sources. See: Kovenock as quoted in John S. Saloma, III, Congress and the New Politics (Boston: Little, Brown and Co., 1969), p. 218. Bauer, Pool and Dexter note that "Congressmen develop an implicit roster of fellow Congressmen whose judgement they respect, whose viewpoint they normally share, and to whom they can turn for guidance on particular topics of the colleague's competence." See: Raymond A. Bauer, Ithiel de Sola Pool, and Lewis Anthony Dexter, American Business and Public Policy (New York: Atherton Press, 1963), p. 437.

[18]Kingdon, Congressman's Voting, p. 227.

[19]Davidson, Kovenock, and O'Leary found that "the most frequently mentioned problems were associated with the complexity of decision-making: the lack of information." The problem of deficient information for decision-making was cited by 62 percent of their sample--the most frequently mentioned complaint. See: Roger H. Davidson, David M. Kovenock, and Michael D. O'Leary,

<u>Congress in Crisis: Politics and Congressional Reform</u> (Belmont, California: Wadsworth Publishing Co., 1966), pp. 75-78.

[20]Turner, <u>Party and Constituency</u>, p. 34.

[21]Clausen, <u>How Congressmen Decide</u>, p. 14.

[22]Davidson, <u>The Role</u>, p. 117.

[23]Theodore J. Lowi, "American Business, Public Policy, Case Studies, and Political Theory," <u>World Politics</u> 16 (1964): 677-715; T.J. Lowi, "Distribution, Regulation, Redistribution: The Functions of Government," in <u>Public Policies and Their Politics</u>, ed. R. Ripley (New York: Norton, 1966), pp. 27-40; T. J. Lowi, "Four Systems of Policy, Politics, and Choice," <u>Public Administration Review</u> 32 (1972): 298-301.

[24]Lowi, "American Business," pp. 689-90.

[25]Aage R. Clausen, <u>How Congressmen Decide: A Policy Focus</u> (New York: St. Martin's, 1973) and Aage R. Clausen and Richard B. Cheney, "A Comparative Analysis of Senate-House Voting on Economic and Welfare Policy, 1953-1964," <u>American Political Science Review</u> 60 (1966): 138-152.

[26]Roger W. Cobb and Charles D. Elder, <u>Participation in American Politics</u> (Boston: Allyn, 1972).

[27]Lewis A. Froman and Randall B. Ripley, "Conditions for Party Leadership," <u>American Political Science Review</u> 59 (1965): 52-63.

[28]Charles O. Jones, "Speculative Augmentation in Federal Air Pollution Policy-Making," <u>Journal of Politics</u> 36 (1974): 438-64.

[29]Warren E. Miller and Donald E. Stokes, "Constituency Influence in Congress," <u>American Political Science Review</u> 57 (1963): 45-56.

[30]David E. Price, "Policy-Making in Congressional Committees: The Impact of Environmental Factors," <u>American Political Science Review</u> 72 (1978): 548-74.

[31]Randall B. Ripley, <u>Congress: Process and Policy</u> (New York: Norton, 1975).

[32]Randall B. Ripley, "Congressional Party Leaders and Standing Committees," Review of Politics 36 (1974): 394-410.

[33]Randall B. Ripley and Grace A. Franklin, Congress, the Bureaucracy, and Public Policy (Homewood, Ill.: Dorsey, 1976).

[34]James Q. Wilson, Political Organizations (New York: Basic Books, 1973) and Wilson, American Government: Institutions and Policies (Lexington, Mass.: Heath, 1980).

[35]David J. Vogler, The Politics of Congress, 2nd ed. (Boston: Allyn, 1977).

[36]Miller and Stokes, "Constituency Influence," p. 56.

[37]Clausen, How Congressmen, Chapter 9.

[38]Froman and Ripley, "Conditions," p. 52.

[39]Ibid., p. 63.

[40]Ripley, Congress, p. 211.

[41]Ripley, "Congressional Party Leaders."

[42]Price, "Policy-Making," pp. 36-41.

[43]Vogler, Politics of Congress, p. 297.

[44]Ripley and Franklin, Congress, p. 166.

[45]Jones, An Introduction to the Study of Public Policy, 2nd ed. (North Scituate, Mass: Duxbury, 1977), p. 218; and Jones, "Speculative," p. 449.

[46]Wilson, Political Organizations, p. 330.

[47]Ibid., p. 331.

[48]Cobb and Elder, Participation, pp. 96-97.

[49]Truman, Congressional Party, p. viii.

[50]Turner, Party and Constituency, pp. 103-104.

[51]Kingdon, Congressmen's Voting, pp. 54 and 140.

[52]Matthews and Stimson, Yeas and Nays, pp. 62-70.

[53]John Kingdon, "Models of Legislative Voting," Journal of Politics 36 (1977): 564.

[54]Nelson W. Polsby, Congress and the Presidency, 2nd ed. (Englewood Cliffs, N.J.: Prentice-Hall, 1971).

[55]Ernest S. Griffith, Congress: Its Contemporary Role, 3rd ed. (New York: New York University Press, 1961), pp. 50-51.

[56]Douglas Cater, Power in Washington (New York: Vintage Books, 1964), pp. 17-21.

[57]James L. Freeman, The Political Process: Executive Bureau-Legislative Committee Relations, rev. ed. (New York: Random, 1965), p. 6.

[58]Edward Schneier, "The Intelligence of Congress: Information and Public Policy Patterns," The Annals of the American Academy of Political and Social Science, 388 (1970), p. 17.

[59]Mayhew, Congress, p. 141.

[60]Jackson, Constituencies, pp. 1-8.

[61]Donald R. Matthews and James A. Stimson, "Decision-Making by U.S. Representatives: A Preliminary Model," in Political Decision-Making, ed.

S. Ulmer (New York: Van Nostrand Reinhold, 1970), pp. 18-23.

[62]Reference note 2.

[63]Meller, "Legislative Behavior," p. 251.

[64]Eulau and Hinckley, "Legislative Institutions," p. 179.

[65]Herbert F. Weisberg, "Evaluating Theories of Congressional Roll Calls," American Journal of Political Science, 22 (1978): 574.

[66]W. Wayne Shannon, "Congressional Party Behavior: Data, Concept and Theory in the Search of Historical Reality," Polity 6 (1974), p. 284.

[67]Ernest Nagel, "The Logic of Historical Analysis," in The Philosophy of History in Our Time, ed. H. Meyerhoff (New York: Doubleday, 1959), pp. 203-04.

[68]Adam Przeworski and H. Teune, _The Logic of Comparative Inquiry_ (New York: Wiley-Interscience, 1970), p. 12.

[69]Richard Hofferbert, "State and Local Policy Studies," in _Political Science Annual_, ed. T. Robinson (Indianapolis: Bobbs-Merrill, 1971), p. 63.

[70]Cobb and Elder, _Participation_, pp. 94-96; Lewis A. Froman, Jr., "The Categorization of Policy Contents," in _Political Science and Public Policy_, ed. A. Ranney, p. 50; Paul Dornan, "Whither Urban Policy Analysis? A Review Essay," _Polity_ 9 (1977), 503-27; Wilson, _Political Organizations_, pp. 328-30; and George D. Greenberg, Jeffrey A. Miller, Lawrance B. Mohr, and Bruce C. Vladeck, "Developing Public Policy Theory: Perspectives from Empirical Theory," _American Political Science Review_ 71 (1977): 1534-36.

[71]Greenberg, et al., "Developing Public Policy Theory," p. 1536.

[72]Lowi, "Four Systems," pp. 304-06. Of special interest is Table III on p. 306 of that publication where he compares distributive, redistributive, and regulative legislation in terms of the number of amendments offered, the percent passed, and the percent of significant amendments passed over the sponsor's objections.

[73]Miller and Stokes, "Constituency Influence."

[74]Clausen, _How Congressmen_.

[75]Clausen and Cheney, "Senate-House Voting."

[76]For examples of an application of Lowi, see: Dean Schooler, _Science, Scientists, and Public Policy_ (New York: Free Press, 1971); M. Chandler, W. Chandler, and David Vogler, "Policy Analysis and the Search for Theory," _American Politics Quarterly_ 2 (1974): 107-18; and C. D. Tubbesing, "Predicting the Present: Realigning Elections and Redistributive Policies," _Polity_ 7 (1975): 478-504.

CHAPTER II

CONTEXTUAL THEORY: AN EXPLICATION, RATIONALE,
AND OPERATIONALIZATION

This chapter aims to improve upon contextual
approaches to legislative decision-making.
Specifically, it will state the major propositions
that inhere in contextual approaches and discuss them
in terms of democratic theory, elaborate on the
reasons why the stated relationships can be expected,
present the research design that operationalized and
tested the major hypotheses drawn from the formally
stated theory, and describe the procedures through
which the research design was implemented and data
collected.

Theoretical Explication: Issue-based Variations in Legislative Decision-making

The basic intellectual construct of the
contextual approach is that legislative decision-
making is a highly variable task that is best
understood as a process involving several different
patterns of behavior. In other words, Congressmen
reach decisions by employing and relying on a variety
of decision processes, rules and aids that vary by
circumstances, conditions, and contexts. Thus, for
those who use this approach, the study of congressional behavior and decision-making is better served
by a dynamic approach that synthesizes several
different models than by a static model that stresses
generalizations.

As noted in Chapter I, a major limitation of the
contextual approach is the lack of explicated
theory. This section will attept to formally state
the theory implied by contextual approaches.

The specific theory ("theory": taken in the
strict sense to mean an explanation of directional
relationships among dependent and independent
variables[1]) which is implicit in the major contextual schemes is, succinctly stated, that "issue
characteristics" (independent variable) strongly
affect decision-making behavior in Congress (dependent variable). Issues having characteristics commonly considered to make for low-profile problems
(e.g., technicality, complexity, low visibility, low
conflict, low salience, routineness) are associated

with narrow decision referents and specialist-dominated decision-making processes. On the other hand, issues with the opposite characteristics (e.g., nontechnical, nonroutine, high conflict, high visibility, high salience, comprehensiveness) are associated with broad, or expanded, forms and styles of legislative behavior.

This theory is not, of course, explicitly stated in a single piece. But, despite the enormous diversity of work in the contextual school, it is clear that the basic approach of most scholars who have a conditional perspective at least implicitly posits the theory that the "issue characteristics" of a bill will determine both how it is handled and responded to by the legislature (macro aspect) and how individual legislators reach a decision on it (micro aspect). Although Lowi posits a link between policy type and political arena, subsequent critiques by Ripley and Franklin, Vogler, Jones, Cobb and Elder, and Price make it clear that the major relationship in contextual schemes is one between issue characteristics and policy relationships. Ripley and Franklin conclude that "The argument has been made ...that different relationships have varying degrees of importance in determining final policy actions depending on the kind of issue at stake."[2] Vogler discusses how on some types of issues pressure groups and their lobbyists are influential; on others they are not.[3] Jones draws relationships among "issue-area characteristics," on one hand, and "institutional characteristics," decision-making characteristics" and "policy characteristics" on the other.[4] Contextual literature implies that how decision-makers define an issue will determine how they will react to it. Few authors follow the Lowi scheme which holds that decision-making is affected by policy substance. In fairness to Lowi, however, his three-fold scheme does imply an issue-based model. Certainly, distributive, regulatory, and redistributive policies can be distinguished in terms of issue dimensions. Lowi's distributive issues are very similar to low-grade issues, while redistributive issues might be considered hot, with regulatory issues somewhere in between.

The clearest expression of the proposition that the characteristics of an issue will sharply influence how a member makes up his mind is found

both in Cobb and Elder and in Price. For Cobb and
Elder, the less routine, technical, complex,
specific, and immediately relevant an issue is, and
the more visible, controversial, costly, comprehensive, and significant it is, the more likely the
issue will be resolved in an expanded or larger
public.[5] When the opposite conditions are
present,the decision is likely to be thrashed out
within a narrow or specific public comprised
primarily of those affected or those for whom the
decision is immediately relevant. In Price's words,
"the degree of conflict an issue is thought to entail
and its perceived salience to the electorate . . .
influence both the distribution of legislators'
policy-making 'investments' and the extent to which
they take their bearings from broader interests."[6]

For democratic theory, the implications of
contextual theory are to reaffirm the contention of
E.E. Schattschneider,[7] V.O. Key,[8] David
Truman,[9] and Robert Dahl[10] that the American
system, if not always actually democratic, is
democratic on important or "hot" issues and, more
importantly, potentially so on almost all issues.
True, certain kinds of low-grade decisions may be
reached with reference to only those who are most
immediately affected, with broader choice and
countervailing pressure not always present. But,
contextual theory assumes checks will become
available if dissatisfaction with prevailing policies
escalates controversy to the extent that "potential"
or "latent" groups are activated and mobilized and
that, to paraphrase Dahl, "homo civici" become "homo
politici."[11] In sum, America is democratic not
because all decisions are made according to the
precepts of democratic pluralism, but because (a) the
widespread and diverse nature of political resources
makes it possible to resolve issues in a competitive
manner if sufficient opposition should develop and
(b) political elites are restrained by the political
power of broader publics in that elites must
constantly anticipate the reactions of broader
publics when making narrow or specific policy.

Theoretical Rationale: Variable Decision Modes as a
Strategy for Coping with "Constrained" Rationality

A theory is more than a statement of relationship
among variables. It is an explanation of the
relationship. It offers the reasons why certain

31

relationships should be expected. As noted in Chapter 1, contextual literature lacks a formal rationale. The purpose of this section is to formulate a theoretical justification for the contextual approach to the legislative process.

The specific rationale for the contextual theory of legislative behavior is provided by four different literatures: (1) organization decision-making with its emphasis on decision constraints and decision rules, (2) legislative behavior's notion of cue-taking, (3) E.E. Schattschneider's thesis concerning the "scope of conflict," and (4) micro investment theory. Combining the concepts of "decision constraints," "variable decision rules," Schattschneider's "contagion of conflict" theory, and "investment incentives" provides a reasonable explanation for the theoretical expectations of the contextual approach. The specific rationale, as gleaned from these literatures, is as follows: decision-making constraints within Congress lead members to employ various decision rules that vary according to the inducements to participation present in different decision arenas.

The theory may be explained as follows. Members face more than 1,500 recorded floor roll-call votes each session in Congress. Those votes, as Matthews and Stimson emphasize, are cast under conditions of constrained rationality due to the large number of decisions, the varied scope of these decisions, the technical complexity of many bills, the presence of time limitations, and the limitations of staff assistance.[12] To cope, members classify the 1,500 votes into different issue contexts or categories, devising a different shortcut or decision rule for each context. In Fredrick Cleaveland's words, issue contexts affect "the way members of Congress perceive a policy proposal that comes before them, how they consciously or unconsciously classify it for study, and what group of policies they believe it related to."[13] To Cleaveland, "such issue contexts strongly influence legislative outcomes because their structure helps determine the approach for analysis . . . as well as the advice and expertise that enjoys privileged access."[14] In contextual writings the inference is that some votes, which members might consider hot or high-profile, provide incentives for member involvement. These are votes high in political stakes. They are votes on which members experience pressure and on which they themselves feel concerned and interested. Other votes, which might be considered low-profile or "low-grade," are basically disinteresting to them due to the lack of perceived political stakes.

The reason why low-profile decisions are expected to be based on narrow or specialist referents, while broad decision referents will provide bearings for controversial, hot issues, is that only a few actors are involved in noncontroversial issues, but many actors are involved in controversial ones. Presumably, on low-grade issues that do not interest a member, do not entail political pressure and high decision costs, and generally are not well known, the member is willing to base the decision on the "specialist" or on "narrow" criteria. So-called hot issues, in comparison, provide sufficient incentives for "broader" behavior. In other words, on controversial issues, Congressmen, reflecting expanded inputs and knowing that many are watching, feel compelled to cast their vote decisions in terms of broader, perhaps more political, criteria. On the other hand, on noncontroversial issues, where few are heard from and few are watching, deference to specialists or narrow criteria may be appropriate.

Theoretical Operationalization: A Variation on a Theme of John Kingdon's "Congressmen's Voting Decisions"

The ultimate validity of an analytical theory is determind by the extent to which it comports with reality. To insure that this criterion is satisfied, it is imperative that dependent and independent variables be specified and operationalized and the presumed relationship tested with "hard" data. This section will relate the procedures with which the contextual theory of legislative decision-making was operationalized and tested.

The unit of analysis of this study is recorded floor votes in the U.S. House. The appropriateness of studying floor votes and their validity as indicators of the congressional decision-making process has been a topic of some contention in the literature. Criticisms are made contending that roll calls reflect very little about the Congress. There are three formidable arguments along these lines. First is the position that seems to inhere in "policy" case studies. It is that struggles at the subcommittee and committee levels concerning the wording of a particular bill are more important in determining congressional outputs than a floor vote. Second, as T.V. Smith emphasizes, each bill involves a number of "issues," and it is difficult to determine which issue is decisive for the member.   In his words,

> The predicament of the legislator is that every vote is a dozen votes upon as many issues all wrapped up together...and given a single number. . . . To decide what issue of the many hidden in each bill one wants to vote upon is delicate, but to make certain that the vote will be actually on that rather than upon another issue is indelicate presumption.[15]

Third, as Anderson, et al. note in their Legislative Roll-Call Analysis, focusing on the final vote of a member on a given bill may mask some very important and relevant legislative activity on the part of that member, activity that may in fact be at variance with his roll-call commitment.

> Although methods of roll-call analysis provide information about the voting behaviors of legislators, one cannot with confidence infer from information about voting behavior to information about the behavior of legislators in other phases of the legislative process. For example, the fact that a legislator is discerned to vote in a highly partisan way does not necessarily indicate anything about the partisanship of his behavior off the floor of the legislative chamber.[16]

Despite these criticisms, this research is based on recorded floor votes. In doing so, it is assumed that the floor vote, although obviously an incomplete and imperfect data source, merits the attention of students of legislative decision-making because it is a publicly recorded decision point that is used to "legitimate" public policies. As Truman notes, "Like statistics on elections, they [the roll-call votes] represent discrete acts the fact of whose occurrence is not subject to dispute."[17] Although, an

34

articulate member of Congress did offer during the
course of interviewing:

> Why are you studying floor votes? I don't
> think they reflect the things thought to be
> important around here. You should be asking
> about subcommittee and committee participa-
> tion and how offices are set up to handle
> constituent services. Those things reflect
> real member priorities.

And although some recent empirical evidence indicates
that members spend less time on lawmaking than on
constituency service,[18] the nearly 1,500 recorded
votes that members are now asked to make each session
of Congress and the 318 hours the House devotes to
them (approximately one-sixth of the total time in
session)[19] must loom as an important concern for
the individual Congressman. The importance of
roll-calls to members is certainly indicated by the
awareness of members that their votes are monitored
and by their efforts to achieve a certain kind of
record. Moreover, on close votes, floor decisions
determine the direction of public policy. Thus,
although the student of legislative decision-making
should not relegate himself exclusively to floor
decisions, roll-call floor votes provide a salient
data source. At the very least, they constitute a
hard decision point at which all members, regardless
of committee assignment, must commit themselves.

The instrument employed for gathering data to
test the guiding hypothesis of this book is a
variation of the interview questionnaire used by
Kingdon in Congressman's Voting Decisions.[20]
Kingdon asked rotating, stratified, random samples of
House members how they reached a decision on specific
floor votes cast within the past week--i.e., members
were asked to recount the various factors and forces
that led to their eventual decision. At least three
distinct advantages seem to be offered by Kingdon's
research approach.

First, in comparison with roll-call analysis
(previously, the major source of legislative behavior
data), the Kingdon method presents a most direct way
of observing congressional decisionmaking. As
Anderson, et al. note:

35

"techniques of roll call analysis themselves
do not explain to the researcher the patterns
he may discern in voting. . . . They do not
provide information about the factors or
variables operating in a situation that
explain or account for these variations."[21]

In Ripley's words,

Typically, these studies examine the
relationship between potential cues and roll
call voting on the floor. They do not prove
causality in the sense that a member
consciously searches for a cue, receives it,
and behaves accordingly; instead they
infer that patterns of behavior reflect
patterns of cue-giving and cue-taking.[22]

In contrast, Kingdon's cue study provides an
instrument for obtaining data firsthand from
decision-makers themselves concerning how they made
up their minds. As such, it avoids the risky
enterprise in roll-call studies of attempting to
infer, extrapolate, or second-guess on questions
pertaining to legislator decision processes.

A second advantage of the Kingdon approach stems
from its "issue-by-issue" orientation. By studying
aspects of a legislator's decision-making behavior on
a vote-by-vote basis with open-ended questions,
Kingdon overcomes the major weaknesses of static
designs that, as noted in Chapter 1, plague
legislative behavior research of role conceptions and
decison modes.

Third, the Kingdon approach affords the
opportunity for the researcher to tap salient aspects
of the political culture of political leaders and
elites as related and reconstructed by leaders and
elites. The fact that scholars have failed to do
this in the past is seen by some as an inherent
weakness of political science research on Capitol
Hill. As James S. Young notes in his The Washington
Community,

Political science has yet to confront
squarely the proposition that the governing
group in Washington . . . has an inner life
of its own--a special culture which carries
with it prescriptions and cues for behavior

that may be far more explicit than those originating outside the group, and no less consequential for the conduct of government.[23]

The advantage of Kingdon's data collection procedure is that it provides glimpses into their world in the words of members. By interviewing the member in a face-to-face situation, the researcher has an opportunity to tap the member's attitudes, certainly a better opportunity than with mailed or "dropped off" questionnaires that members routinely delegate to staffers.

Despite these major assets, a close inspection of Kingdon's work reveals, at least for our purposes, three shortcomings that limit its utility in a search for issue-based patterns of legislative decision-making.

The first problem pertains to the nature of the questions Kingdon asked and the nature of the inferences he drew from them. Table 2.1 displays Kingdon's interview schedule. As can be seen, it appears that Kingdon is asking questions about information sources, communications, and cognitive procedures. In his text, however, he draws conclusions about the relative influence of various actors operating within the legislator's "force field." This poses several problems. "Information," "communications," and "influence" constitute very different aspects of a decisionmaker's cognitive map. The fact that a Congressman agrees with an actor who has access to him and gives him information is no indication of the actor's influence on the Congressman. Also, some actors (e.g., groups, parties) can be influential via other agents (e.g., constituency). For example, "party," although not frequently mentioned as a decision-making influence in the Kingdon study, may nonetheless be influential through the medium of state delegation. State delegations, which are frequently cited as an influence, are in fact party groupings of representatives from the same state. The fact that they are influential indicates that party as a label has an impact on voting, although not necessarily through leaders. Likewise, the position of interest groups, which is also not frequently mentioned, may be "carried" into decision-making through other members who lobby on behalf of group interests.

Table 2.1

Kingdon Questionnaire

1. (Cite the vote picked.) How did you go about making up your mind? What steps did you go through?

2. Were there any fellow congressmen that you paid attention to? If no: I don't mean just following them; I mean looking to them for information and guidance. If yes: Who? Why them?

3. What did the party leadership do? How about informal groups within the party? (e.g., Democratic Study Group)

4. Did you talk to staff people about this?

5. What do you think your constituents wanted you to do on this? How was your mail?

6. Did anyone in the administration or executive branch contact you?

7. Did you hear anything from any organizations?

8. Was there anything that you read that affected how you saw it?

9. At any point along the way, were you ever uncertain about how to vote

Source: Kingdon's Congressmen's Voting Decisions, p. 287.

Finally, the questionnaire fails to distinguish between what Kovenock refers to in his "Communications Audit" as factual information and evaluative information (i.e., information used for making judgments).[24]

A second problem which limits the use of Kingdon for a contextual study is that no systematic data is provided on how Congressmen perceived or defined the issue. With the exception of Kingdon's own perceptions concerning the relative public salience of the various pieces of legislation studied, no attention is given to the characteristics of different issues.[25] Moreover, Kingdon chose only those votes that were (to him) politically "important" and "interesting." All of these were, in Kingdon's words, "big votes." There was no attempt to insure a representative sample of legislation. As he notes, deliberately excluded were "the vast number [of votes] that appeared to be noncontroversial and routine.[26]

A third limitation is the absence of a formal analysis of the legislative backgrounds of the sampled legislation (e.g., committee vote, type of rule, amendments over committee objections, party leadership activity, other House action, degree and kind of presidential involvement). At the very least, such information is required to identify various patterns of legislative decision-making. If the contextual theory is valid, it is reasonable to expect that differences in legislative backgrounds will be related to differences in micro decision processes.

Table 2.2 presents the questionnaire used here in this study of the conditional nature of congressional decision-making. It differs from Kingdon's decision-making approach in two respects. First, various components of actor cognitive map are separated rather than intertwined. Second, actors were asked to define the characteristics of the issue on which they made a decision.

To operationalize the dependent variable of legislator behavior and decision-making process, a distinction was made among four components of the member's cognitive map: (1) force field or policy arena, (2) information sources, (3) decision modes and determinants, and (4) role conception. Each

Table 2.2

Questionnaire

1. Re the _____ vote, who did you hear from or talk to concerning how to vote?

2. Was there anyone else you paid attention to?

3. I imagine that these kinds of communications and information sources are helpful to you in different ways.

   a) Who was helpful in informing you about the facts of the bill?

   b) In your estimation who/what was most decisive in helping you make up your mind?

4. What kind of issue do you feel this is?

   a) Do you feel it is complex? y   n
   b) Do you feel it is technical? y   n
   c) Is there a lot of conflict and disagreement on this bill? y   n
   d) Is it major legislation? y   n
   e) 1) Is this legislation important to the people of your district? y   n
      2) Are they aware of it? y   n
   f) Did you receive a lot of mail on it? y   n
   g) Do you feel that your vote on this could affect (1) your renomination
                                                            y   n
                                                        (2) your reelection?
                                                            y   n
   h) Do you feel that this is a routine matter? y   n
   i) How strongly do you personally feel on this issue? 1 2 3
   j) When did you make up your mind on this issue?
   k) Is it a tough decision? y   n

5. When making up your mind on this piece of legislation what did you rely o constituency wishes, your own opinion, or something else

6. Was your focus the national interest, local interest, both?

7. How informed do you feel about the issues raised in this legislation?
   1 not at all   2 somewhat   3 very well

8. Did you put much thought into it?

refers to a different aspect of micro decision-
making. Each has been used in various studies of
decision-making and, therefore, each seems appropriate for an investigation for a contextual effect
within the Congress.

Table 2.3 summarizes these four components of
cognitive map and the aspect of decision-making to
which they refer.

Force fields, or "field of forces" as Kingdon
refers to them,[27] describe who the member heard
from or paid attention to in the course of the
decision. This concept is similar to that of "policy
arena" as used by Lowi. Both focus on the input a
member receives on a given issue. Both refer to
those actors a legislative decision-maker feels were
relevant to his decision--i.e., those whose position
he actively considered when making up his mind. To
tap this notion of force field, policy arena, and
relevant actor, questions #1, "Re the _____ vote,
who did you hear from or talk to concerning this
vote?" and #2, "was there anyone else you paid
attention to?" were employed.

Information sources, as used here, pertain
directly to what Kovenock refers to as "factual
premises."[28] They are communications and contacts
that provide information about the specific wording
and facts of a bill and the issue raised by them.
To study this component of cognitive map, question
#3a was used: "Who was helpful in informing you
about the facts of the bill?"

As an aspect of cognitive map, "decision
referents" or "determinants" refer to those forces,
factors, and actors that were decisive in leading a
member to make up his mind. They are the "evaluative
premises" in Kovenock's lexicon. They are the "shortcuts" or "rules" that the member uses when reaching a
decision. Question #3b, "In your estimation who/what
was most decisive in helping you make up your mind?"
was used to study this aspect of decision-making.
Although it is beyond the scope of this inquiry to
assess patterns of "influence," this question seems
to probe influence in a more direct fashion than
Kingdon's correlations of member-actor agreement.

Table 2.3

Four Components of the Member's Cognitive Map

Component	Decision-Making Aspect
Force Field/Policy Arena	Communications Input--Attempts to influence to which member pays attention in making a decision
Information Sources	Actors/Sources from which member learns about the factual aspect of a bill
Determinants	Actors/Decision Rules on which members rely when making a decision
Role	Broad Philosophical Perspective with which members observe the representational aspects of a bill

Role conceptions are broad orientations members have toward the legislative system and their place in it. They are the basic perspectives with which legislators view their decision processes. Questions #5, "When making up your mind on this piece of legislation what did you rely on: constituency wishes, your own opinion, perhaps a combination of both, or something else?"[29] and #6, "Was your focus the national interest, local interest, both?" were used to gather data on congressional role perceptions.

The real advantage of using four different components of decision-makers' cognitive map is that it affords the opportunity to identify actor involvement and importance more fully. Kingdon's general model looks at actor influence in a general way.[30] It seems reasonable to expect, however, that the importance of various actors may vary according to different aspects of cognitive map--i.e., actors who may not serve as a decision cue may nonetheless be important as an information source. The four-fold distinction employed here is capable of detecting the range of contributions each actor makes to legislative decison-making.

To operationalize the independent variable of "issue contexts" in an abstract fashion--i.e., with maximum generality--issue dimensions were studied. Several prominent attempts have been made to differentiate various issue dimensions.[31] An integration of these works reveals at least ten dimensions on which issues are thought to vary: (1) technicality, (2) complexity, (3) specificity, (4) routineness, (5) visibility, (6) temporal relevance, (7) controversiality (which includes actor involvement), (8) social significance, (9) decision costs, and (10) electoral salience. In this study, there was an attempt to operationalize all ten dimensions.

Data were obtained from perceptual, objective and subjective sources. Perceptual data were gathered with the questionnaire. Questions #4 (a through k) and #8 were used to obtain the member's definition and perception of the "issue characteristics" of the particular vote at hand.

Objective data sources refer to various parliamentary and nonparliamentary aspects of a bill obtained from documents and other public sources. Source material includes committee report,

Congressional Record for the day of debate,
Congressional Quarterly and National Journal
coverage, copies of the bill and its rule, and
personal research. Legislative background data coded
for each examined vote are: type of rule, margin of
rule adoption, type of vote, margin of passage, party
unity for both Democrats and Republicans, index of
party likeness, number of amendments passed over
committee objections, committee vote, and party
endorsements. Other examples of objective indicators
are: mention as a story in the Washington Post and
Congressional Quarterly, amount of money involved and
projected time as obtained from the committee report
on each bill, the President's position on the
legislation as obtained from Congressional Quarterly,
and listing as a "main issue facing the country
today" in a Yankelovich poll.[32]

     "Researcher subjective" sources involve the
attribution of characteristics to the vote by the
researcher on the basis of interview sessions with a
committee staff person close to the bill. Specific
characteristics investigated in this fashion were the
role of Congress vis-a-vis the presidency on the
issue (i.e., initiator, modifier/broker, or
facilitator/ratifier[33]), the repetitiveness of the
issue, the specificity of the issue, and the degree
of policy change that would result from the bill.
Although categorizations of this type are strictly
judgemental, they have been commonly accepted by
students of the policy process.[34]

     Table 2.4 presents a summary of the indicators of
issue characteristics employed in this study.
Indicators are displayed by type, issue dimension
measured, and data source. Appendix A details the
presumed hot/low profile values of each.

     This research design also employed controls for
member backgrounds and constituency characteristics.
Background characteristics used were party, regional
section, length of service,[35] membership on the
Republican policy committee or Democratic steering
and policy committee,[36] ratings by certain interest
groups (ADA, ACA, CORE, and Chamber of Commerce) for
the second session of the 94th Congress,[37] party
unity scores, bipartisan support score, conservative
coalition score for both the second session of the
94th[38] and the first session of the 95th,[39] and

Table 2.4

Summary of Issue Characteristics Indicators

Type of Indicators	Issue Dimension Measured	Data Source
Perceptual (Questionnaire)	Complexity	Question #4a (complexity)
	Technicality	Question #4b (technicality)
	Controversiality	Question #4c (conflict)
	Salience	Questions #4e1 (constituency importance) and #4i (personal feelings)
	Social Significance	Question #4d (major status)
	Routineness	Question #4h (routine matter)
	Visibility	Questions #4f (mail) and #4e2 (constituency awareness)
	Decision Cost	Questions #4g1 (renomination effect) #4g2 (reelection effect), and #8 (thought)
Objective, Legislative Background	Political Heat	Type of Rule (e.g., closed, modified open, open)
		Rule Margin (CQ)
		Democratic Unity)
		Republican Unity) Computed from
		Index of Likeness) CQ data
		Amendment over Committee Objections (interviews)
		Committee Vote (committee report)
		Minority Report (committee report)
		Presidential Involvement (CQ)
		Democratic Policy Endorsement (policy committee)
		Republican Policy Endorsement (policy committee)
		Role of Congress (legislative history)

Table 2.4--Continued

Type of Indicator	Dimension	Data Source
	Visibility	CQ Box Score
		CQ Story
		Washington Post Box Score
		Washington Post Story
	Social Significance	Standing in Polls as a Major Issue Facing the Country (Yankelovich Poll)
		Money (Committee report)
		Time Frame (Committee report)
Researcher Subjective	Newness/ Recurringness	Interviews with Committee Staff
	Change	Interviews with Committee Staff
	Specificity	Interviews with Committee Staff

presidential support scores for the first session of the 95th.[40]

Constituency characteristics employed were the percent of the constituency that is urban, the percent of the population that falls within a standard metropolitan statistical area (SMSA), the percent nonwhite, the percent of families earning $15,000 or more, the percent of families below the low-income level, the percent of white-collar workers, and the percent of owner-occupied units.[41] Also used were political characteristics of the district such as the percentage with which the member won the last election and whether or not, in the case of freshmen, the district was a "switch" type--i.e., if party control of the district changed hands.[42]

Appendix B details the operationalization of control variables. Each of them was entertained as possible, alternative explanations to the contextual theory. As noted in Chapter I, the basic thrust of static research designs implicitly seems to be that the most meaningful variations in legislative behavior occur among different types of legislators. In other words, all legislators utilize the same basic process. But, for reasons that can be attributed to differences in background, different kinds of legislators will have different kinds of normative premises, and, therefore, they will make different decisions, although the basic decision process itself is universal. If the static approach is valid, we should expect these control variables to account for most of the meaningful variance in decision-making behavior. If, on the other hand, the contextual approach is valid, most variance should occur according to differences in issue contexts.

Data Collection Procedures: An Inside Strategy

Data were collected over a four-month period beginning the first week of March 1977 and ending the first week of July 1977. Allowing for two, week-long recess periods (Easter and Memorial Day), 15 weeks of intensive interviewing was undertaken. In that period 81 different members were interviewed, 31 different floor votes were studied, and 361 questionnaires were completed.

The most formidable problem confronted was that of gaining access to members. There are several reasons why it is difficult to obtain interviews. First, members receive numerous requests for meetings by those seeking to influence or sell, by those with a problem to solve, or by those just wanting to visit. Second, there are enormous institutionalized demands on the time of members. As several prominent congressional scholars noted in conversations with this author, within the last 10 years these demands have increased immensely.[43] Third, within the last decade, political scientists and their students have flocked to the Hill, resulting in an often-outworn welcome for political researchers bent on gathering attitudinal data from members.[44] Finally, as Kingdon emphasizes "Asking a Congressman to divulge how he went about casting a vote in a specific instance is a potentially touchy subject."[45] To cope with the problem of access, an inside strategy within the U.S. House was pursued.

For two reasons, the House was the sole focus rather than both the House and the Senate. First, it was felt that Senators, as the result of state-wide responsibilities, greater visibility, and more committee assignments, would simply be more difficult to have access to. Second, the House and Senate are so different as institutions that comparisons would be extremely difficult if data were collected from both houses. (A note on comparisons with the Senate is contained in the postscript to this book.)

After consultation with several experienced researchers,[46] it was decided that having a member sponsor the research would minimize the risks of being turned down or referred to staff. Accordingly, the support of Congressman Jim Lloyd (D., Calif.) was requested and graciously granted. Congressman Lloyd made office facilities available and, most important, had a member of his staff--Marsaleete Harmon--make appointments with members in the Congressman's name. Although it might be arued that Mr. Lloyd's sponsorship might have contaminated the sample by yielding responses mainly from his friends and ideological counterparts, his moderate Democrat stance, position as zone whip for California, and his status as an officer within both his class and state delegation seemed to assure and in fact did provide balanced access. (See Appendix C)

In undertaking the research, two very critical sampling procedures were performed: (a) the sampling of members, and (b) the sampling of decisions or votes.

To sample members, Kingdon's strategy of rotating sub-samples was followed. Kingdon used four samples of 15 members each, rotated on a weekly basis. Three advantages are present in this procedure. First, 15 interviews seem to be all a researcher can hope to accomplish within a week. Second, by rotating weekly, no member will be interviewed more than once a month. In Kingdon's words, "Under such conditions, very little response fatigue--annoyance, contamination, interviewer effects--was in evidence."[47] Third, frequent brief visits develop a sense of familiarity and trust with the respondent that may produce a higher response rate for appointments and greater candor in subsequent interview sessions. Sampling procedures are detailed in Appendix C.

One final point should be emphasized concerning the sampling of members. The sample is randomly chosen and stratified, but no pretense of representativeness is made. It is not a probabilistic sample, and, therefore, in the process of data analysis, the usual inferential measures and statistical manipulations do not apply. Data will be analyzed, however, in the tradition of great classics in legislative behavior research by Kingdon, Fenno,[48] and Deckard:[49] impressionistic searches for "the feel" and "the blood" of Congress on the basis of summary statistics that measure for broad tendencies.

To sample votes an effort was made to obtain as much diversity as possible. As noted above, Kingdon excluded "noncontroversial" and "routine" votes. As he stated, his study is based on "some of the major issues of the decade."[50] Here, because of the desire to test the notion that different kinds of issues are associated with different decision behaviors, it was necessary to obtain a diversified assortment of votes. To promote a mix of the routine with the major issues, a member of Mr. Lloyd's staff--Ms. Lisa Phillips--was consulted each week. On each Friday, Ms. Phillips, who assists the Congressman in his performance of zone whip duties, would recommend one each of a controversial or major or important vote and a routine matter from the past week's schedule. These would then be the subject of

49

the next week's interviews. Two pieces of legislation were studied for each of the 16 weeks during
which research was conducted, with the exception of
one week cut short by a recess. In that case only
one vote was studied. This yielded a sample of 31
different votes. Appendix D displays a synopsis of
the sampled votes together with the number of
interviews collected for each vote. Those votes
considered "major" or "important" were the House
ethics code, President Carter's proposed tax cuts,
the Rhodesian chrome ban, common situs picketing,
strip-mining regulation, defeated budget targets, the
Clean Air Act, the creation of the Energy Department,
the Hyde (anti-abortion) amendment, the congressional
pay raise, the repeal of the Hatch Act, federal
regulation of debt collection practices, a proposed
Department of Health, Education, and Welfare ban on
saccharin, and Presidential reorganization
authority. The remaining 17 votes were considered
less important.

Summary and Findings Concerning Issue Characteristics

The theory that different kinds of issues are
related to differences in decision-making behavior
implies three important ancillary assumptions: (1)
that legislators themselves think in terms of issue
contexts and characteristics; (2) that different
categories of legislators similarly perceive
different kinds of issues; and (3) that certain issue
characteristics will factor together in a
dichotomized fashion as either hot or high-profile
issues and low-grade or low-profile issues.

Data for investigating the validity of these
propositions were provided by two questionnaire
sources. The first is a general, open-ended question
(#4) that asked the member to describe in his own
words what kind of issue he felt was at stake: "What
kind of issue do you feel this is?" The second data
source is the series of short, closed-answer
questions that appear as #4a-i, and 4k and #7. Also
analyzed were the objective and subjective measures
of issue characteristics and the control variables.

Neither space nor emphasis permit a thorough test
of these assumptions. Such a test is available from
another source.[51] However, for the purposes of our
study of the context of congressional decision
behavior a summary is most useful.

50

First members develop categorizations and classificatory schemes that they use to differentiate various broad types of legislation. In other words, they identify different decision settings. Some votes are controversial; others are nonconflictual. Some votes are tough; others are simple. Some votes are emotional, visible, and atypical; others are nonemotional, nonvisible, and typical. Some votes involve intense political pressure; others are devoid of pressure. There are routine votes, recurring votes, monumental and watershed votes, and votes of conscience. Members themselves use the hot/low-profile distinction.

Second, the data show that members themselves differentiate among votes with general concepts. This is demonstrated by both responses to the general question asking members to describe the kind of issue at hand and in their differentiation of votes on the basis of the various, specific perceptual dimensions.

Third, although not all members were in agreement concerning the specific characteristics of each vote, most defined the issue similarly. The data show evidence that several variables--most notably length of service, committee membership, party, and electoral security--have some but not much impact on issue definition. Thus, although most Congressmen will tend to see the same issue in the same way--indicating different kinds of issues--how a specific member defines a vote may be colored not only by issue contexts in Congress but also, at times, by his partisanship, status in the legislature, district political situation, and involvement with the bill itself.

Finally, contrary to the expectations of many authors, the data do not show a high degree of interrelationship among issue characteristics. Indicators do not linearly clump nor correlate together in neat clusters of issue contexts as many authors have presumed. Evidently, members' perceptions of some dimensions are unrelated to their perceptions of others. Although there is some relationship among characteristics in terms of a hot/low-profile continuum, there are numerous instances where a relationship does not appear or where there is association in the direction opposite

our expectations. As such, subsequent analysis
will treat each indicator as a separate factor.

The task at hand, then, is to determine if the
variations in issue definition are associated with
patterned differences in members' cognitive maps.
The fact that different members will often perceive
issues differently provides justification for
examining the relationships between perceptual
characteristics and decision-making behavior. By
correlating perceptual characteristics with
decision-making behavior, one is actually searching
for decision-making patterns on the basis of the
member's definition of the kind of issue at hand.

Summary and Conclusions

A recent emphasis in legislative behavior
literature contends that Congressmen reach decisions
differently in different kinds of situations. It is
the notion that there are different decision "tracks"
or "arenas" in Congress that are related to different
patterns of decision-making behavior. A close review
of this work reveals serious shortcomings in both
conceptualization and research. The purpose of this
chapter has been to formally state the contextual
theory and to provide a research design for
operationalizing and testing it. If the basic
assumptions of the contextual scheme are correct,
legislative behavior is best understood not with a
general or static model but with a conditional
perspective that is based on an issue-by-issue
approach and grounded in an appreciation of issue
characteristics.

Table 2.5 highlights the major features of the
research design. As can be seen there, the major
theory with which a search for a context will be made
is one of varying specialist influence. It
hypothesizes that low-grade issues will involve
narrow "policy arenas" and specialist- or
subgovernment-dominated decision-making processes,
while hot issues will involve "broad" or "expanded"
legislative behavior responses. Hot issues, high in
political incentives, provide sufficient inducements
for member involvement. Under hot conditions,
members are likely to make a decision on the basis of
their ideology. Conversely, low-grade issues,
lacking incentives, are apt to be based on shortcuts,

52

Table 2.5

Synopsis of Research Design

Topic:
The contextual aspects of Congressional decision-making.

Problem:
Immediate--Replication of Kingdon's study employing revised questionnaire in order to search for possible contextual patterns in the Congress.

Theoretical (place to return)--Conditional nature of the democratic process in the U.S. Congress.

Importance of the Topic:
Re the functioning of the democratic process, the conditions under which the legislature functions in its classic sense of debating, deliberating, checking and balancing specialists, utilizing expanded cue and information networks and broadened role conceptions.

Focus:
Patterned differences in issue characteristics, legislative backgrounds, force fields, information and cue networks, decision processes, and role conceptions.

Theory:
A legislator's policy relationships are a function of issue contexts. Issues are said to vary on the following dimensions: technicality, complexity, specificity, routineness, visibility, temporal relevance, controversiality, decision cost, and social significance. The more routine, technical, complex, specific, and the less visible, controversial, costly, and significant an issue is, the more likely legislators are to depend on specialists. This is because, in the absence of strong political pressure, legislators will defer to specialists (within and outside the legislature) as a decision short cut. When the opposite issue characteristics are present, we expect low specialist dependence, an expanded policy arena, and a broader role conception.

Central Research Question:
Do issue characteristics affect the policy arenas, information sources, decision modes, and role conceptions of legislators?

Hypothesis:
Variations in the configuration of issue characteristics will be related to differences in force fields, information sources, decision processes, and role conceptions, with low grade issues associated with narrow forms of legislative behavior and hot issues associated with expanded or broad behavior.

53

Table 2.5-(continued)

Null
Hypothesis: Jackson: "Decision-making is largely invariant by
                     type of legislation."

Alternative   Actor differences, not issue differences, account for
Hypothesis: major variations in legislative behavior.

Variables: 1. Dependent--Decision-making processes as observed in
                         force fields, information sources, decision modes,
                         role conceptions.
                     2. Independent--Issue characteristics (objective and
                         subjective measures), legislative backgrounds.
                     3. Control--Member and constituency characteristics,
                         majority/minority status.

Data: Interviews, documents and records.

Method: Investigate the extent to which patterns of the dependent
                     variable are associated with patterns of the independent
                     variable. Examine which of the objective and subjective
                     issue characteristics are most associated with variations
                     in the independent variable.

Possible Policy   Specify the conditions under which Congressmen exhibit
Relevance: various forms of legislative behavior.

Unit of   Recorded floor votes, U.S. House of Representatives.
Analysis:

Task: To determine if our understanding of legislative be-
                     havior, as derived from static models and general
                     propositions, is enhanced by a contextual, "issue-
                     based" approach.

*John E. Jackson, "Statistical Models of Senate Role Call Voting,"
American Political Science Review, 65 (1971), 468.

such as deference to the perceived knowledge and expertise of others.

The theoretical rationale for the contextual scheme of legislative behavior and its predicted relationships is provided by four different literatures: (1) organization decision-making theory, (2) legislative behavior, (3) democratic theory, and (4) micro investment theory. Specifically, the rationale is as follows: because of decision-making constraints, legislators employ various decision rules according to the incentives for involvement present in different political arenas.

This study will test the concextual theory with data provided through a research strategy fashioned after John Kingdon's. Kingdon obtained data directly from members. They were asked to reconstruct their decision process on specific votes. The questionnaire used here differs from Kingdon's in three respects. First, data were collected on four different aspects of decisionmaking behavior: communications, information sources, decision modes, and role orientations. Second, issue characteristics were systematically studied. Various perceptual, objective, and subjective data sources were used as indicators of issue characteristics. Third, both hot and low-profile votes were studied.

Subsequent chapters will analyze interview data collected using four rotating, stratified samples. Chapters III through VI will analyze findings pertaining to the four aspects of members' cognitive map. Chapter III will focus on force fields, chapter IV on information sources, chapter V on determinants and decision modes and chapter VI on role orientations.

If the hypothesis is true, the expectation here is that on low-grade issues (i.e., issues that are technical, complex, specific, routine, nonvisible, temporally relevant, noncontroversial, nonsocially significant, low in decision cost, and low in electoral salience, Congressmen (a) will have narrow, specialist-dominated force fields, (b) will have low information as a result of perfunctory scan and low volume of information, (c) will rely on specialists, and (d) will employ a trustee orientation. On hot issues (i.e., votes that are nontechnical, noncomplex, nonspecific, nonroutine, visible,

55

nontemporally relevant, controversial, socially significant, high in decision cost, and electorally salient), Congressmen (a) will have full and broad force fields, (b) will have high information volume, (c) will employ ideological decision rules, and (d) will have a district role orientation. The rationale for each of these specific expectations will be detailed in subsequent chapters. For now, suffice to say that each proposition constitutes a reasonable deduction from the contextual theory.

Although this research will be "hypothesis-oriented" in that a search for the hypothesized directional relationships will guide data analysis, it should be mentioned in concluding this chapter that the study will also be explorative. Throughout, our guiding questions will be: (1) Does legislative behavior vary according to issues? (2) Does decision-making differ from issue type to issue type? In sum, what follows will be a search for "issue-based" patterns of legislative behavior and decision-making.

NOTES FOR CHAPTER II

[1]This meaning of theory is taken from the following methodo-
logical primers;" William Buchanan, Understanding Political
Variables, 2nd ed. (New York: Scribner's, 1974), pp. 7–10; Alan
C. Isaak, Scope and Methods of Political Science, rev. ed. (Home-
wood, Ill.: Dorsey, 1975), pp. 136–39; Abraham Kaplan, The
Conduct of Inquiry (Scranton, Pa.: Chandler, 1964), chapter VIII;
Eugene J. Meehan, The Theory and Method of Political Analysis
(Homewood, Ill.: Dorsey, 1965), pp. 128–34; Vernon Van Dyke,
Political Science: A Philosophical Analysis (Stanford: Stanford
University Press, 1960), pp. 38–41.

[2]Randall B. Ripley and Grace A. Franklin, Congress, the
Bureaucracy and Public Policy (Homewood, Ill.: Dorsey, 1976),
p. 166.

[3]David J. Vogler, The Politics of Congress, 2nd ed. (Boston:
Allyn, 1977), p. 297.

[4]Charles O. Jones, "Speculative Augmentation in Federal Air
Pollution Policy-Making," Journal of Politics 36 (1974): 440–46.

[5]Roger W. Cobb and Charles D. Elder, Participation in
American Politics: The Dynamics of Agenda-Building (Boston:
Allyn, 1972), p. 110 and chapter 6.

[6]David E. Price, "Policy-Making in Congressional Committees:
The Impact of 'Environmental' Factors," American Political Science
Review 72 (1978): 572.

[7]E. E. Schattschneider, The Semi-Sovereign People (New York:
Holt, 1960).

[8]V. O. Key, Jr., Public Opinion and American Democracy (New
York: Knopf, 1965).

[9]David B. Truman, The Governmental Process, 2nd ed. (New
York: Knopf, 1971).

[10]Robert A. Dahl, A Preface to Democratic Theory (Chicago:
University of Chicago Press, 1956); and Robert A. Dahl, Who
Governs? (New Haven: Yale University Press, 1961).

[11]Dahl, Who Governs?, pp. 223–28.

[12]Donald R. Matthews and James A. Stimson, Yeas and Nays
(New York: Wiley, 1975), pp. 14–17.

[13]Fredrick N. Cleaveland, "Legislating for Urban Affairs: An Overview" in Congress and Urban Problems ed. by F. N. Cleaveland (Washington, D.C.: Brookings, 1969), pp. 356-57.

[14]Ibid., p. 357.

[15]T. V. Smith as quoted in William Keefe and Morris S. Ogul, The American Legislative Process, 4th ed. (Englewood Cliffs, N.J.: Prentice-Hall, 1977), pp. 259-60.

[16]Lee F. Anderson, Meredith W. Watts, Jr., and Allen R. Wilcox, Legislative Roll-Call Analysis (Evanston: Northwestern University Press, 1965), p. 11.

[17]David B. Truman, The Congressional Party (New York: Wiley, 1959).

[18]These data were obtained from Frank Verderame, "The Electoral Con," a paper presented to Claremont Men's College. This was based on 301 returned questionnaires from Congressional offices. The data showed that 75 percent of the responding offices stressed public relations/constituency services over legislative activities. Only 4 percent stressed law-making and only 14 percent acknowledge a 50/50 prioritizing.

[19]These figures were obtained from U.S. Congress, House, Commission on Administrative Review, Scheduling the Work of the House, H. Doc. 95-23, 95th Cong., 1st Sess. (Washington, D.C.: Government Printing Office, 1977).

[20]John W. Kingdon, Congressmen's Voting Decisions (New York: Harper and Row, 1973).

[21]Anderson, Watts, ad Wilcox, Roll-Call Analysis, p. 10.

[22]Ripley, Congress, p. 71.

[23]James S. Young as quoted in Matthews and Stimson, Yeas and Nays, p. 150.

[24]David Kovenock, "Influence in the U.S. House of Representatives: A Statistical Analysis of Communications," American Politics Quarterly 1 (1973): 410-13.

[25]Kingdon, Congressmen's Voting, p. 20.

[26]Kingdon, Congressmen's Voting, pp. 292-93.

[27]Ibid, pp. 230-32, 234-35, 304.

[28]Kovenock, "Influence in the U.S. House," pp. 410-13.

[29]This is the question that Jones used to tap representative roles among members of the House Agriculture Committee. Charles O. Jones, "Representation in Congress: The Case of the House Agriculture Committee," American Political Science Review, 55 (1961): 365.

[30]Kingdon, Congressmen's Voting, p. 20 and Appendix E, passim.

[31]Cobb and Elder, Participation, pp. 96-102; Lewis A. Froman, Jr., and Randall B. Ripley, "Conditions for Party Leadership," American Political Science Review 59 (1965): 62; Price, "Policy-Making," pp. 45-46; and Warren E. Miller and Donald E. Stokes, "Constituency for Party Leadership," American Political Science Review 57 (1963): 53-54.

[32]Yankelovich poll on "The Main Issues Facing America Today," Time, 25 December 1977, p. 12.

[33]These distinctions are adapted from David E. Price, Who Makes the Laws? (Cambridge, Mass.: General Learning Press, 1972), pp. 290-91.

[34]See, for example, Dean Schooler, Science, Scientists and Public Policy (New York: Free Press, 1971), p. 64; Ripley and Franklin, Congress, pp. 16, 167-69; Price, Who Makes, pp. 290-91; and R. K. Yin and K. A. Heald, "Using the Case Survey Method to Analyze Political Studies," Adminstrative Science Quarterly 20 (1975): 372.

[35]This information was obtained from Congressional Directory.

[36]Congressional Quarterly Weekly Report, Supplement to 35 (April 30, 1977).

[37]Congressional Quarterly Weekly Report 35 (Feb. 5, 1977), pp. 220-21.

[38]1976 Congressional Quarterly Almanac 32 (Washington, D.C.: Congressional Quarterly, Inc., 1977), pp. 1000-11.

[39]Congressional Quarterly Weekly Report 36, (Jan. 7, 1978), pp. 3-8 and (Jan. 14, 1978), pp. 79-88.

[40]Congressional Quarterly Weekly Report 36 (Jan. 7, 1978), pp. 14-15.

[41]This information was obtained from Congressional District Data Book, 93rd Congress (Washington, D.C.: U.S. Government Printing Office, 1973) and its supplements for California, New York and Texas.

[42]Congressional Quarterly Weekly Report 34 (Nov. 6, 1976), pp. 3147-54.

[43]See Norman Ornstein, "What Makes Congress Run," Washington Monthly, Dec. 1973, pp. 4749 for an excellent description of how Congressmen have become busier since the 1970 Congressional Reorganization Act. As Ornstein noted in a conversation with this author, "The Congressman of today is much busier than the one interviewed by Clapp or Matthews or Kingdon."

[44]Kingdon, Congressmen's Voting, p. 285.

[45]Ibid.

[46]The author wishes to acknowledge the valuable counsel given to him with regard to inteviewing by Professors Holbert Carroll, Charles O. Jones, John W. Kingdon, Morris S. Ogul, Bert A. Rockman and James A. Stimson, and Walter Beach of the American Political Science Association.

[47]Kingdon, Congressmen's Voting, p. 278.

[48]Richard F. Fenno, Jr., "U.S. House Members in Their Constituencies," American Political Science Review 71 (1977): 883-917 (see especially p. 884).

[49]Barbara Deckard, "State Party Delegations in the U.S. House of Representatives: A Comparative Study of Group Cohesion," Journal of Politics 34 (1972): 199-222 (see especially p. 201).

[50]Kingdon, Congressmen's Voting, p. 28.

[51]David C. Kozak, Contexts of Congressional Decision Behavior, Unpublished Ph.D. dissertation, University of Pittsburgh, 1979.

CHAPTER III

THE CONDITIONAL NATURE OF CONGRESSIONAL
COMMUNICATIONS

Actors both external and internal to the legislature attempt to influence congressional decision-making. Congressional party leaders, interest groups, the President, bureaucrats, staff, and constituents, as well as other members, make deliberate attempts to shape congressional outcomes.[1] In an effort to study lobbying, political scientists have focused on communications within the Congress. They have examined who Congressmen hear from or pay attention to as they attempt to reach a decision on a floor vote. Their research has supported two major conclusions. First, for most votes, Congressmen hear from few sources to which they actually pay attention, and as Dexter has emphasized, "A Congressman hears most often from those who agree with him."[2] Second, in Kingdon's words, ". . . fellow Congressmen appear to be the most important influence on voting decision, followed by constituency."[3]

The purpose of this chapter is to investigate the conditional nature of these conclusions.

Congressional Communications:
The Member's Force Field

To understand congressional communications, political scientists have used Kingdon's concept of "field of forces," Lowi's notion of "policy arenas," and Ripley and Franklin's "policy relationships." All of these focus on who members hear from or turn to in the course of making up their minds on floor votes.

The force field or policy arena of a member refers to incoming communications received by the member from the political environment. As a concept, force field focuses on all the meaningful inputs a member considers on a policy question.

A member's force field connotes an aspect of a member's decision process that is different from information sources, decision rules, and role. As a measure of input, force field is the component of a member's cognitive map that gives the broadest possible picture of a Congressman's policy relationships. It refers to all those people who the member feels made an attempt to influence him and to whom he paid attention when deciding. It includes all the factors relevant to the member's decision. Also, force field is a good indication of lobbying activity in Congress. In comparison, information sources and decision rules, as components of cognitive map, pertain to the member's selective use of other actors. Information sources are those actors that members turn to for learning the facts of a bill. Determinants are those actors that a member relies on as a decision aid or shortcut. Role is the member's general conception of how a particular decision relates to the member's overall perspective on representation.

On the basis of the research, seven general conclusions can be drawn with regard to the communications that members receive concerning legislative matters.

Finding 1: "Members hear from relatively few actors when casting a floor vote."

The average volume of communications that a member can recall paying attention to on given votes is quite low. For the 361 decisions studied here, the average was three contacts per vote. Table 3.1 is a frequency distribution of the volume of communications. As noted there, for 8 percent of the decisions studied, members did not receive any input. For only a small proportion of decisions did members recall more than six communications.

Finding 2: "Staff, constituents and other members make the most input."

Staff, constituents and other members are the actors most frequently mentioned by members as providing noteworthy input to congressional decision-making. Provided in Table 3.2 are the percentage of times each of the major potential communicators was listed by members as they responded to the question, "Who did you hear from, pay attention to, in making this decision?" It can be seen there that, contrary to Kingdon, a member's personal staff was the most frequent source of input. Staff was followed by individual constituents (as distinguished from organized interest groups in the district and inspired mail) and then by other Congressmen, both

62

Table 3.1

Frequency Distribution of Volume of Communications: the Percentage of
Interviews in which Members Mentioned Various Numbers
of Communications

Number of Communications	Percent of Total
0	8%
1	15
2	17
3	19
4	14
5	15
6	8
7	1
8	1
9	1

Table 3.2

Percentage of the Interviews in Which Each Actor Was Mentioned by
Members in Response to the Question "Who Did You Hear
From, Pay Attention to, Consider Concerning
This Decision?"

Actor	Responses
Personal Staff	42%
Individual Constituents	37
Committee Members	36
Other Members	36
State Delegation	31
Group Constituents	26
Private Groups	22
Committee Chairman	20
White House	14
Media	14
Party Leader	13
Inspired Mail	8
Public Interest Groups	5
Committee Staff	5
Public Sector Groups	3
Ranking Minority	3
Bureaucrats	3

those on the committee and those from the ranks of the general membership.

The following are general findings concerning each potential source of decision input.

Personal Staff

As the largest single input (42 percent mention), personal staff seemed pervasive in congressional decision-making. For floor votes, the staff position most often referenced was a legislative assistant or "LA." There seemed to be two major ways in which staff provides an input for decision-making. First, for a few, staff is a definite lobbying force. Illustrating this were comments to the effect, "I was lobbied hard on this by my staff" and "The staff gets their say like anyone else at the legislative meeting. They are frequently advocates." Second, and what seems to be the most prevalent approach, staff acts as an information conduit for the member. Examples of this were the statements, "My staff's job is not to argue with me but to boil it down for me and try to give me both sides" and "Staff's job is to tell me what people are saying."

Which staff style is utilized seems to depend on the individual member's conception of the role of staff in his decision process.

Constituents

Individual constituents, as opposed to constituent groups and inspired mail from the constituency, were mentioned 37 percent of the time.

The most frequently mentioned means of citizen input were the mail, telephone calls, personal visits, and informal conversations. Also mentioned as sources of citizen input to decision-making were a) polls through which the member solicits communications from the district and b) empathy the member has for district interests and issue positions. With regard to the latter, members noted that because of their contacts with their constituents, they can generally predict what people want, and they take this into consideration. One member said, "When you talk to people on weekends all year, you can tell what they are for or against. You know them, and it impacts on you."

65

Members made six points concerning general constituency input. First, few issues really activate
constituents. In the words of one Congressman, "Most
legislation is nonmaterial for the average citizen.
I hear very little from them." Members noted that
most often they hear from segments of the electorate--
those with a special interest in a given piece of
legislation. Second, the more the member is
committed to a vote and the more his position is
known, the less he will hear from constituents.
Third, even when citizen contacts and mail are low,
members still pay attention. As one member noted,
"Even when there are a few letters, if it's not
organized I'll pay attention." Fourth, mail is
usually processed by personal staff. The usual
procedure is for staff to open and handle it and
forward representative samplings to the member.
Fifth, when ordinary citizen contacts are high, in
the words of a member, "Real pressure is on." And
sixth, most of the contact members have with
constituents concerning legislation is only
indirectly related to specific votes. For example,
as one member stated, "The pay raise and ethics votes
are referenced only in passing as constituents talk
about corruption in government, excessive benefits,
and Wayne Hays. Likewise, those who made an input on
the government reorganization authority and the
ethics votes linked it to the broader question of red
tape in government."

Committee Members

The rank and file members of the parent committee
reporting a bill were mentioned as an input 36
percent of the time. Congressmen noted that their
contacts with those on the committee are both
antecedent from and proximate to the actual vote, as
committee members attempt to influence the floor
member both in advance of the vote and on the floor
immediately prior to the vote.

In advance of the vote, noncommittee members hear
from committee members through three means. First,
members hear from those on committee via a "dear
colleague" letter. Through these communications,
committee members attempt to lobby others concerning
a piece of legislation just completed or still being
processed in committee. Second, the official
committee report, forwarded to all members prior to
the time of the vote, lists the positions of

committee members. This offers the member the opportunity to learn the stand of committee members. But, as one member noted, "Usually, you'll already know. You'll hear about a committee member's position either through a dear colleague or informal talk." Third, committee members make contact through informal, ad hoc groups. Many members noted that they hear from committee members at weekly or biweekly meetings of their class (i.e., members of the same party elected to Congress the same year), state delegation, or ideological clique (e.g., Society of Statesmen).

Committee members are heard from at times more proximate to the vote through either debate or an institutionalized advocacy/adversary system at the doors leading to the House floor. As several members contended, if a member is present during debate, he will hear from committee members, because they normally dominate debate. If he is not present for debate but comes to the floor to cast a vote when the bells beckon, he will encounter committee members at the doors. Committee members pro and con are usually present at the doors and in the cloakrooms in order to lobby members. For this reason alone, as one member noted, "Predictably you will hear from those on committee."

Other Members

Thirty-six percent of the time, members mentioned that Congressmen other than those on committee, in the leadership structure, or in the state delegation made an input to them.

The occasions for member communications and interactions are lunch, dear colleague letters, walks to the floor, class meeting, debate, cloakroom and floor conversations, and discussions with others with whom the member serves on committee.

The input of members to other members is a natural occurrence within the Congress. As one member noted, "We talk informally so often that it's hard not to pay attention to another member."

There are two occasions when other members are likely to be considered an input to decision-making. The first occurs when certain members, although not a committee, are considered to have expertise on an issue: "On energy I go to Emery and on something like saccharin I talk to several of the members who are doctors." The second involves the politics of pork barrel ("Pork will put the pressure on. You'll hear from tham all when their districts' interests are at stake.")

State Delegations

Recently, political scientists have examined the role of state delegations in congressional decision-making.[4] They have discovered that state delegations are a major influence. The interviews here also found state delegations to be important. For 31 percent of the decisions studied, state delegation members made an input.

In line with studies of state delegations, these interviews revealed an enormous variety of practices through which delegation members communicate. For some of the larger delegations, a formal meeting is held and presided over by the most senior member, commonly referred to as "the dean." The dean establishes an agenda, and various matters of interest to the delegation are brought up. Other delegations enjoy a more informal conclave--perhaps over lunch in the House dining room. Smaller, two or three member delegations are often involved in steady communications.

Group Constituents

In 26 percent of the cases covered, members acknowledged an input from an organized interest in the constituency. Members said that they heard from the Chamber of Commerce on strip mining, from environmentalists on porpoise protection, from producers of chrome products on Rhodesian chrome, and from bill collectors in their district on debt collection practices.

Many members noted that a lot of lobbying is done by municipal officers who serve in communities affected by a vote. A good example is the school lunch vote. As one member noted, "We all heard from the school lunch people in our districts." Several members offered that groups in the district are often contacted on the member's initiative. "We'll often call interest groups and public officials to find out

68

what they want and how they feel they will be
impacted."

National Private Interest Groups

National private interest groups were mentioned
as having made an input to which the member actually
paid attention on 22 percent of the decisions studied.

Most of the contacts involved issue-specific
groups: home builders on the housing (HUD) votes,
the National Organization of Women (NOW) and the
American Medical Association (AMA) on the Hyde
(anti-abortion) Amendment, United Auto Workers and
auto dealers on clean air, steel companies on
Rhodesian chrome, tuna men on the marine mammal
protection bill, pharmaceutical houses on saccharin,
and AFL-CIO on Hatch and common situs.

Members made three points concerning nationl
interest groups. First, national interests usually
make only subtle contact. As one member emphasized,
"Interest groups don't make a strong push." Second,
groups target for pressure those members thought to
be uncommitted or wavering. According to one member,
"You don't get pressure if they know where you
stand. If you're a swing vote, they'll zero in on
you." Finally, members noted that an often-used
strategy by national interest groups is to approach
Congressmen through groups in the constituency. In
this vein, Congressmen noted that they were
approached by tuna producers in their district with
regard to the marine mammal protection act, by
district auto dealers on the clean air act, and by
groups of workers on common situs picketing. In each
of these instances, those interviewed felt that these
locally initiated contacts were the result of a
concerted national effort. The wisdom of doing this
seems verified by one member's statement that "I
don't pay attention to any of these interest groups
unless they are in my district."

Committee Chairman

Although many members acknowledged that the
chairman of the committee from which legislation
originated does exercise enormous influence over a
bill, for only 20 percent of the decisions studied
did members cite the chairman as a relevant input.
This rather low level of input may reflect increasing

subcommittee dominance. Conversations with members
revealed that they often paid more attention to the
chairman of the parent subcommittee than the chairman
of the full committee.

White House

The President or the White House staff was judged
to be an input on only 14 percent of the votes that
were studied. Most often, the input was through
White House legislative liaison staff. Not
infrequently, however, members did acknoweledge that
the President's position was considered, because they
"paid attention to major aspects of his program."
For example, a member noted that he related President
Carter's human rights position to the Rhodesian
chrome vote. Others related the energy and tax votes
to the Carter platform.

The relatively-infrequent mention of the
President as a decision input runs counter to past
scholarly assessments that there is increasing
presidential hegemony on Capitol Hill.[5] Yet
several members, including a member of the majority
party leadership, argued that the President was still
getting organized and for that reason the role of the
White House in congressional decision-making is
probably underestimated by data collected at the
outset of a new administration. Others argued that
the White House was crippled early on by its
preoccupation with the Burt Lance affair.

Media

Recently, media influence on the affairs of
government has been a much discussed topic.[6] In 14
percent of the interviews, members mentioned the
media as a force to which they paid attention. When
discussing the media, Congressmen acknowledged that
input occurs primarily as the result of members
"following issues in the press or on TV."

Party Leaders

In some cases, those interviewed had difficulty
determining who specifically is a party leader. For
example, one member stated that "John Moss and Mo
Udall are leaders in our party," although neither
were formal party leaders. However, for our

purposes, a party leader is thought to be a member in the formal, official hierarchy.

For only 13 percent of the decisions studied here did members mention that party leaders provided an input to which they paid notice. This is extremely low and, as will be argued subsequently, really does not give an accurate indication of the extent of party influence in Congress. Although many members acknowledged that they heard from party whips who are stationed at the House doors along with committee members to provide the party's position on a vote, few members define this as input to their decision. When leaders were mentioned, those who were most commonly mentioned were the Speaker, zone whip, and, for Republicans, the chairman of the Republican Policy Committee. Contacts occurred through both face-to-face and written communications.

Inspired Communications

Members receive a high volume of inspired mail. These kinds of communications are instigated by organized interests and are usually post cards.[7] In only 8 percent of the decisions studied here did members acknowledge paying attention to or turning to such communications.[8]

The reason so few mentioned inspired mail is the general aversion one finds in Congress to this form of political communication. When they detect an organized effort, members maintain they ignore it. A Republican stated, "That junk from the John Birch Society and other issue-oriented stuff is generally dismissed."

Public Interest Groups

Much has been made of the emergence of public interest groups, such as the Ralph Nader organization and Common Cause, as a formidable political force. Surprisingly, for only 5 percent of the cases did members recollect an input from these kinds of groups. When a public interest group was mentioned, it was usually a Common Cause chapter in the district.

Committee Staff

Committee staff was mentioned on only 5 percent of the decisions. Several members mentioned that

71

committee staff was a potential source of input for members, since on each bill committee staff are present for the floor vote to answer questions during debate.

Public Sector

Both Suzanne Farkas's <u>Urban Lobbying: Mayors in the Federal Arena</u>[9] and Donald Haider's <u>When Governments Come to Washington</u>[10] document the increased lobbying activity of public sector lobbyists--i.e., national representatives of subnational governments and organizations of public employees and local government officials. Several such contacts were mentioned in this study. Several mentioned being approached by public employee and postal unions on the Hatch Act. Others recalled communications from city and county organizations of mayors and managers with regard to the housing and countercyclical votes. Generally, contact from such groups was minimal. Only 3 percent of those interviewed recalled a public group input on the examined decision.

Bureaucrats

Despite the growth of legislative liaison activities of federal agencies, few members mentioned bureaucratic input.[11] On only 3 percent of the decisions was the input of bureaucrats recalled. When bureaucrats were mentioned, it was frequently in connection with a visible political appointee whose testimony during committee hearings was recalled. Sometimes, however, an agency position was mentioned, as with the Army Corps of Engineers on the water projects vote and the Department of Health, Education, and Welfare on the school lunch bill.

Ranking Minority

The position of ranking minority member on a congressional panel has assumed great importance in recent years. The last few Congresses have witnessed much wrangling in the ranks of the Republican party concerning how the ranking minority member should be selected. Yet, those interviewed in this study mentioned the ranking minority only 3 percent of the time.

Miscellaneous Communications/Inputs

In addition to the traditional list of actor influences, this study uncovered a number of miscellaneous sources of input. They are: The General Accounting Office, Library of Congress, Congressional Budget Office, family and friends, The Brookings Institution, the Coalition of Industrial/Northeastern States, Supreme Court rulings, and a member's past experience or own position the last time the legislation was handled by Congress. Although none of these miscellaneous inputs were mentioned more than one percent of the time, they do illustrate the plethora of forces to which a member pays attention when reaching a decision.

Finding 3: "There are different types of congressional communications."

Interviews revealed two ways in which communications can be differentiated. First, a distinction can be made on the basis of when the input was received. There are inputs proximate to the time of the vote, such as the partisan members who man the doorways, and inputs more antecedent to the decision, such as constituency mail, staff briefing, and correspondence from interest groups. Second, communications vary according to whether or not there is an attempt to exert pressure. Some inputs involve active attempts to sway and influence. Examples are lobbying activities by those competing for a member's attention, such as other members, the President, constituents, and interest groups. Other inputs do not involve intense pressure. Rather, they are initiated or solicited by members. They are best thought of as a member's self referents for decision-making. Examples are perceptions of constituency interests, opinions obtained through member sponsored polls, inquiries a member makes to a trusted colleague, staff work on an issue, and communications received from congressional agencies such as Library of Congress, Congressional Budget Office, and General Accounting Office.

Finding 4: "The volume of communications varies by vote."

The Lowi scheme and other contextual approaches assume that congressional inputs are better described with conditional propositions than with generalizations. With regard to the volume of communications a member receives, it is inferred that more actors are heard from on politically hot issues than on those of a low-profile variety. For example, for Lowi, distributive issues constitute a very narrow policy arena in which only those affected communicate.[12] For Cobb and Elder,[13] and for Price,[14] hot issues will involve "expanded publics" and "broader" inputs.

A test of this proposition is based on the mean number of communications for all decisions in this study (i.e., an average of three inputs for each decision). For each vote and for each value of the perceptual, objective, and researcher/subjective indicators, the percentage of respondents with contacts above the mean was computed. Both tests support the proposition.

Table 3.3 contains the percentage of communications above the mean for each of the sampled 31 votes. It shows that the volume of communications does vary by vote. Many of the hot issues--ethics, tax, common situs, clean air, Hatch Act, saccharin, water projects, and pay raise--involve at least 60 percent above mean contacts. For six low-key votes-- supplemental housing, FAA, Romanian earthquake relief, EPA, snow removal fund, school lunch--contacts are below the mean. For another three--NASA, marine mammal, and foreign aid--the percentage of communications volume above the mean is below 20 percent. These votes are perhaps good examples of what one member described as "quiet issues." "You hear from nobody. You usually go to the floor and shoot from the hip."

Thus, the breakdown of the volume of communications by vote does generally support the contextual theory. There are several exceptions. Two hot issues--strip mining and the Energy Department votes--had only 31 percent above the mean input. The highly emotional Hyde anti-abortion amendment had less than 50 percent above the mean. The low-profile, routine HUD Authorization had a surprisingly high 58 percent of the respondents with above mean contacts. Evidently, an intense dispute on HUD concerning the specific provisions of the distribution formula was associated with above average communications. In general, however, hot

Table 3.3

The Volume of Communications by Vote:
The Proportion of Respondents Who Reported
Three or More Contacts, Per Vote

Hot Votes:

House Ethics Code	79%
Tax Simplification and Rebate	70
Rhodesian Chrome Ban	55
Energy Department Establishment	31
First Budget Resolution (defeated)	46
Debt Collection Practices	18
Common Situs Picketing	62
Presidential Governmental Reorganization Authority	23
Strip Mining Regulation	31
Clean Air Act	73
Hyde Anti-Abortion Amendment	43
Repeal of the Hatch Act	62
Saccharin Ban	64
Water Projects Fight with President Carter	77
Pay Raise	83

Low-Profile Votes:

Nuclear Carrier Recission	46%
Goldwater Housing Amendment	0
NASA Authorization	20
FAA Authorization	0
Snow Removal Funds	0
Public Works Conference	33
Countercyclical Aid Reauthorization	39
HUD Authorization	58
Marine Mammal Protection	17
House Assassination Committee Reauthorization	39
Romanian Earthquake Relief	0
Arab Boycott	50
First Budget Resolution (passed)	50
Foreign Aid Reduction	9
School Lunch Authorization	0

issues are associated with above average contacts, while low-profile votes have relatively empty force fields.

Finding 5: "Volume of communications varies by issue characteristics."

The volume of communications a member receives markedly varies according to issue characteristics. Seventy-four percent of the distributions in Table 3.4 involve variations of 9 percent or more among issue characteristics' values (i.e., there is at least a 9 percentage variation in the percent of members with above average contacts on, for example, votes defined as "complex" in contrast with those defined as "noncomplex").

The variations in the volume of communications generally conform to the expectations of the contextual theory. Under most hot conditions, members receive more input while under most low-profile conditions they receive less.

There are several findings in Table 3.4 contrary to the contextual model. For instance, members receive more communications on issues that are considered complex and technical than they do on hot issues (i.e., those "noncomplex" and "nontechnical"). Decisions considered complex and technical have a higher percentage of members with above mean communications than those considered "not complex" and "not technical," indicating that more actors try to influence members on complex and technical decisions than when the opposite is true. Those votes not mentioned in the polls as an important national issue actually have slightly more above average contacts than those mentioned. Also, some distinctions on the basis of issue characteristics fail to produce any meaningful variations in congressional input. For example, none of the subjective indicators reveals a meaningful difference. There are minimal differences when communications volume is arrayed by salience, feeling, party unity, index of difference, amendment over committee objection, committee vote, minority report, and time frame.

Most of the distinctions, however, support qualifications concerning congressional communications in the predicted direction.

76

Table 3.4

Values of Issue Characteristics Associated
With Above and Below the Mean Communication
(Correlates Based on a Variation of 9 Percent or More;
mean =   3   or more contracts.)

Above the Mean Volume	Below the Mean Volume

Perceptual Indicators

Complex (LP)	Noncomplex (H)
Technical (LP)	Nontechnical (H)
Conflict (H) o	No conflict (LP) ●
Major status (H)	Not major (LP)
Salience (H)	Not salient (LP)
Constituency awareness (H)	No constituency awareness (LP)
Heavy mail (H) ●	No heavy mail (LP) ●
Renomination effects (H) ●	No renomination effects (LP)●
Reelection effects (H) ●	No reelection effects (LP)●
Nonroutine (H) ●	Routine (LP) ●
Tough (H) ●	Not tough (LP) ●
Thought (H) ●	No thought (LP) ●

Objective Indicators

Below the mean rule margin (H) ●	Above the mean rule margin (LP) ●
Defeated (H) ●	Close, comfortable margin (LP) ●
Before the mean Dem. unity (H)	Above the mean Dem. unity (LP)
Below the mean Rep. unity (H)	Above the mean Rep. unity (LP)
Minority report (H)	No minority report (LP)
CQ story (H) ●	No CQ story (LP) ●
Wash Post box score (H) ●	No Wash Post box score (LP)●
Congress as initiator (H) ●	Congress as ratifier (LP) ●
CQ box score (H)	No CQ box score (LP)
Wash Post Story (H)	No Wash Post story (LP)
Pres. involvement (H)	No Pres. involvement (LP)
Dem. policy endorsement (H) ●	No Dem. policy endorsement (LP) o
Above the mean money (H) ●	Below the mean money (LP) ●

Subjective Indicators

Change (H)	No change (LP)

 H = Presumed hot value
LP = Presumed low-profile value
 ● = variation of 20 percent or greater

In sum, Table 3.4 reveals that important qualifications concerning how many communications members receive can be made on the basis of various indicators of issue characteristics. These data, combined with those already discussed in Table 3.3 support the conclusion that the volume of communications a member receives concerning a vote is more precisely described with categorical concepts than with the general proposition that "Congressmen hear from few sources." On hot issues they hear from more and on low-profile issues they hear from fewer. Certain hot values of perceptual and objective indicators of issue characteristics are associated with relatively full force fields. The opposite is true for many low-profile values.

Finding 6: "The actors from whom a member hears vary according to the kind of decision at hand."

Contextual approaches posit that low-profile issues involve very narrow policy arenas in which members hear from only those affected by the vote. Hot issues involve input from much broader publics.[12] Accordingly, for low-profile issues, the expectation is that interest groups and Congressmen on the relevant committee will be the actors most frequently mentioned. In contrast, hot issues should involve party leaders, constituents, and the President.

Table 3.5 is the breakdown of sources of input by vote. It shows that the actors Congressmen hear from depends on the issue at hand. An actor-by-actor description illustrates variable patterns of congressional input.

Personal Staff

The mention of personal staff ranges from in excess of 70 percent on the Federal Aviation Administration (FAA) and tax votes to less than 10 percent of the Goldwater amendment and the snow removal funds vote. The highest incidence of personal staff input occurred on three kinds of votes. First, votes that were hot but also complicated tended to involve a lot of staff input (tax, budget, clean air, saccharin, Rhodesian chrome, and water projects). Perhaps explaining this is the statement by one member, "On controversial issues that are somewhat complicated, I put staff to work.

Congressional Communications by Vote: Distribution by Vote of Responses to the Question "Who Did You Hear From, Pay Attention To?"

Actor	House Ethics Code	Tax Simplifi- cation	Rhodesian Crome	Energy Dept. Establishment	First Budget Res. (defeated)	Debt Collection
Personal Staff	43% *	70%	55%	44%	82%	64%
Individual Constituents	50	40	45	31	9	36
Committee Members	7	40	9	56	45	27
Other Congressmen	65	30	36	19	27	36
State Delegation	50	60	18	25	54	27
Group Constituents	21	20	18	13	9	18
Private Groups	0	0	45	19	0	27
Committee Chairmen	57	0	9	25	36	9
White House	0	50	45	31	0	0
Media	0	30	55	25	9	0
Party Leaders	50	20	9	0	55	0
Inspired Mail	7	0	9	0	0	0
Public Interest Groups	57	0	0	0	0	0
Committee Staff	7	20	0	6	0	0
Public Sector Groups	0	0	0	0	0	0
Ranking Minority	14	0	9	6	18	0
Bureaucrats	0	0	17	0	0	0
Type of Vote:	Hot	Hot	Hot	Hot	Hot	Hot

*Percentages represent the proportion of interviewees on that vote mentioning that actor

Table 3.5 (Continued)

Actor	Common Situs	Gov't Reorg.	Strip Mining	Clean Air Act	Hyde (Anti-Abortion) Amend.	Repeal of Hatch Act
Personal Staff	46%	23%	38%	53%	21%	31%
Individual Constituents	69	23	15	34	71	62
Committee Members	46	8	8	67	14	38
Other Congressmen	70	23	15	40	21	23
State Delegation	46	15	23	53	21	38
Group Constituents	46	8	0	100	43	31
Private Groups	85	8	46	53	0	46
Committee Chairmen	31	54	38	40	0	8
White House	8	54	15	0	0	8
Media	31	39	8	20	14	8
Party Leaders	22	8	8	0	0	0
Inspired Mail	69	0	0	7	29	46
Public Interest Groups	0	0	23	27	0	0
Committee Staff	0	8	0	0	0	0
Public Sector Groups	0	8	8	0	0	23
Ranking Minority	8	0	0	0	0	8
Bureaucrats	8	0	0	0	0	0
Type of Vote:	Hot	Hot	Hot	Hot	Hot	Hot

80

Table 3.5 (Continued)

| | Vote | | | | | | |
Actor	Saccharin Ban	Water Projects	Pay Raise	EPA Auth	Nuclear Navy	Goldwater Housing Amend.	NASA Auth
Personal Staff	46%	47%	22%	80%	27%	0%	50%
Individual Constituents	100	59	89	0	9	20	20
Committee Members	46	71	28	20	18	20	40
Other Congressmen	73	94	0	20	18	40	20
State Delegation	36	47	78	20	36	0	0
Group Constituents	18	53	6	0	0	40	0
Private Groups	18	24	6	0	0	20	0
Committee Chairmen	0	6	0	0	55	20	10
White House	0	77	0	0	73	10	0
Media	27	12	29	0	46	0	10
Party Leaders	0	0	89	0	18	0	0
Inspired Mail	9	6	0	0	0	0	0
Public Interest Groups	0	12	6	0	0	0	0
Committee Staff	0	0	0	0	0	0	10
Public Sector Groups	0	0	0	0	0	0	0
Ranking Minority	0	0	0	0	0	0	0
Bureaucrats	9	0	0	0	36	0	10
Type of Vote:	Hot	Hot	Hot	Low Profile	Low Profile	Low Profile	Low Profile

Table 3.5 (Continued)

Actor	FAA Auth	Snow Removal	Public Works Conference	Countercyclical Aid Auth	HUD Auth	Marine Mammal	House Ass. Comm. Auth
Personal Staff	13%	9%	22%	85%	58%	25%	46%
Individual Constituents	0	0	33	8	17	42	38
Committee Members	38	0	11	31	50	67	77
Other Congressmen	0	18	22	23	33	17	39
State Delegation	0	0	44	31	42	0	31
Group Constituents	0	18	44	69	75	8	0
Private Groups	0	0	0	8	17	58	8
Committee Chairmen	12	0	11	8	25	25	39
White House	0	0	11	0	0	0	0
Media	0	0	22	0	0	0	23
Party Leaders	0	0	11	8	8	0	0
Inspired Mail	0	0	33	0	0	8	8
Public Interest Groups	0	0	0	23	0	0	23
Committee Staff	13	9	0	15	17	0	0
Public Sector Groups	0	0	0	8	8	0	0
Ranking Minority	0	0	0	8	0	8	0
Bureaucrats	0	0	0	8	0	0	0
Type of Vote:	Low Profile	Low Profile	Low Profile	Low Profile	Low Profile	Low Profile	Low Profile

82

Actor	Romanian Earthquake Relief	Arab Boycott	First Budget Res. (passed)	Foreign Aid Reduction	School Lunch Authorization
Personal Staff	30%	30%	50%	36%	25%
Individual Constituents	10	60	0	0	0
Committee Members	20	30	87	36	38
Other Congressmen	0	40	50	36	0
State Delegation	20	10	37	9	13
Group Constituents	0	40	0	9	37
Private Groups	0	40	26	0	0
Committee Chairmen	20	10	38	0	13
White House	0	0	0	0	0
Media	10	20	13	0	0
Party Leaders	10	0	37	18	0
Inspired Mail	10	0	13	0	0
Public Interest Groups	0	0	13	0	0
Committee Staff	0	10	0	0	0
Public Sector Groups	0	0	0	0	0
Ranking Minority	0	0	0	0	13
Bureaucrats	0	0	0	0	0
Type of Vote:	Low Profile	Low Profile	Low Profile	Low Profile	Low Profile

83

I want them to give a briefing on both sides of the issue." Second, staff input was high on low-profile issues that were hard to understand: National Aeronautics and Space Administration (NASA), Environmental Protection Agency (EPA), and debt collection practices. Third, in the words of one member, "Staff gets put to work on votes that might specifically affect the district." Grant programs such as the HUD and countercyclical votes were judged by members to involve a high rate of staff input. Staff input was lowest on a) votes with little lead time (Goldwater amendment, snow removal, and nuclear navy), b) routine bills (FAA, public works, marine mammal, and school lunch), and c) those hot issues on which the member is likely to have a fairly well developed position (Government reorganization, Arab boycott, strip mining, Hyde, Hatch, and pay raise).

Individual Constituents

The mention of individual constituents varies from 89 percent on the pay raise vote to no mention on the school lunch vote. Individual constituents were heard from most frequently on certain hot issues: common situs picketing, Arab boycott, Hyde, Hatch, water projects, saccharin, and the pay raise. This reflects a Congressman's observation that "If it (a vote) gets publicity, you'll hear from people on it." Citizen input was lowest on routine issues (NASA, FAA, Romanian earthquake, EPA, counter-cyclical, HUD, and school lunch) and short suspenses (foreign aid, snow removal, nuclear navy, and Goldwater amendment). Also, certain hot but technical issues--perhaps the kind of issues that do not generate citizen interest--were associated with low-citizen input. They were government reorganiza-tion, strip mining, budget, and clean air.

Members acknowledge that constituency can be a latent input since members consider how the interest of the constituency will be affected by a given vote. As one noted, "On all votes, I ask myself, 'How will this affect programs and policies in my state?'"

Committee Members

The input of committee members varies greatly, from an 87 percent mention on the second budget vote to mention by no interviewees on the snow removal vote. It was highest on two kinds of issues: those that were hot but somewhat technical (tax, common situs, Energy Department, budget, HUD, clean air, and water projects) and those that were low-grade, esoteric, and obscure (NASA, HUD, and marine mammal). Votes on which committee members were infrequently mentioned are those that came up quickly in a parliamentary fashion and the committee was not fully mobilized (nuclear navy, Goldwater amendment, Romanian earthquake, snow removal, and public works conference) and those issues that "were around for awhile" (Rhodesian chrome, government reorganization, EPA, debt collection practices, strip mining, HUD, and Hyde amendment).

Several members provided an explanation for these patterns. One noted that "Committee members must be paid attention to on technical amendments. After all, they are usually proposed on the floor by members who get shot down in committee." Another noted that "On marine mammal protection, I had to pay attention to McCloskey who's on the committee. He was one of the major contestants." Another noted that when there is an attempt to significantly amend a bill (an occurrence for most major bills), the sponsor of the amendment (usually a member of the committee) will approach the floor member. In the member's words, "On something like the Energy Department bill the sponsor--in this case John Moss--will talk to me."

Other Members

The mention of other members not on the committee nor in the state delegation ranges from a high of 73 percent on the saccharin vote to a low of no mention on the FAA vote. Other members became an input when the issue was extremely hot such as ethics, common situs, the budget, saccharin, and water projects. In the words of a member, "When the heat is on, everybody talks to everyone else to find out what they are doing." Input from other members was the lowest on many routine bills (NASA, FAA, Romanian earthquake, EPA, snow removal, marine mammal, and school lunch) and bills on which members may already have staked out a position or conviction (strip mining, Hyde, Hatch, and the pay raise). With regard to this latter category, most members realize that "It's no use lobbying; most have already made up their minds."

State Delegation

The mention of state delegation as a decision input ranges from 80 percent on the pay raise to no mention on the NASA and FAA votes. The frequency of communications within state delegations was highest on two kinds of bills: some really hot issues (ethics, tax, common situs, the budget, clean air, and the pay raise) and those votes that involved grants and pork barrel projects (public works, countercyclical, HUD, and water projects). With regard to the hot issues, members seem to check how the delegation votes. As one member related, "On real issues, I want to see how others in the state voted." For grant and pork barrel bills, members communicate to maximize the gains for their state. A member stated, "We talk together to insure a good deal for the state." State delegation was weakest as an input on routine bills (marine mammal protection and authorizations for NASA, FAA, EPA and school lunch), bills with short parliamentary suspenses (Goldwater amendment, snow removal, foreign aid amendment), and old bills (Rhodesian chrome, government reorganization, debt collection, Arab boycott, and Hyde). Members also noted that state delegation is not usually an input if state interests are not involved.

Group Constituents

Groups within the constituency were mentioned by as many as 100 percent of the interviewees on clean air and by no member on the nuclear navy vote. Organized groups of constituents were heard from on two basic types of legislation: (1) certain hot votes (clean air, water projects, strip mining, common situs and Arab boycott) relevant to certain local interests and (2) votes affecting grant programs (Goldwater amendment, public works, countercyclical and HUD) that have existing constituencies. Group contacts appeared less frequently on almost all of the routine issues and on hot votes that lacked specific constituencies: e.g., the budget and pay raise.

Private Interest Groups

The input of private national groups varied from 58 percent mention on marine mammal to no mention on both the ethics and the nuclear navy vote. The issues on which national private interests were most frequently heard from are common situs ("I felt constant pressure on that one"), Arab boycott, strip mining, marine mammal protection, clean air, Hyde, and Hatch. Most of these were hot issues on which individual citizens also made significant input. But, on marine mammal there was not significant citizen communication. The tuna lobby was the only input external to Congress. Interest groups were mentioned less on many routine bills (NASA, FAA, House assassinations, Romanian earthquake, EPA, public works, countercyclical, HUD, and school lunch), bills with short suspenses (nuclear navy, snow removal, public works, and foreign aid) and several hot bills (ethics, government reorganization, and the pay raise) that seemed to lack a defined group interest.

Committee Chairman

The input of the committee chairman to the floor voting member's decision-making process is highly variable. On some issues such as ethics, nuclear navy, and Government reorganization, more than 50 percent mentioned the chairman. On 14 votes (Rhodesian chrome, NASA, EPA, debt collection practices, Arab boycott, snow removal, counter-cyclical, foreign aid, tax, Hyde, Hatch, saccharin, water projects, and pay raise), the chairman's input was 10 percent or less.

Mention of the chairman usually depends on the visibility of his involvement and his dominance as a competitor. On ethics, the navy vote, and the reorganization act, he was a major, visible competitor. For example, on government reorganization, one member noted that "I followed closely the position of Jack Brooks. He was the President's major adversary on it, and I looked to him to work things out." On those issues on which the chairman is only infrequently mentioned, the chairman was one of many competitors attempting to shape a piece of legislation on the floor. Specifically, with regard to Rhodesian chrome, debt collection practices, and Arab boycott, controversy primarily involved rank-and-file members on and off committee.

White House

The input of the President to congressional
decision-making varied from 77 percent mention on the
water projects vote to no mention on the ethics
vote. It was greatest on those issues on which the
President chose to get involved. The nuclear navy,
tax, Rhodesian chrome, government reorganization,
Energy Department, and water projects votes had above
average mention of the President due to the fact that
the Carter Administration chose to stake its prestige
on them. Others had low presidential involvement
because the presidency was not involved.

Media

The media were mentioned by 55 percent of the
interviewees on Rhodesian chrome and by no
interviewees on 11 votes. Mention of the media was
most prevalent on certain hot issues such as tax,
Rhodesian chrome, government reorganization,
saccharin and the pay raise. On these issues,
members felt that past or future media coverage of an
issue were forces to be considered. Also, the media
were frequently mentioned on one routine issue--the
nuclear navy vote--which had been debated in a
general way in the press many times prior to the
specific vote. Most hot and routine votes did not
involve significant press coverage.

Party Leaders

Party leaders were mentioned by as many as 89
percent of the interviewees on the pay raise and by
no members on the Goldwater amendment. Party leaders
were mentioned most on votes on which the majority
party staked its prestige: ethics, the budget and
the pay raise. As one member related, "I really
heard from party people on those votes through the
whip. They really worked the pay raise and the
closed rule for the ethics vote." A Republican noted
that "On a vote like the budget, most Republicans
will turn to the Republican Policy Committee to see
what they have to say." Party inputs were lowest on
routine, low-grade issues (no member mentioned party
leaders on Goldwater, NASA, FAA, House
assassinations, EPA, debt collection, Arab boycott,
snow removal, marine mammal, and school lunch) and,
surprisingly, on many hot issues (no mention of
leader input on Rhodesian chrome, Energy Department,

clean air, Hatch, Hyde, saccharin, and water projects). This indicates that party leaders are very selective when investing their prestige. They provide guidance on only those issues they want to feature as the party's hallmark.

Inspired Mail

Only three votes were associated with any significant degree of inspired mail: common situs picketing, Hyde amendment, and Hatch act. For the rest of the votes, there was no mention of this kind of input.

Public Interest Groups

The input of these associations was generally very low except on reform (ethics) and environmental legislation (strip mining and clean air).

Committee Staff

Committee staff was practically irrelevant on the hot, important issues. No member mentioned the staff employees of committees on common situs, strip mining, the budget, clean air, Hyde, Hatch, saccharin, pay raise, and water projects. Also, light input was made on routine issues (no mention on nuclear navy, Goldwater amendment, Romanian earthquake, EPA, debt collection, marine mammal, foreign aid, and school lunch) and older issues (no mention on Rhodesian chrome, strip mining and clean air). Several votes did involve above average input from committee staffers: tax, House assassinations, and several grant programs such as public works, countercyclical, and HUD. Tax was a difficult issue to understand, and several members mentioned that they solicited the advice of committee staff. House assassinations was a rare issue where an imbroglio surrounded staffers. For the grant program, a member mentioned he talked to staffers "if I have a problem deciphering how the darn thing will impact on my district."

Public Groups

These groups made themselves felt most often on grants (school lunch, HUD, and countercyclical) and general governmental issues (government reorganization and Hatch).

Ranking Minority

Although the ranking minority member is generally
not frequently mentioned, there are certain votes
where he made a sizable input. The bills on which
ranking minority members were mentioned most are
ethics and the budget. On more than half of the
sampled votes, no member listed the ranking
minority. Many of these votes are generally
low-profile, but some--such as clean air, Hyde
amendment, pay raise, and strip mining--are hot
issues.

Bureaucrats

Bureaucrats or federal officials were recorded as
having the highest frequency of contact on two
votes: nuclear navy and saccharin. In both cases,
members mentioned that they paid attention to the
position of bureaucrats with expertise on these
controversial, technical matters.

To conclude the discussion of Table 3.5, these
findings support the notion that input into member
decision-making varies according to the type of
legislation at stake. Although there is not a neat
dichotomization between hot and low-profile decisions
along the lines predicted by the theory of major
authors who employ a contextual approach, there are
general tendencies in this direction. Reading down
the columns of Table 3.5 rather than across the rows,
reveals that most of the issues that can be
considered low-profile (nuclear navy, NASA, FAA,
House assassinations, Romanian earthquake, EPA, debt
collection, foreign aid, school lunch, and marine
mammal) involved sizable input from committee
chairmen, committee members, and personal staff.
Many hot issues (ethics, tax, Rhodesian chrome,
common situs, clean air, Hyde, Hatch, saccharin, and
pay raise) involved input from broader sources that
include individual citizens, group constituents,
interest groups, and, in some cases, party officials
and the White House. This conclusion is strongly
supported in Table 3.6, which shows the input of each
actor by volume of communication. When
communications are below average, personal staff and
committee members were the two most frequent inputs.
When communications are above average, individual
constituents and state delegation members were the
most frequently mentioned actors. Evidently, there

Table 3.6

Sources of Congressional Communications Arrayed
by Volume of Contacts

Actor	Below Average Contacts /	Above Average Contacts
Committee Chairman	(13%	29%)*
Ranking Minority	0	6
Committee Members	(23	54)·
State Delegation	(11	59)·
Party Leader	(4	26)·
Other Congressmen	(21	56)·
Personal Staff	(31	57)·
Individual Constituents	(21	59)·
Inspired Mail	(4	14)
Group Constituents	(14	41)·
Private Groups	(10	33)·
Public Interest Groups	(1	11)
Bureaucrats	1	5
White House	(9	21)
Media	(9	28)

*Proportions represent the percentage of interviews in which members
mentioned contact with the actor
( ) = A variation of 10% or greater
  · = A variation of 20% or more
 / = Below and above average contacts were computed on the basis of a
mean of three communications for each decision.

are two broad types of decision arenas in Congress.
There are quiet, internal issues where members
receive input only from staff or committee members,
and there are expansive issues that involve input
from constituents and state delegation members.

A more precise description of patterns of
congressional input uncovered in Table 3.5 may be
provided by a four-category classification scheme:
routine issues, grant programs, hot issues, and
specialized, hot issues. Routine issues primarily
involve staff and committee input. Contrary to the
expectations, those affected do not make a substan-
tial input on these votes. That is not to say that
the affected are not influential. It is to say,
merely, that they do not register in the component of
cognitive map referred to as force field. Grant
programs and public works programs involve staff and
state delegation input plus contacts with specific
clientele within the district. Hot issues (Hyde,
Hatch, pay raise, ethics, and saccharin) involve
input from a variety of forces including private
interest groups, constituents, party leaders, and the
White House. Specialized, hot issues are hot as well
as complex and technical. Examples are Arab boycott,
budget, energy, clean air, strip mining, and common
situs. These involve expanded input combined with
significant mention of committee members and
constituent groups.

Finding 7: "The input of various actors to
congressional decision-making varies according to
issue characteristics."

A breakdown of communications by perceptual,
objective, and researcher-subjective indicators of
issue characteristics reveals some variation. In
some instances, there is very little variation in
actor input by the issue characteristics. In other
instances, meaningful differences appear. Overall,
65 of the distributions involve meaningful
variations--i.e., variations of 20 percent or more in
the mention of input sources among various values of
an issue characteristic indicator.[15] (For example,
a distribution would be considered meaningful if
committee members were mentioned a minimum of 20
percent more when the issue is defined as complex as
opposed to not complex.)

Thus, the involvement of each actor in the decision-making process has certain correlates. Table 3.7 displays the issue characteristics associated with the mention of various actors. This table shows that different inputs are more likely to occur under certain issue conditions than when the opposite conditions are present.

The presentation of force field inputs by issue characteristics in Table 3.7 shows that, under characteristics presumed to be hot, members are more likely to mention the White House, state delegation, party leaders, other members, and constituents. Committee chairmen and members, group constituents, staff and private national interests make input (i.e., are heard from and paid attention to and thus are part of the member's decision-making field) under some low-profile conditions.

In conclusion, when combining the arrays of input by issue characteristics with the distribution of communications by vote, basic tendencies in the direction of the contextual theory can be observed. Members mention different sources of decision-making input in different decision contexts. Under low-profile conditions, they have narrow force fields, hearing mainly from only those affected. Under hot conditions they experience broader inputs. One qualification is in order. On low-profile issues, personal staff is mentioned in addition to groups and committee members. With this qualification in mind, the expectations of the contextual approach are verified.

Summary and Conclusions

Previous studies of congressional communications have yielded two generalizations commonly cited in the literature of congressional decision-making. The first can be inferred from Dexter's research. It is that members receive a low volume of communications, usually only from those with whom they already agree. The second is Kingdon's finding that constituents and other members are the actors who most frequently provide inputs to the decision processes of members.

This chapter has shown that who Congressmen hear from or pay attention to depends on the kind of vote

93

Table 3.7

Values of Issue Characteristics Associated with Mention of Input
Sources (These correlates are based on variations of
20 percent or more)

Chairman	Committee Member	State Delegation
CQ Box Score (H)	Closed rule (H)	Non-routine (H)
Congress ratifies (LP)	Amendment over committee (H)	Tough (H)
No Amendment over committee (LP)	Congress modifies (LP)	Thought (H)
		Closed rule (H)
		Below average rule margin (H)
		Defeat (H)
		CQ story (H)
		Washington Post story (H)
		Below average Republican unity (H)

Table 3.7--Continued

Inspired Mail	Group Constituents	Private National Groups	Media
Mail (II)	Salience (II)	Complex (LP)	Above average money (II)
	Mail (H)	Renomination effects (H)	
	Tough (H)	Reelection effects (H)	
	Thought (H)	Non-routine (H)	
	Minority report (H)	Thought (H)	
	Congress modifies (LP)	CQ Box Score (H)	
	Above average time (H)	Congress modifies (H)	White House
	Presidential involvement (H)	Above average time (H)	Open rule (II)
		Democratic endorsement (H)	Presidential involvement (H)
		Presidential involvement (H)	Policy change (H)

Public Interest Groups

No correlates

95

Table 3.7--Continued

Party Leader	Other Members	Personal Staff	Individual Constituents
Feelings (H)	Constituency awareness (H)	Complex (LP)	Conflict (H)
Closed rule (H)	Below average rule margin (H)	Thought (H)	Constituency awareness (H)
Below average rule margin (H)	Defeated (H)	Closed rule (H)	Mail (H)
Defeated (H)	Congress initiates (H)	Minority report (H)	Non-routine (H)
Above average Republican unity (LP)		Mention in polls (H)	Feelings (H)
No Democratic endorsement (LP)		Above average money (H)	Modifies open rule (H)
			Below average rule margin (H)
			Defeated (H)
			CQ Story (H)
			Presidential involvement (H

H = Presumed hot value
LP = Presumed low-profile value

96

involved. There are multiple patterns of congressional input.

The volume of communications a member receives concerning floor votes is not always low as Dexter infers. The volume of input to member decision-making is highly variable. Some votes involve a low volume of contacts, while others involve a high volume. High-profile votes are associated with more input than low-profile votes. Variations in volume are also related to issue characteristics. This evidence helps to corroborate a member's view that:

> There is no law of congressional commun-
> ications. If there is an existence of
> contrary approaches on a bill, you do talk
> to a lot of people on it. When a lot of
> people are interested, when the range of
> opinion is wide, many attempt to talk
> to you and you have no alternative but to
> talk to them. On big, important bills, you
> will always hear from people.

Variations also occur with regard to the specific actors from whom members hear when making a decision. Contrary to Kingdon's findings, the personal staff of members, not other members and constituents, provide the most frequently mentioned input. But input from staff is highly variable. In excess of 70 percent of the respondents mentioned a decision input from staff on the tax and EPA votes, while less than 10 percent mentioned staff on the Goldwater amendment and the snow removal funds vote. This kind of variation was found to hold true for all communication sources.

Under certain conditions, confirming Kingdon's findings, members hear mainly from constituents and other members. Under other conditions, however, they hear from many different actors. The greatest variation in sources of communications occurs among routine issues, grant programs, hot issues, and specialized, hot issues. Also, each communication source has certain issue characteristic correlates. For each communications source, there are certain values of perceptual, objective, and subjective indicators of issue characteristics under which the source is more likely to make an input. These patterns generally conform to the expectations of

those authors who have a conditional approach. Hot
characteristics are related to broader inputs (party,
committee chairman, state delegation, constituents),
while some low-profile characteristics (complexity,
technicality) are associated with communications from
narrower, more affected sources (group constituents,
national private interests, committee members).

All of this suggests that to understand
congressional communications, one should have an
appreciation for policy differentials in Congress.
There are different arenas of decisionmaking in
Congress. There are "quiet, internal issues" on
which there is little pressure and on which few are
heard. There are also extremely visible decisions
that attract heavy mail, press coverage, and party
and presidential involvement. General propositions
about congressional communications necessarily gloss
over these differences.

Finally, interviews with members reveal two
important qualifications with which to conclude this
discussion of members' force fields. First, "Just
because you hear from somebody during the course of a
decision and pay attention to them, doesn't mean you
agree with them or are influenced by them." In other
words, although a member may mention an actor as a
source of communication or input, that actor may not
be part of the member's decision equation. Second,
actors who are influential in the legislative process
are not necessarily present in a member's force
field. As one member stated, "You don't run into
much pressure here. It's exercised subtly and
indirectly, frequently down at the subcommittee
level."

[1]This list parallels the one found in John W. Kingdon, Congressmen's Voting Decisions (New York: Harper & Row, 1973), p. 20.

[2]Lewis Anthony Dexter, The Sociology and Politics of Congress (Chicago: Rand McNally, 1969), p. 159. Also see Lewis Anthony Dexter, "The Job of the Congressman," Readings on Congress, ed. by R. E. Wolfinger (Englewood Cliffs, N.J.: Prentice-Hall, 1971), p. 81.

[3]Kingdon, Congressmen's Voting, p. 22.

[4]See A. R. Clausen, "State Party Influences on Congressional Behavior," Midwest Journal of Political Science 16 (1972): 77-101; B. Deckard, "State Party Delegations in the U.S. House of Representatives: A Comparative Study of Group Cohesion," Journal of Politics 34 (1972): 199-222; A Fiellin, "The Functions of Informal Groups in Legislative Institutions," Journal of Politics 14 (1962): 72-91; J. H. Kessel, "The Washington Congressional Delegation," Midwest Journal of Political Science 8 (1964): 1-21; and David B. Truman, "The State Delegation and the Structure of Voting in the United States House of Representatives," American Political Science Review 50 (1956): 1023-45.

[5]See Lawrence Chamberlain, The President, Congress and Legislation (New York: Columbia Univ. Press, 1946) and Samuel P. Huntington, "Congressional Responses to the Twentieth Century," in The Congress and America's Future, 2nd ed., ed. by David B. Truman (Englewood Cliffs, N.J.: Prentice-Hall, 1973).

[6]See Delmer D. Dunn, Public Officials and the Press (Reading, Mass.: Addison-Wesley, 1969); Douglas Cater, The Fourth Branch of Government (Boston: Houghton, 1959); Bernard C. Cohen, The Press and Foreign Policy (Princeton, N.J.: Princeton Univ. Press, 1963); Dan D. Nimmo, News Gathering in Washington (New York: Atherton, 1964); and Daniel P. Moynihan, "The Presidency and the Press," Commentary 51 (1971): 41-52.

[7]Malcolm E. Jewell and Samuel C. Patterson, The Legislative Process in the United States, 3rd ed. (New York: Random, 1977), p. 30.

[8]This corroborates a finding by Charles L. Clapp, The Congressman: His Work as He Sees It (Washington: Brookings, 1963), p. 189.

[9]Suzanne Farkas, _Urban Lobbying: Mayors in the Federal Arena_ (New York: New York Univ. Press, 1971).

[10]Donald Haider, _When Governments Come to Washington_ (New York: Free Press, 1974).

[11]See Abraham Holtzman, _Legislative Liaison: Executive Leadership in Congress_ (Chicago: Rand McNally, 1970).

[12]See Lowi Table, chapter 1 of this work.

[13]Roger W. Cobb and Charles D. Elder, _Participation in American Politics: The Dynamics of Agenda-Building_ (Boston: Allyn, 1972).

[14]David E. Price, "Policy-Making in Congressional Committees: The Impact of Environmental Factors," _American Political Science Review_, 72 (1978), 548-74.

[15]For communications, the 20 percent spread is used for significance because numerous 9 percent differences were present. Correlates for information sources and search and decision determinants, where there are fewer differences, are based on 9 percent.

CHAPTER IV

THE CONDITIONAL NATURE OF THE CONGRESSIONAL
INFORMATION PROCESS

How Congressmen inform themselves on floor votes has been a matter of recent scholarly interest. Basically, this interest stems from the realization that, as Saloma states, ". . . information is a form of power . . ."[1]

Studies of congressional information flows and information processing have yielded several general conclusions. First, Congressmen have a pressing need for information. As Deckard notes, "All Congressmen, the most senior as well as the freshmen, are faced with a perpetual need for information at as cheap a cost in time as possible."[2] And, as Congressman Udall has written,

> In order to make decisions on increasingly complex and constantly changing issues, to respond to a melange of requests from constituents, to keep abreast of the activities of the Congress itself--all require constant acquiring and sifting of information.[3]

Second, to cope with information problems, Congressmen devise various routine shortcuts. Stevens et al. argue that "The insight gained from recent research is that certain institutional forms and practices have developed in the House that provide the Congressman with 'shortcuts' toward gaining the information he needs."[4] Third, Congressmen have need for various types of information. As Ornstein notes, there are five distinct patterns of information: content-descriptive, procedural-technical, institutional-political, constituency-political, and ideological.[5]

With specific regard to the micro aspects of congressional information gathering--that is to say, the behavior of the individual legislator as he processes information--important generalizations have been drawn concerning information sources, information search, and information adequacy. Concerning information sources, the major research finding has been that other members are the major source of a Congressman's information. Kovenok discovered that information inputs coming directly from members of the House were three times as great as from other sources.[6] Bauer, Pool, and Dexter note that "Congressmen develop an implicit roster of fellow-Congressmen whose judgment they respect, whose viewpoint they normally share, and to whom they can turn for guidance on particular topics of the colleague's competence."[7]

Concerning the search for information, the finding has been that most members usually engage in what Kingdon refers to as problemistic search. ". . . Congressmen confine their searches for information only to the most routine and easily available sources."[8] Usually, they consult only a few regular sources.

Concerning the adequacy of congressional information, the major finding has been that members suffer from a general shortage or inadequacy of information. Davidson, Kovenock, and O'Leary found that "The most frequently mentioned problems were associated with the complexity of decision-making: the lack of information . . ."[9] The problem of deficient information for decision-making was cited by 62 percent of their sample--the most frequently mentioned complaint.[10] Janda notes that "Students of the legislative process have identified the information problem as a major factor in the decline of modern legislatures."[11] Saloma highlights various problems of information such as decentralized control, dependence on the executive, and contradictory information.[12]

The purpose of this chapter is to investigate the contextual applicability of these conclusions concerning Congressmen and information. To do this, three propositions--derived from the conditional theory of the legislative process--were examined.

The first proposition is that "Information sources vary according to the kind of issue at hand." The thesis of the conditional scheme is that specialized interests will dominate on low-grade kinds of votes, while more visible issues will involve broader political interests. With regard to the information sources of Congressmen, the inference is that Congressmen receive information primarily from narrow or affected sources on low-grade issues, while on hot issues information comes from broader

sources. In sum, information sources vary according
to the kind of vote at hand.

The second is "The volume of information (defined
as the number of sources) a Congressman refers to
varies according to the kind of issue involved." The
inference of the conditional theory is that on
low-grade issues members rely primarily on narrow
sources of expertise and involvement and make only a
perfunctory scan of information. They usually lack
sufficient interest to search beyond the few sources
of information provided by those proximately
involved. According to this line of reasoning, the
scan of information will be much more intense on
major issues. Highly visible votes will involve
extraordinary information searches, with reference to
many sources.

The third proposition is as follows: "The
member's perception of the adequacy of information
varies according to the kind of issue at hand." On
low-profile votes, only those proximately involved
are informed. The average floor voting member, due
to the lack of personal interest, does not feel
particularly well informed. On hot, burning issues,
which are frequently raised in intense political
discourse, the member will be relatively well
informed.

It should be noted that factual information, or
what David Truman calls technical knowledge (in
comparison to political knowledge), will be the kind
of information emphasized in this chapter.[13] Focus
will be primarily on how members inform themselves
concerning "...the content of a policy issue."[14]
In sum, to use Kovenock's distinction, this chapter
will stress the sources of factual decision premises
while the following one will be devoted to the source
of evaluative, political premises.[15] As noted in
the introduction to chapter III and in chapter II,
information sources constitute the member's more
selective use of communication inputs.

Finding 8: "There are many information sources
for congressional decision-making."

Congressional information stems from what
Saloma refers to as a system of "multiple information
channels."[16] Table 4.1 presents a frequency
distribution of sources mentioned by members

Table 4.1

Aggregate Frequency Distribution of Information Sources:
the Percentage* of Interviews in Which Members Mentioned
Various Information Sources
in Response to the Question:
Where Did You Get Your Information?

Source	Responses
Personal Staff	33%
Democratic Study Group	30
Party Whip Notice	22
Floor Debate	18
Media/Reading	18
Committee Report	14
Committee Members	13
Other Members	9
Last Time Through	8
Committee Membership	6
Committee Chairman	5
Constituents	5
Interest Groups	5
Personal Experience/Learning	5
Dear Colleague Letter	5
State Delegation	4
Party Leader	4
Committee Staff	3
White House	3
Membership on Related Committee	2
Environmental Study Group (ESG)	2
Republican Ad Hoc Group	1
Steering/Policy Committee Membership	1

*Percentages are based on an N= of 361 interviews

throughout the 361 interviews in response to the question, "Where did you get your information--i.e., where did you turn to find out about the facts of the bill?" As displayed there, 14 different sources were mentioned at least 5 percent of the time. Seven were mentioned in more than 10 percent of the interviews. The findings in Table 4.1 corroborate Clapp's finding that

> legislators use many sources in the course of their deliberations . . . such as . . . individual colleagues, informal organizations of Congressmen to which a legislator belongs, committee and personal staffs, the hearings and reports of committee, pressure groups, executive departments, the mail, and floor debate.[17]

Finding 9: "Some sources are relied on for information more than others."

In Kingdon's words, ". . . certain actors in the legislative system are more prominent in the decision-making of Congressmen than others."[18] In this study, the most frequently mentioned information source is personal staff followed by publications of the Democratic Study Group (DSG), party Whip Notices, floor debate, media and general reading, committee reports, and committee members. These findings provide several surprises. Contrary to both Kingdon[19] and Matthews and Stimson,[20] other members (including both members on the relevant committee and those not on it) are not the most frequently mentioned source of information. Also, despite the emphasis in recent publications on the information value of "books and scholarly studies,"[21] congressional research and investigatory agencies[22] (such as General Accounting Office, Congressional Budget Office, and Office of Technological Assessment), and Information Technologies[23] (such as the Legislative Reference Service of the Library of Congress), few members mentioned them as a significant source of information.

It should be emphasized that some sources of information such as personal staff, DSG publication, Whip Notices, and the committee report perform what both Kingdon[24] and Schneider[25] refer to as a filtering or "gate keeper" function. These sources act to synthesize and forward information from a number of diverse sources.

Finding 10: "There are different categories of congressional information sources."

Major congressional information sources can be grouped as follows: personal contacts with other members, impersonal contact with other members, in-house publications, personal staff, outside sources, and members' experience and reading. Members provided a number of insights concerning the utility and contributions of these major sources.

Members as Information Sources

Information concerning a floor vote comes from committee chairmen, committee members, other members, party leaders, and state delegation members.

Committee chairmen, cited 5 percent of the time, were mentioned as an information source in instances where the chairman was an obvious, dynamic actor such as were Morris Udall on strip mining, Robert Giaimo on the budget, and Louis Stokes on the Assassinations Committee.

Committee members were mentioned 13 percent of the time. Other members note the information utility of committee members in two ways. First, those on committee are often turned to for clarification of bills that originate from their committee. As one member described: "I'll seek committee people out if I don't understand. If I have no trouble, no questions--there's no need to visit with them." Another noted, "I usually talk to committee proponents to get a clearer view." Second, committee members "at the door" often provide information. The function of committee members positioned as such is "to discuss. They do not tell you how to vote." One freshman Republican illustrated the use of committee members at the House door with his reconstruction of his decision with regard to the FAA authorization. "I walked on the floor cold on that one. I got all of my information by asking a committee member at the door." Many members emphasized the selective use of committee members. Again and again members noted how they turn to committee members in whom they have confidence. In the words of one member, "I usually talk to friends on the committee to find out about the bill."

Other members not on the committee were mentioned in 9 percent of the decision cases. Other members mentioned as an information source are (1) class members, (2) those who closely monitor floor debate for Republicans, (3) those who offer amendments ("I talked to Baucus to find out how his amendment would affect the Strip Mining Bill"), (4) those who have pork barrel projects at stake in any given vote (especially on the snow removal and water projects votes), and (5) those with recognized expertise on an issue (e.g., the Michigan delegation on clean air, doctors on saccharin). Many members pointed out that their fellow members are a natural source of information. As one noted, "You always survey the guys to find out about things that seem to be ambiguous."

Party leaders were mentioned in only 4 percent of the cases. Three forms of contact were mentioned. One is through official leadership positions issued on major issues. Democrats disseminate leadership positions in the form of published endorsements of the House Democratic Steering and Policy Committee. Republican leaders have two forums: publications of the House Republican Policy Committee and publications of the Republican Research Committee. These endorsements and stands primarily provide "general information. They do not advise." As one Republican described Republican party pronouncements, "They are factual materials that help a guy make up his mind. Usually you'll go with them unless there is an overriding philosophical or local interest."

A second way in which party leaders provide information is meetings with party whips. As a Democratic zone whip noted, "These meetings are used primarily to get information out through the whip network."

A third type of party leader information input is through doorman and cloakroom recordings. The leadership of both House parties station partisan members of the doorkeeper's staff at all entrances to the House floor. These doorkeepers closely follow parliamentary developments and are prepared to give both a synopsis of the facts of a bill under consideration and the party's stand on it. Also, both leaderships provide telephone information lines in their cloakrooms so members away from the floor at the time of a vote can call to find out "what is up."

State delegations were reported in fewer than 5 percent of the interviews, despite the fact that several studies have emphasized the "information sharing" utility of state delegations.[24] Members mentioned several occasions in which delegations provided information: reliance by delegation members on a member of the delegation ("On those kinds of things we all turn to _____"); delegation meetings where each member briefs the delegation on developments in his committee ("These rundowns by committee are really helpful"); and, finally, consultation by delegation members with U.S. Senators from the same state.

Impersonal Contact with Other Members

Impersonal contact that members have with other members also provides information for floor voting. Two very noteworthy impersonal contacts are "dear colleague" letters and debate.

Dear colleague letters are mentioned overall in approximately 5 percent of the decision cases. These communications are sent to all colleagues by a member--on or off the parent committee--concerned with a particular bill. The letters give a concise, but biased, statement of the issue and the member's position on it. Although some members said that these kinds of communications are "simply too much to read, I don't have the time," many members mentioned their utility for "getting the pros and cons." One member stated that "due to their information value and the political situation around here, I always read them to see who is doing what."

General floor debate on a bill was mentioned as an information source in 18 percent of the interviews. Academic literature tends to downplay the importance of debate. Clapp notes that "Legislators commonly believe that debate is more important in terms of public education than for member education."[27] Matthews argues that debate "lacks drama and excitement. . . .most members have already made up their minds."[28] Nevertheless, many members interviewed in this study stressed the informativeness of debate. A freshman Democrat stated that "Listening to debate affords a way to hear the arguments." A senior southern Democrat mentioned the information value of debate as follows: "From debate I learn what a bill and its amendments do. Nine times out of ten, if you have a question on a bill, someone will answer it during debate." The information value of debate is also emphasized by widespread support by members for closed circuit telecasting of debate into House offices. As one member noted, "The TV allows me to conduct business in my office without missing the value of debate." Finally, it should be noted that committee members indirectly provide information through debate, since they usually serve as floor managers for a bill and thus dominate debate.

In-House Congressional Publications

Members identified three in-house congressional publications that have an information value: committee reports, party Whip Notices, and DSG materials.

The report a committee issues on a bill was mentioned as a source in 14 percent of the decisions. The report describes the purpose and scope of the bill and the reasons for its recommended approval. Generally, a section-by-section analysis is set forth in detail, explaining precisely what each section is intended to accomplish. Also, the report lists all changes the proposed bill will make in existing law, cost estimate, and new budget authority.[29] Finally, the report records the views of the committee majority together with any concurring, dissenting, or minority views.

Many members noted that the report is invaluable as an information source. "It is just a good background summary of the bill," one member stated. Several members mentioned that members can determine their need for further study by examining the report. In one member's words, "If there are minority or dissenting views, that indicates to me that there was trouble in committee and there is likely to be a floor fight. For that reason I conscientiously read them." This member also noted that members probably don't have to read the report to get the information from committees. "You'll get the points of view of the committee from committee members on the floor."

Party information packets distributed through whip networks are mentioned in 22 percent of the interviews, the third most frequently mentioned information source. Both parties distribute packages of information to their members. The Democrats title their packet Whip Advisory. It is prepared a week in advance, and members receive it usually the Friday before each new legislative week. It consists of a schedule of all bills to be called up to the floor for the following week, together with a synopsis of each bill. The synopsis lists the floor manager of the bill, gives a title by title summary of the bill, a background of the bill, dissenting views, and estimated cost. Republicans call their notice, Legislative Digest. It is published under the auspices of the House Republican Conference. Like the Democratic Whip Advisory, it provides a schedule and summary of bills. The Republicans supplement the Legislative Digest with publications from the minority leader's office entitled Legislative Alert. These are in-depth studies of major bills prepared by minority counsels to the parent committee. It should also be noted that the Democratic and Republican packages are made available on the floor as well as through the mail. Many members--especially those who seem to be on the fringes of their parties acknowledged that they try to read information packages from both parties.

Members were effusive in their praise of the information value of the DSG. Several Republicans confided that they belonged to the DSG solely to receive the information packets. As one Republican noted, "It's the best information source up here." A Democrat pointed out that "It is a quick summary of issues that is put forth without pressure." Another Democrat said that "It is useful in telling us what is coming up, that it's coming up, and what consent and suspension stuff and amendments entail." Of a different order one member observed, "When the membership of a committee splits, the DSG is good for an objective statement of pros and cons." Members frequently mentioned the information value of the special reports on the strip mining and clean air bills. These special reports seem obligatory reading for members. "If it's something I feel the DSG will cover and review, I go to it," one member stated.

Publications of the DSG rank as the second most frequently cited information sources, having been mentioned by 30 percent of the interviewees.

Originally, the DSG was intended as a counterbalance to the conservative coalition.[30] The DSG constituted an attempt--and there is some evidence available to conclude that it has been moderately successful[31]--to develop higher voting cohesion among liberal Democrats. The contemporary DSG, although continuing these efforts, has also secured a reputation on both sides of the aisle and among those of all persuasions as the congressional information source par excellence. It has approximately 230 members.

DSG distributes four different publications: Legislative Report, Daily Report, Special Reports, and Fact Sheets. Legislative Report is issued weekly. It gives a complete schedule of the upcoming week's activities together with a summary of all bills. The particular utility of Legislative Report in comparison to party publications is that it anticipates the amendments that are expected to be offered. It also lists the arguments pro and con for each amendment. In a commentary section, Legislative Report lists the support and opposition of the administration and major interest groups. Daily Report is issued each day and provides a detailed, updated schedule for the particular day plus a last-minute listing of possible amendments. Special Reports are in-depth discussions of issues that, although not presently up, are imminent. They are compiled by the legislative staff of the DSG and are intended to provide background information on the major bills of the session. Fact Sheets are detailed studies of major, controversial pieces of information that are coming up.

Personal Staff

The personal staff of a member was the most frequently cited source, mentioned in 33 percent of the decision cases.

The interviews revealed three uses of personal staff in information gathering: filtering and preparing, researching, and following debate.

The usual information input of staff is through the preparation of information packages and briefing papers. In this way, staff filters and distills information received from DSG, committee, other members, interest groups, party organizations, the Administration, and constituents. The following comment from a member serves to illustrate this staff function: "The staff breaks down a bill for me. They digest the information forwarded from the DSG, sponsors, and constituency mail and then size it up."

Other members pointed to a research contribution. One member noted that

> I don't get briefed by staff. I pick up basic information on the floor, especially in conversations with other members and the party stuff they have on the floor. For me, staff contributes by looking into questions.

Another member, a Republican, stated that, my staff "goes on the assumption that I've read 'Legislative Alert.'" Their job is to get into it. If there is controversy in the report, that serves as a red flag to get to work on it." Another mentioned that he used staff to research things in which he gets interested and involved. "On those kinds of things where I see a problem, I put them to work. On the pay raise deal I had them do research on salary systems." Several members noted that staff research usually involves consultation with committee people and committee staffs and the staffs of other members, especially those in the state delegation and those with whom the member has ideological compatability.

A final information contribution of staff stems from assigning staff to follow debate (on closed circuit TV) on hotly contested issues when the member cannot be present. Several members noted the utility of doing this when they are in committee and unable to be on the floor. In one member's words, "This way I can keep abreast of developments in the committee of the whole and the business of amendments."

Outside Sources

Constituents and interest groups constituted the only real outside actors contributing information, and this contribution must be regarded as minimal since both were mentioned equally--only 5 percent of the time. The White House, a potential outside source, was mentioned only 3 percent of the time.

Members noted that information from the constituency is only rarely forwarded by average citizens. In fact, the only information input from individual constituents seems to come through member's district opinion polls. These tell the member what constituents know and think about bills. Information from constituents usually comes from groups in the district that are somehow affected by the bill in consideration--e.g., local public officials on grant programs, district industrial plants and auto dealers on clean air, and postal workers on Hatch Act revisions.

Although Clapp,[32] Jewell and Patterson,[33] Milbrath,[34] and Tacheron and Udall[38] have written of the information value of interest groups, it is surprising to discover that groups and their lobbyists are mentioned for only 5 percent of the decisions.

The few who did mention interest groups viewed them as providing information in one of two ways. First, as a senior Republican noted, "Pressure groups help by providing background materials." Such background information on bills is often routinely forwarded to members through the mail." Second, hearing from competing interest groups on a policy question provides the pros and cons of an issue. Those situations where groups were mentioned as information sources mainly involved narrow groups on specific issues such as tuna fishermen, grocers, and the Heinz Corporation on marine mammal protection; right to work committees and labor on common situs; coal companies on strip mining; government labor unions on the Energy Department; United Auto Workers on clean air; National Organization of Women (NOW) on the Hyde Amendment; postal workers on the Hatch Act; and pharmaceutical concerns and the American Diabetic Association on saccharin. In commenting on interest groups and legislation, many members corroborated the notion of Bauer et al. that interest groups deal only

113

with legislators who are already sympathetic with the
group's objectives.[38]

Member's Experience and Reading

Members noted that information is often provided
by their general learning and experience, their
experience with a similar bill in a previous session
of Congress, and their general reading.

Five percent listed personal experience.
Personal experience was felt to be helpful in the
following ways. First, "Expertise accumulated before
one comes to Congress can be relied on." Second,
experience that results from a member's following of
a policy issue for several years can be a source of
information. In this way, one member felt
sufficiently informed on the FAA vote since he had
"followed FAA matters for years." Another felt that
his interest in foreign policy provided sufficient
background on the Miller amendment. Finally, a
member's involvement with a bill provides him with
information. Several members, not on the parent
committee of a bill, emphasized that, due to
constituency or personal interest, they had become
active at the committee stage of a bill, giving
testimony, debating, or following the hearings. This
kind of involvement was felt to provide "all the
guidance one needs."

The experience one has with a policy issue "the
last time it was through" was cited in 8 percent of
the interviews. For experienced members, routine
authorizations and appropriations and bills such as
those pertaining to strip mining, countercyclical aid, common situs, and the Hyde amendment
that have "been around for awhile" pose no
information problems. As one member noted, "These
things tend to be the same as before--I don't have to
look into them again." Another emphasized that "When
they have been around for a few years, I have low
information needs. I know what the bill is." Even
in the case of amendments, prior experience is
helpful. "If you've experienced it once before, you
know what the major issues are and you can let your
personal experience guide you--even on the
amendments."

Media and general reading were mentioned in 18
percent of the interviews. Those who mentioned the

114

media felt that the media provided them with background information on the ethics bill and on the saccharin debate. The media most frequently mentioned were the <u>Washington Post</u>, <u>the Wall Street Journal</u>, and <u>Congressional Quarterly</u>.

Miscellaneous

In addition to the above noted sources, a number of miscellaneous information sources were identified, although none by any great number of members. These miscellaneous sources of information include the following: committee staff ("especially the staffers on subcommittee who wrote the bill--more than anyone they can help members understand what the bill does"), membership on another committee (Ways and Means and budget committee members mentioned they received information on major bills by virtue of their membership on those committees), copies of the actual bill and amendments, class organizations, Republican ad hoc groups (such as the Society of Statesmen and the Republican Study Committee), study organizations such as the Democratic Research Orgaization that services southern Democrats, the bicameral, bipartisan "Environmental Study Group," and the liberal "Members of Congress for Peace through Law." Republicans noted that their party's practice of scheduling and stationing younger members on the floor as monitors was an additional source of information for the monitor and others who turned to him.

Also mentioned were the White House and federal bureaucrats. The White House was seen as a source of information on the Energy Department vote and on the HUD vote where the Carter administration provided the breakdown of aid by states and congressional districts for alternative allocation formulae. Bureaucrats were viewed as helpful on school lunch (HEW), saccharin (HEW, FDA), and the water projects votes (Army Corps of Engineers).

Finally, sponsorship of a bill and, more important, membership on the parent committee are seen as sources of information. Carroll has argued that less than a majority of the membership of a committee's membership are "efficient" in terms of the committee's business.[37] For those who are, however, hearings and the testimony of witnesses is a valuable information resource. In the words of one

member, "If I pay attention on committee, I have no
reason to read party, committee or group synopses."

Finding 11: "Congressional information sources
can be differentiated by directness and proximity."

Congressional information sources can be
differentiated on two bases: directness and
proximity. With regard to directness, there are 1)
direct contacts that involve a personal, direct face
to face relationship between the member and the
source and 2) indirect sources that involve
impersonal relationships. With regard to proximity,
some sources provide information to the member at a
point most proximate to the time of the decision
while others are antecedent. Table 4.2 shows the
classification of major sources according to these
two variables.

Finding 12: "Some information sources synthesize
the position of others."

As the above discussion illustrates, DSG
publications, Whip Notices, the committee report and
staff inputs act as carriers for information provided
by other sources. Both DSG and Whip Notices give the
committee position. DSG provides positions taken by
interest groups and by the Administration. The
committee report contains the positions of key
Congressmen and interest groups. Staff input often
involves consultation with the committee and the
staffs of other members, constituents, and
bureaucrats. As such, these sources constitute
collective channels of information.

Finding 13: "Information sources vary according
to the kind of issues at hand."

Several members argued that they did in fact
use the same information sources for each and every
vote. One member described his standard procedure:
"My staff gives me a packet for each bill that's up.
It contains a copy of the bill, the report, DSG, and
samples of correspondence we've received on it."
Another described a routine search process: "The day
before the vote, I'll look at the bill, the Report,
the Whip and DSG summaries, legislative staff
summary, a sample of the mail, and staff assessments
of district relatedness."

Table 4.2

Classification of Major Congressional Information
Sources by Proximity and Directness

	Directness	
	Personal	Impersonal
Proximate	Committee Chairman Committee Members Other Members Party Leaders State Delegation Personal Staff	Doormen Caucus Recording Debate
Antecedent	Committee Members Other Members State Delegation Personal Staff Interest Groups Constituents	DSG Publications Whip Notice Media/Reading Committee Report Policy Committees Dear Colleague

Proximity

Other members acknowledged a normal scan for information but noted that some votes fall outside the realm of the routine. As one member emphasized, "Not all votes are normal. You use different sources on different votes." For another, "Ninety percent of my decisions do not involve substantive information. But, 10 percent do."

Table 4.3 is a listing of information source by vote. It clearly shows that there is a good deal of variation in the mention of sources from vote to vote. There are votes on which normal sources (i.e., those most frequently mentioned such as DSG, staff, Whip Notices, and committee report) are relied on and other votes where atypical sources come into play. Moreover, reliance on normal sources varied from issue to issue. DSG is mentioned as an information source by 67 percent of the interviewees on the Clean Air Act and by no member on the saccharin vote. The mention of staff varies from a high of 67 percent on HUD to no mention on FAA, public works conference, and the second budget. Whip notices are mentioned by as many as 83 percent on the second budget vote and by no member on the ethics and the NASA votes. The committee report is cited as an information source by 50 percent of the interviewees on marine mammal and by none on ethics and the nuclear navy.

Personal staff, DSG publications, Whip Notices, and committee reports are mentioned on practically all votes but were cited less on two types of votes: those that might be considered visible and salient and those that had been seen before. In both cases members had low information needs since they already had something on which to rely.

Personal staff contributed the most on those votes that were either extremely controversial and complex (Rhodesian chrome, budget I, foreign aid, clean air, Hatch Act, and saccharin) or low-grade and complex (NASA, EPA, marine mammal) or involved grant programs (countercyclical, HUD, and school lunch). Personal staff was mentioned least on votes that members usually knew something about from conversations with other members (ethics, nuclear navy debate, government reorganization, House assassinations, public works, the second budget resolution, the Hyde Amendment, and the pay raise).

Information Sources by Vote: The Percentage of Interviews in Which
Members Mentioned Various Information Sources on Different Votes

VOTE

SOURCE	Ethics	Tax Simpli- fication	Rhodesian Chrome	Energy Dept. Establishment	First Budget Res. (defeated)	Debt Collection
Personal Staff	14%	30%	46%	31%	46%	36%
DSG	29	40	18	31	36	36
Whip Notice	0	40	9	38	45	36
Floor Debate	7	0	18	38	36	27
Media Reading	14	20	18	38	0	0
Committee Report	0	20	9	19	27	18
Committee Members	0	20	27	25	9	18
Other Members	0	0	27	0	9	0
Last Time Through	0	0	27	0	0	27
Committee Chairman	43	0	0	0	0	0
Constituents	7	0	0	13	0	0
Interest Groups	7	0	0	6	0	0
Personal Experience (Learning)	0	0	18	6	0	0
Dear Colleague Letter	0	0	0	0	9	9
State Delegation	14	0	9	0	0	9
Party Leader	29	10	0	0	18	0
Type of Vote:	Hot	Hot	Hot	Hot	Hot	Hot

*Percentages represent the proportion of members on that vote mentioning that information source

119

TABLE 4.3 (Continued)

SOURCE	VOTE						
	Common Situs	Govt Reorg	Strip Mining	Clean Air Act	Hyde (Anti) Abortion Amend.	Repeal of Hatch Act	Saccharin Ban
Personal Staff	31%	8%	23%	47%	21%	46%	46%
DSG	15	23	31	67	36	39	0
Whip Notice	15	15	23	27	29	23	0
Floor Debate	8	8	0	20	29	46	9
Media Reading	0	23	0	13	21	15	73
Committee Report	23	15	8	27	21	31	0
Committee Members	8	0	8	20	0	8	9
Other Members	8	15	8	40	7	0	9
Last Time Through	23	0	39	13	36	8	0
Committee Chairman	0	8	15	7	0	0	0
Constituents	0	0	0	13	7	0	0
Interest Groups	23	0	8	20	0	15	46
Personal Experience (Learning)	15	0	0	0	21	15	0
Dear Colleague Letter	0	0	0	0	0	15	9
State Delegation	0	0	0	7	7	0	0
Party Leader	0	0	8	7	0	0	0
Type of Vote:	Hot	Hot	Hot	Hot	Hot	Hot	Hot

120

TABLE 4.3 (Continued)

SOURCE	Water Projects	Pay Raise	EPA Auth	Nuclear Navy	Goldwater Housing Amend.	NASA Auth	FAA Auth	Snow Removal
				VOTE				
Personal Staff	35%	22%	60%	9%	30%	60%	0%	27%
DSG	53	17	60	36	20	20	25	9
Whip Notice	29	6	40	18	30	0	13	9
Floor Debate	19	0	0	36	60	20	0	55
Media Reading	47	39	0	0	0	0	0	9
Committee Report	0	0	0	0	20	10	13	0
Committee Members	12	6	20	9	10	10	25	0
Other Members	29	0	0	27	30	0	0	9
Last Time Through	0	0	20	0	0	0	0	0
Committee Chairman	6	0	0	9	10	10	0	0
Constituents	6	11	0	0	0	0	0	9
Interest Groups	0	0	0	0	0	0	0	0
Personal Experience (Learning)	6	11	0	0	0	0	0	0
Dear Colleague Letter	12	0	0	18	10	0	13	9
State Delegation	6	6	0	0	0	0	0	0
Party Leader	0	0	0	9	10	0	0	9
Type of Vote:	Hot	Hot	Low Profile	Low Profile	Low Profile	Low Profile	Low Profile	Low Profile

TABLE 4.3 (Continued)

			VOTE			
SOURCE	Public Works Conference	Countercyclical Aid Auth	HUD Auth	Marine Mammal	House Assn. Comm. Auth.	Romanian Earth-quake Relief
Personal Staff	0%	77%	67%	50%	8%	30%
DSG	33	8	25	17	0	40
Whip Notice	22	15	17	33	15	30
Floor Debate	33	15	8	25	0	0
Media/Reading	22	0	0	17	23	0
Committee Report	44	8	8	50	0	0
Committee Members	11	0	8	33	31	10
Other Members	0	8	0	17	0	10
Last Time Through	0	15	0	0	0	10
Committee Chairman	11	0	0	0	0	0
Constituents	0	8	0	8	0	0
Interest Groups	0	0	0	25	0	0
Personal Experience/ Learning	0	8	8	8	8	0
Dear Colleague Letter	0	8	8	0	0	0
State Delegation	0	15	17	0	0	0
Party Leader	0	0	0	0	8	0
Type of Vote	Low Profile	Low Profile	Low Profile	Low Profile	Low Profile	Low Profile

122

TABLE 4.3 (Continued)

VOTE

SOURCE	Arab Boycott	First Budget Resolution (passed)	Foreign Aid Reduction	School Lunch Authorization
Personal Staff	20%	6%	55%	50%
DSG	40	25	46	25
Whip Notice	40	63	18	25
Floor Debate	20	0	9	13
Media/Reading	10	0	18	13
Committee Report	30	13	9	25
Committee Members	10	38	9	13
Other Members	20	0	0	0
Last Time Through	20	13	9	0
Committee Chairman	0	13	0	0
Constituents	0	0	0	0
Interest Groups	0	0	0	0
Personal Experience/ Learning	0	0	9	13
Dear Colleague Letter	20	13	18	0
State Delegation	0	13	0	13
Party Leader	0	13	0	0
Type of Vote	Low Profile	Low Profile	Low Profile	Low Profile

DSG input was highest on issues that were hot but complex (tax, Arab boycott, clean air, and water projects) and those low-grade votes for which little information was available (Romanian earthquake, EPA, and foreign aid). It was the lowest on relatively straightforward hot issues and all types of issues for which information was plentiful.

Whip Notices were mentioned most on fiscal votes (tax, budget), Arab boycott, and EPA; infrequently on ethics, saccharin, the pay raise, Rhodesian chrome, and amendments (nuclear navy, snow removal, and foreign aid reductions).

Debate was most mentioned as an information source on those bills that were handled on short suspenses (amendments such as nuclear navy, Goldwater, and snow removal) and those bills that tended to involve a high level of disagreement (Energy Department, the first budget vote, and the Hatch Act revisions).

Media reading was an information factor on the highly visible votes: tax, common situs, Energy Department, Hyde, saccharin, water projects, and pay raise.

Committee reports were frequently mentioned when the committee was divided (common situs, public works, marine mammal, and the Hatch Act) or when the committee evinced unanimity on a controversial matter (Arab boycott). Reports were not perceived as an important information source on major issues (ethics, Rhodesian chrome, strip mining, Energy Department, saccharin, water projects, and the pay raise) on which the member himself was already likely to be informed and those low-grade votes on which he might have received a synopsis of committee action from another source (nuclear navy, NASA, FAA, EPA, Romanian earthquake, House Assassinations Committee, snow removal, countercyclical, HUD, and foreign aid).

Other sources, not so prominent in the total breakdown of sources, were mentioned with a high frequency on certain bills, indicating that the information contributions of various atypical sources are highly contextual. Committee members were mentioned when they themselves became major combatants on the floor: assassinations committee, marine mammal protection, and the second budget vote. Other members not on the committee or in the state delegation were most prominently mentioned on both the clean air act and the Goldwater amendment--two instances of attempts by floor members to override the committee. Experience the last time up was viewed as important by some on four votes: Rhodesian chrome, debt collection practices, strip mining, and the anti-abortion amendment. Committee chairmen were mentioned in 43 percent of the interviews concerning the ethics vote. Personal experience was mentioned in approximately one-fifth of the interviews concerning both Rhodesian chrome and the Hyde anti-abortion amendment--issues that had been faced in the previous Congress. Dear colleague letters were judged as an information source on the foreign aid cut vote. Constituents were mentioned as an information source in 47 percent of the interviews on saccharin. Constituents were also slightly mentioned on other hot bills such as the Energy Department bill, clean air, and the Hatch revisions. Interest groups were mentioned by approximately 20 percent on common situs, marine mammal, and clean air--issues where groups did make a determined effort to influence Congress. State delegation members were most prominent as an information source on two major grant programs: countercyclical and HUD. Party leaders were perceived by many as informative on the ethics vote.

To summarize the distribution of sources by vote, data presented in Table 4.3 shows that there is significant variation, according to vote, in member use of various normal as well as atypical information sources. Normal sources (DSG, party material, staff, committee report) are used if the member has an information need--i.e., if the vote is both unfamiliar to him and at least somewhat important. These normal sources are supplemented by atypical sources under various special circumstances.

Testing the specific relationships of the proposition (that low-profile votes will be dominated primarily by narrow sources of information, while hot issues will involve broader input) with Table 4.3 provides results that are inconclusive. Supportive is the finding that extremely high profile votes--strip mining, clean air, Hyde, and water projects--involve high levels of input from the member's own general reading of media. Nonconfirming is the finding that on low-profile votes such as

NASA, FAA, EPA, HUD, countercyclical, marine mammal, and school lunch, information is provided not by committee members or affected interest groups, but by DSG, Whip reports, and staff. Although, as argued above, these normal sources may very well be based on subsystem sources.[38]

The arrays by issue characteristics do not show a marked variation in information sources by issue characteristics. Only 11 percent of the arrays involve distributions where the mention of a source varies more than 9 percent under different values of the same issue characteristic.

These variations of 9 percent or greater do permit the identification of some correlates of information sources--i.e., the values of issue characteristics under which a source is more likely to be mentioned than not. Table 4.4 presents these significant correlates of each information source.

With regard to the specific relationship between type of source and kind of vote, the breakdown of sources by issue characteristics offers only mixed support for the proposition. Supportive is the fact that committee members, presumably a narrow information source, are more apt to be mentioned on complex and technical votes. Yet, contrary to the proposition, Whip notices and DSG publications, presumably broader sources (although as mentioned earlier, they may in fact be based on the committee), are also prevalent in many low-profile situations. Also disconfirming are the following findings: a) Whip notices are more often mentioned on issues involving low constituency awareness and the absence of perceived renomination and reelection effects and b) DSG is mentioned when the issue is defined as complex, technical, and not involving constituency awareness or renomination or reelection effects.

In sum, the data in Table 4.4 show that the use of information sources varies according to only some issue characteristics. Variation in members' mention of information sources occurs more by vote than by issue characteristics.

To conclude the discussion of information sources, tests show that members mention different information sources on different pieces of legislation. Evidently, different issues pose

Table 4.4

Values of Issue Characteristics Associated with Mention of Different Information Sources
(These Correlates are Based on Variations of 9 Percent or More)

Committee Chairman	Committee Member	Debate	Whip Notice	Committee Report
No correlates observed	Complex (LP) Technical (LP) Closed rule (H) Congress modifies (H)	No renomination effects (LP) Routineness (LP) Above average rule margin (LP) Above average policy time (H) Presidential involvement (H)	Salient (H) Constituents unaware (LP) No renomination effects (LP) Closed rule (H) Above average rule margin (LP) Minority report (H) Democratic endorsement (H) Mention in polls (H) Presidential involvement (H)	Congress as modifier (H) Above average policy time (H) Above average Republican unity (LP) Amendment over committee objection (H) Republican endorsement (H)

State Delegation

No correlates mentioned

Party Leader

Closed rule (H)

Table 4.4--Continued

Other Members	Staff	Media	DSG	Last Time
Above average rule margin (LP)	Complex (LP)	Constituency aware (H)	Complex (LP)	Minority report (H)
No Republican endorsement (LP)	Constituency not aware (LP)	Mail (H)	Technical (LP)	Congress as Initiator (H)
Policy change (H)	No strong feeling (LP)	Tough (H)	No constituency awareness (LP)	Above average policy time (H)
Constituency	Thought (H)	Modified open rule (LP)	Mail (H)	Not new (H)
Constituency awareness (H)	Open rule (LP)	Defeated status (H)	No renomination effects (LP)	
Mail (H)	Above average rule margin (LP)	Committee consensus (LP)	Tough (H)●	
Thought (H)	Congress modifies (H)	Washington Post story (H)	Thought (H)	
Interest Groups	No presidential involvement (LP)	No Republican endorsement (LP)	Minority report (H)	
CQ box score (H)		New (H)	Below average Democratic unity (H)	
Personal Experience		Specific (LP)	Democratic endorsement (H)	
Mail (H)			No presidential involvement (LP)	
Dear Colleague			Change (H)	
No presidential involvement (LP)				

H = Presumed hot value
LP = Presumed low-profile value
● = Variation of 20 percent or more

128

different information needs for the member that
cannot be satisfied by consistently referencing a
single source or a set of sources. In most
instances, normal information channels suffice.
Under several special circumstances, however, members
turn to atypical sources. Few relationships exist
between source and issue characteristics.

Finding 14: "The volume (the number of sources)
of information a Congressman refers to (although
generally low) varies according to the kind of issue
involved."

Kingdon concludes that most Congressmen ". .
. engage in an extended search for information only
rarely . . ."[39] In other words, most members use
the same search procedures on most issues.

In describing their own information procedures,
several members corroborated the notion of a single
process. When asked "From where did you obtain
information?," several answered, "the usual process"
or "the normal procedure." The following quotes are
examples of members' descriptions of standardized
procedures for all decisions:

> If I do anything, I take a passing look at
> DSG.
>
> For most votes, you know all you have to to
> make a yea or nay decision. There is no
> need for extended research.
>
> I rely totally on DSG, Library of Congress
> stuff and Ways and Means staff.

I read the Whip Advisory on everything and get it
all from there.

The conditional approach implies a process that
is much more variable. It is inferred that low-grade
issues involve no more than perfunctory search, but
hot issues witness an extraordinary, broader search
for information. Kingdon accepts the notion of a
variable search process. In his words, "There is
more reading, talking, and seeking out of information
during consideration of the highest-salience issues
than with other issues."[40] But, this occurs only
rarely for the member "only when confronted with some
unusual problems."[41]

Several members spoke of a more pronounced variation in information scan, as shown by the following statements:

> To inform myself, I merely go to two or three on each side and hear what they have to say. If I'm confused, I go to two or three more.

> Intense conflict clearly raises a different perspective. Routine matters involve different information gathering procedures than those not so routine. On those not so routine you must visit with other members.

> For every vote you try to get all the facts. Sometimes you can do this by just going to DSG publications. At other times, especially when the vote is controversial and my constituency is involved or affected, I go to committee members, state delegation members, and, if I have to, to debate.

> What is a routine information procedure on one issue may not be routine for another. What's routine for one member may not be routine to another because of interest and involvement.

To address the disparity between the routine and variable perspectives, two tests were made.

First, the number of information sources cited in each interview session were counted and categorized as being above or below the mean number of contacts (the average for all respondents was approximately three information sources per vote). The distribution of above and below mean sources were then cross-tabulated by vote and issue characteristics' indicators. It was felt that if the conditional theory is correct, the number of members having above mean sources should vary from issue to issue, with hot issues involving a preponderance of above mean sources.

The second test involves inspection of the responses of all members for whom four or more questionnaires are available. It was felt that if the contextual approach is valid, the responses of those who were interviewed numerous times should evince diversified search procedures, as seen in the mention of different sources on different votes.

Table 4.5 displays a general frequency distribution of all sampled members for all issues. Overall, most members relied on only one or two sources when making a decision, giving superficial support to the perfunctory scan generalization. It is interesting that for 7 percent of the decisions, no information source was mentioned. In these cases, members acknowledged that "There wasn't much on it."

Cross-tablulations by both votes and by issue characteristics reveal meaningful variation in information search.

Table 4.6 shows that how many information sources members refer to depends on the vote at hand. The percent of members with above mean information sources varied from vote to vote, from a high of 80 percent on clean air to a low of 13 percent on the FAA vote. For eight of the votes studied--including some of the more controversial ones such as the Arab boycott, Energy Department, clean air, Hyde, Hatch, and water projects--more than half of those interviewed had above mean information sources. In contrast, for 12 votes, less than 30 percent of the interviewees had above mean information sources. The 12 are basically of three types: 1) low-grade votes (FAA, House Assassinations, NASA, Romanian earthquake, public works, and HUD), 2) votes with short parliamentary deadlines (nuclear navy, snow removal, and saccharin), and 3) hot votes for which the member is usually already fairly well informed (pay raise, ethics, and the budget).

Tables 4.7 to 4.9 show the issue characteristics correlates of information volume. Fifty percent of the distributions involve variation in above mean information sources in excess of 20 percent. Most of the correlates of high volume information are hot characteristics. Exceptions are those votes defined as complex and technical. Arrays by these characteristics also reveal that extended search occurs on both hot and low-profile issues. Although one member insisted that "On old issues, there just isn't an information need," this study shows no difference in terms of information volume between old and new policy questions.

131

Table 4.5

Frequency Distribution of Information Sources; the Percentage of
Interviews in which Members Mentioned Various Numbers
of Information Sources

Number of Sources	Percent of Total
0	7%
1	29
2	26
3	23
4	10
5	5
6	1

n - 361

Table 4.6

The Volume of Information by Vote:
The Proportion of Respondents Who Reported
Three or More Contacts, Per Vote

Hot Votes:

House Ethics Code	29%
Tax Simplification and Rebate	40
Rhodesian Chrome Ban	46
Energy Department Establishment	56
First Budget Resolution (defeated)	36
Debt Collection Practices	55
Common Situs Picketing	31
Presidential Governmental Reorganization Authority	70
Strip Mining Regulation	31
Clean Air Act	80
Hyde Anti-Abortion Amendment	50
Repeal of the Hatch Act	77
Saccharin Ban	27
Water Projects Fight with President Carter	65
Pay Raise	22

Low-Profile Votes:

Nuclear Carrier Recission	18%
Goldwater Housing Amendment	66
NASA Authorization	30
FAA Authorization	13
Snow Removal Funds	18
Public Works Conference	22
Countercyclical Aid Reauthorization	46
HUD Authorization	17
Marine Mammal Protection	58
House Assassination Committee Reauthorization	8
Romanian Earthquake Relief	20
Arab Boycott	60
First Budget Resolution (passed)	25
Foreign Aid Reduction	36
School Lunch Authorization	38

Table 4.7

Values of Issue Characteristics
Associated with Above and Below the
Mean Information Search (correlates based on
a variation of 9 percent or more;
mean = three or more sources)

	Above the Mean Search	Below the Mean Search
Perceptual Indicators	Complex (LP) Technical (LP) Conflict (H) Heavy Mail (H) Tough (H)	Not complex (H) Not technical (H) No conflict (LP) No Mail (LP) ● Not tough (H)
Objective Indicators	Open Rule (LP) Above Average Rule Margin (LP) Minority Report (H) Congress as Initiator (H)● Above Average Timeframe (H) Democratic Policy Endorsement(H)	Closed Rule (H) Below Average Rule Margin (H No Minority Report (LP) Congress as Ratifier (LP) ● Below Average Timeframe (LP) No Dem. Policy Endorsement (
Subjective Indicators	Change (H)	No Change (LP)

H = Presumed hot value
LP = Presumed low profile value
● = variation of 20% or more

134

Table 4.8

Level of Information by Vote: Distribution of Responses, by Vote, to the Question "How Informed Did You Feel?"

Vote

Level of Information	House Ethics Code	Tax Simplification	Rhodesian Crome	Energy Dept Establishment	First Budget Res.(defeated)	Data Collection	Common Situs	Gov't. Reorg.
Not much	0%	20%	9%	0%	0%	9%	0%	15%
Somewhat	14	60	27	50	55	64	33	54
Very well	86	20	64	50	45	27	67	31
Type of Vote:	Hot	Hot	Hot	Hot	Hot	Hot	Hot	Hot

Vote

Level of Information	Strip Mining	Clean Air Act	Hyde (anti-Abortion) Amend.	Repeal of Hatch Act	Saccharin Ban	Water Projects	Pay Raise	EPA Auth.	Nuclear Navy
Not much	25%	20%	0%	0%	0%	0%	0%	0%	0%
Somewhat	42	53	21	46	55	59	6	100	82
Very well	33	27	79	54	45	41	94	0	18
Type of Vote:	Hot	Hot	Hot	Hot	How	Hot	Hot	Low Profile	Low Profile

Table 4.8
(continued)

Vote

Level of Information	Goldwater Housing Amend.	NASA Auth.	FAA Auth.	Snow Removal	Public Works Conference	Countercyclical Air Reauth.	HUD Auth.	Marine Mammal
Not much	10%	56%	60%	18%	33%	8%	17%	8%
Somewhat	80	33	40	46	11	67	33	75
Very well	10	11	0	36	55	25	50	17
Type of Vote:	Low Profile	Low Profile	Low Profile	Low Profile	Low Profile	Low Profile	Low Profile	Low Profile

Vote

Level of Information	House Assn. Committee	Romanian Earth- quake Relief	Arab Boycott	First Budget Res. (passed)	Foreign Aid Cut	School Lunch
Not much	23%	50%	0%	0%	0%	25%
Somewhat	31	40	80	55	40	50
Very well	46	10	20	45	60	25
Type of Vote:	Low Profile	Low Profile	Low Profile	Low Profile	Low Profile	Low Profile

136

Table 4-9

Values of Issue Characteristics Associated with Mention of Different
Levels of Information

(These correlations are based on variations of 9 percent or more)

Not Much	Somewhat	Very Well
No conflict (LP)	Complex (LP)	Not complex (H)
Constituency	No conflict (LP)	Not technical (H)
not aware (LP)	Not major (LP)	Conflict (H)●
No mail (LP)	Constituency not	Major (H)
Routine (LP)	aware (LP)	Salient (H)
No thought (LP)●	No mail (LP)	Constituency aware (H)●
Modified open-rule (LP)	No renomination	Mail (H)
Comfortable margin	effects (LP)●	Renomination effects (H)●
of passage (LP)	No reelection	Reelection effects (H)●
No CQ story (LP)	effects (LP)●	Not routine (H)●
No Washington Post	Routine (LP)	Feeling (H)●
story (LP)	No strong feelings (LP)●	Thought (H)✔
Congress ratifies (LP)	Above average rule	Closed rule (H)●
Above average	margin (LP)●	Below average rule
Democratic party	Close final passage (H)	margin (H)●
unity (LP)	Committee dissensus (H)	Final passage defeated (H)●
	No minority report (LP)	Minority report (H)
	No Washington Post	CQ story (H)✔
	box score (LP)	Washington Post box
	No Republican party	score (H)
	endorsement (LP)	Washington Post
	Presidential	story (H)
	involvement (H)	Congress initiates (H)
		Below Democratic party
		unity (H)
		Below average likeness (H)
		Democratic party endorse-
		ment (H)
		Republican party endorse-
		ment (H)
		Above average money (H)
		No presidential involve-
		ment (LP)●

H = Presumed hot value
LP= Presumed low-profile value
●= Variation of 20 percent or more

The second test--inspection of the information processes of the 51 members for whom there are four or more questionnaires--reveals that 80 percent of the interviewed legislators show what might be described as a diversified information process. They mention different sources and have a different information volume on different pieces of legislation. For only 20 percent of the legislators for whom four or more questionnaires were collected was there anything resembling a routine search procedure--i.e., use of the same sources and the same information scan in most cases.[42]

To conclude the discussion, on some issues members make a perfunctory scan, and on others they engage in extraordinary search. These variations do not neatly coincide according to hot/low profile status. High volume search is associated with hot issues with which members are not personally involved, votes without short parliamentary suspense, and low-profile votes that are complex and technical. On these kinds of votes, members are likely to refer to many sources of information.

Finding 15: "Congressmen generally feel adequately informed when casting floor votes."

Although, as noted at the beginning of this chapter, lack of information is considered a characteristic of the congressional information process, in only 11 percent of the interviews did members note that they felt inadequately informed.

Table 4.10 gives the distribution of responses to the question: "How informed did you feel on this decision?" It shows that most classify their level of information in the "moderate" or "somewhat" category and the "very well" category. Table 4.11 presents a list of verbal descriptions that members offered for each of the response categories available to them for the level of information question. It shows that those classifying their information level as "not much" do not feel informed on the issue and feel their knowledge is below average. Conversely, those classifying their information as "very well" consider themselves to be above average in knowledge, due to either committee responsibilities or intimate involvement. Those classifying their information level as "somewhat" fall somewhere in between. They feel they have enough information to adequately or

138

comfortably make a yea/nay vote. They describe their
level of information as "comfortable," "reasonably
enough," "better than most," "average," "marginal,"
and "superficial."

Finding 16: "The member's perception of the
adequacy of information varies according to the kind
of issue at hand."

The distribution of responses to the
question on level of information by vote reveals that
a member's level of information varies from vote to
vote. Table 4.12 presents this distribution. "Not
much" responses vary from a high of 60 percent
mention on the FAA vote to a low of no mention on
ethics and several other votes. "Very well"
responses vary from 94 percent on the pay raise to no
mention on the FAA vote. Low-profile votes such as
NASA, FAA, and Romanian earthquake are associated
with above average "not much" responses and below
average responses in the "somewhat" and "very well"
categories.

Hot votes such as ethics, Rhodesian chrome,
common situs, Energy Department, the second budget,
Hyde Amendment and pay raise are associated with
inordinately high "very well" responses and no
responses for the "not much" category. Low-profile
or short suspense bills such as nuclear navy,
Goldwater amendment, marine mammal, EPA, and Arab
boycott and complex, technical and specialized votes
such as tax and clean air are associated with below
average "very well" responses.

The reasons for these variations are best
provided in members' words. One member noted,

> We are usually prepared on major bills and
> significant amendments to them. Divisions
> in committee which occur on important
> votes provide safeguards by communicating to
> the member that there will be a fight, and he
> better inform himself. On things not so
> important, you fly by the seat of your
> pants.

Another argued that

> The more controversy, the more you'll know
> about it. If you are to be respected by

139

your colleagues, you should be able to talk
the pros and cons on an issue. When there
is less controversy and emotion and more
complexity, a member is not likely to know.

Another noted that

On major bills you get stuff from the
Library of Congress, the Congressional
Research Organization, and party and
factional groups. There is usually an
abundance of informtion that allows you to
get familiar with basic issues. On minor
issues you just don't get much information.
You often have to guess.

The issue characteristics' correlates of
information level provide overwhelming support for
the directional relationships predicted by the
conditional theory. These correlates, based on
variations of 9 percent or more, are exhibited in
Table 4.13. "Not much" responses are associated with
only low-profile values. All of the correlates of
"very well" responses are, with only one exception,
hot values. Correlates of "somewhat" responses are,
with a few exceptions, low-profile values.

To conclude the discussion on level of
information, Congressmen view their level of
information in varying degrees depending on the kind
of issue involved. On hot issues they feel
relatively well informed. On low-grade votes,
perhaps due to the lack of incentives and interest,
they perceive their information to be relatively
scant.

Summary and Conclusions

Students of Congress have formulated three major
generalizations concerning congressional
information: (1) Kovenock's finding that other
members are the main source of a Congressman's
information, (2) Kingdon's conclusion that
Congressmen confine their information searches to
routine sources and "only rarely" go beyond them, and
(3) Davidson et al.'s conclusion that most members
perceive an information deficiency when voting.

This chapter has examined the contextual nature
of congressional information and has revealed a

process much more variable than implied by previous research. An examination of three aspects of congressional information from the perspective of the member--sources, volume, and adequacy--has revealed that the sources members utilize, their search procedures, and their perceptions of their own level of information vary according to different kinds of votes. Thus, for the congressional scholar, descriptions of congressional information seem better captured by the identification of contexts than by single models.

This chapter has revealed that members rely on many different sources of information. These sources are of both a personal and an impersonal nature and are disseminated both proximate to and antecedent from the vote. The most frequently mentioned sources are personal staff and various in-house publications, not other members as Kovenock has suggested. Use of information sources is variable. Normal sources (those most frequently mentioned such as personal staff, DSG publications, party materials, and the committee report) satisfy usual information needs. Normal sources are supplemented by other actors and sources, however, under special circumstances. Variation in sources is not strongly related to either issue characteristics or to the hot or low-profile distinction. Instead, variable use of information sources seems to be a function of member knowledge and need. If a member is unfamiliar with a vote, but it is somewhat important to him, he will consult with normal sources such as staff and congressional publications. Special contextual circumstances cause him to turn to other sources for various reasons. For example, committee members provide information when they are combatants. Debate is an information source when bills are handled on short suspense.

The search procedures of Congressmen are highly variable. The number of sources a member refers to prior to a floor vote varies from only a few on some votes to many on others. These variations are related to different values of issue character- istics but not solely in the direction of a hot or low-profile distinction. Members search for more information when the issue is hot, when there is not parliamentary suspense, and when there are certain low-grade issues that are hard to understand. Combining these findings with an inspection of questionnaires from members from whom four or more interviews were completed reveals a search process more varied than Kingdon's notion that members only occasionally deviate from routines.

How informed a member feels when casting a vote is also highly variable, and these variations do conform to the distinctions between hot and low-grade issues. In contrast to Davidson et al., members feel at least adequately prepared to cast a vote. On low-profile votes, however, a disproportionate number admit to knowing "not much" on an issue. On hot votes a disproportionate number perceive that they know an issue "very well." There is variation among different values of issue characteristics. These variations conform to a hot or low-profile distinction, with hot characteristics associated with a higher level of perceived information and low-profile characteristics associated with a lower level.

A major research question not examined in this chapter involves the actual sources from which congressional publications and personal staff receive the information that they forward to members. As Schneier notes, "There is a two-step flow of information within the legislature."[43] Yet, the initial source of information was not studied. Statements from various members and interviews with party and group information systems, however, do suggest that most of the information distributed by these sources is based on committee sources. This seems to corroborate Schneier's notion of "functional fragmentation"--i.e., that the information process in Congress is fragmented into policy subsystems.[44] The problem with this kind of system is that, in Schneier's words, "There are few general sources . . . of information."[45] If information is based on the committee system, there is no guarantee that multiple, competing points of view are being heard. Instead, if the committee is the major information source, floor information may be based on a homogeneous group of Congressmen. Committee recruitment patterns are such that members are attracted to a committee primarily because of constituency interests and case work responsibilities. In other words, most committee members are motivated by a sense of service to affected interest groups rather than to service to the public interest. If, then, committees are the

major source of floor information, an effort should
be made to insure broad-based representation on the
committees of Congress.[46]

[1]John S. Saloma, III, Congress and the New Politics (Boston: Little, Brown, 1969), p. 214.

[2]Barbara Deckard, "State Party Delegations in the U.S. House of Representatives: A Comparative Study of Group Cohesion," Journal of Politics 34 (1972): 199-222.

[3]Donald G. Tacheron and Morris K. Udall, The Job of the Congressman (Indianapolis: Bobbs-Merrill, 1966), p. 125.

[4]Arthur G. Stevens, Jr., Arthur H. Miller, and Thomas E. Mann, "Mobilization of Liberal Strength in the House, 1955-1970: The Democratic Study Group," American Political Science Review 68 (1974): 688.

[5]Norman J. Ornstein, "Information Resources and Legislative Decision-Making: Some Comparative Perspectives on the U.S. Congress," Ph.D. dissertation, University of Michigan, 1972, chapter 3.

[6]Kovenock as quoted in Saloma, Congress, p. 218.

[7]Raymond A. Bauer, Ithiel de Sola Pool, and Lewis Anthony Dexter, American Business and Public Policy (New York: Atherton Press, 1963), p. 437.

[8]John W. Kingdon, Congressmen's Voting Decisions (New York: Harper and Row, 1973), p. 227.

[9]Roger H. Davidson, David M. Kovenock, and Michael D. O'Leary, Congress in Crisis: Politics and Congressional Reform (Belmont, Calif.: Wadsworth Publishing Co., 1966), pp. 75-78.

[10]Ibid.

[11]Kenneth Janda, "Information Systems for Congress," in Congress: The First Branch of Government (Washington, D.C.: American Enterprise Institute, 1966), p. 415.

[12]Saloma, Congress, pp. 212-18.

[13]David Truman, The Governmental Process, 2nd ed. (New York: Knopf, 1971), p. 334.

[14]Ibid.

[15]This distinction is used in David Kovenock, "Influence in the U.S. House of Representatives: A Statistical Analysis of Communications," _American Politics Quarterly_ 1 (1973): 410-13.

[16]Saloma, _Congress_, p. 215.

[17]C. Clapp, _The Congressman: His Work as He Sees It_ (Garden City, N.Y.: Anchor, 1963), p. 126.

[18]Kingdon, _Congressmen's Voting_, p. 227.

[19]Ibid., p. 20.

[20]Donald R. Matthews and James A. Stimson, _Yeas and Nays_ (New York: Wiley, 1975), pp. 102-110.

[21]Charles R. Dechert, "Availability of Information for Congressional Operations," in _Congress: The First Branch of Government_, p. 173.

[22]Tacheron and Udall, _The Job_, p. 125.

[23]Saloma, _Congress_, p. 218.

[24]Kingdon, _Congressmen's Voting_, pp. 223-25.

[25]Edward Schneier, "The Intelligence of Congress: Information and Public Policy Patterns," _The Annals of the American Academy of Political and Social Science_ 388 (1970): 16.

[26]See: Deckard, "State Party Delegations."

[27]Clapp, _Congressman_, p. 141.

[28]Donald Matthews, _U.S. Senators and Their World_ (Chapel Hill: Univ. of North Carolina Press, 1960), p. 246.

[29]Charles J. Zinn, _How Our Laws are Made_, rev. by E. F. Willett (Washington, D.C.: U.S. Government Printing Office, 1978), p. 16.

[30]See: Stevens, "Mobilization," and Mark F. Ferber, "The Formation of the Democratic Study Group," in _Congressional Behavior_, ed. by N. W. Polsby (New York: Random, 1971), pp. 249-69.

[31]Stevens, "Mobilization."

[32]Clapp, _Congressman_, pp. 188-89.

[33]Malcolm E. Jewell and Samuel C. Patterson, The Legislative Process in the United States, 3rd ed. (New York: Random, 1977), p. 289.

[34]Lester W. Milbrath, "Lobbying as a Communications Process," Public Opinion Quarterly 19 (1955-56): 32-53; and Milbrath, The Washington Lobbyists (Chicago: Rand McNally, 1963).

[35]Tacheron and Udall, The Job, pp. 140-43.

[36]Bauer, et al., "American Business," p. 351. Also see Lewis A. Dexter, How Organizations are Represented in Washington (Indianapolis: Bobbs-Merrill, 1969), p. 73.

[37]Holbert N. Carroll, The House of Representatives and Foreign Affairs (Pittsburgh: Univ. of Pittsburgh Press, 1966), pp. 27-29.

[38]This researcher's fragmentary investigations of the sources for Whip notices, DSG, and staff input would support the conclusion that most of the input to these sources is based on committee sources.

[39]Kingdon, Congressmen's Voting, p. 227.

[40]Ibid.

[41]Ibid.

[42]A member was considered to have a diversified search process if he exhibited an information process on two or more bills which is different from his search procedures on other votes.

[43]Schneier, "Intelligence," p. 18.

[44]Ibid., p. 17.

[45]Ibid.

[46]For compelling arguments for maximum cross-sectioning of committees, see Lewis A. Froman, The Congressional Process (Boston: Little, Brown, 1967), pp. 193-205, and Roger H. Davidson, "Representation and Congressional Committees," in "Changing Congress: The Committee System" Annals 411 (January 1974): 48-62.

CHAPTER V

THE CONDITIONAL NATURE OF DECISION DETERMINANTS

The most important component of the legislator's decision-making map is, of course, the basis on which the member actually makes the decision. In the parlance of decision theorists, it is referred to as the "normative premise."

To explain why Congressmen vote as they do, political scientists have focused on two major concepts: determinants and roles. Decision determinant refers to the determinative cause of a Congressman's floor vote.[1] Role is the basic orientation with which the legislator approaches his decision responsibilities. In employing both concepts, many analysts seem to imply that a Congressman's decision-making is generally dominated by a single determinant and a single role. This chapter will investigate the variability of decision determinants. The next will examine role variability.

The enormous research efforts undertaken by political scientists to uncover why legislators vote as they do have identified a plethora of forces, factors, and actors that correlate with, cause, determine, or explain the vote. These various determinants can be classified according to four categories, depending on how proximate they are to the vote and whether they are internal or external to the legislature or legislator. Table 5.1 classifies the major, identified causes according to four possible categories.

Actors within the legislature and proximate to the vote who have been identified as influential in congressional voting are committee members,[2] fellow members,[3] party leaders,[4] and a member's personal staff.[5] Internal forces somewhat remote from the vote are party,[6] ideology,[7] legislator's demography,[8] legislative procedures,[9] and norms and folkways.[10] External actors proximate to the vote are constituents,[11] the President,[12] bureaucrats,[13] and lobbyists.[14] Factors external to the legislature and antecedent to the vote are constituency characteristics,[15] media,[16] electoral outcomes,[17] and public opinion.[18]

Table 5.1

Forces, Factors and Actors Variously Identified
As Determinants of Legislative Voting

	External to the Legislature or Legislator	Internal to the Legislature or Legislator	
Proximate to the Vote	Constituents President Bureaucrats Lobbyists	Committee System	
		Fellow Members	
		Party Leaders Personal Staff	{Classes Friends Ideological Groups State Delegations
Distal from the Vote	Constituency Characteristics Media Electoral Outcomes Public Opinion	Party Ideology Legislator's Demography Legislative Procedures Norms/Folkways	

148

Many of the researchers who identify these actors, forces, and factors presume that the determinant which they pinpoint determines most legislative voting. For example, for Turner "party continues to be more closely associated with congressional voting behavior than any other discernible factor."[19] For Matthews and Stimson, as the subtitle of their work states, cue-taking is the "normal" decision-making procedure in the House.[20] For Clausen, most decisions are made on the basis of policy dimensions. In his words,

> legislators reduce the time and energy requirements of policy decision-making by (1) sorting specific policy proposals into a limited number of general policy content categories and by (2) establishing a policy position for each general category of policy content, one that can be used to make decisions on each of the specific proposals assigned to that category.[21]

Kingdon fosters a consensus mode theory. To him,

> Congressmen begin their consideration of a given bill or amendment with one overriding question: Is it controversial? . . . when there is no controversy in the Congressman's environment at all, his decision rule is simple: vote with the herd, . . . If the Congressman does see some conflict in his total environment . . . he proceeds . . . to the next step in the decisional flow chart.[22]

Each of these authors fails to emphasize that different legislators may be influenced by different determinants or that legislators may be alternately affected by various factors, depending on the decision situation.

In contrast, Lowi, Ripley and Franklin, and Price stress the contextual applicability of different decision referents. Lowi, and Ripley and Franklin, for example, argue that different forces are influential on different kinds of decisions. Although they do not specifically address determinants of decision-making from the perspective of the member's cognitive map, these authors imply that on distributive issues members will engage in

cue-taking from committee members, on regulatory
issues they will make ideological decisions, and on
redistributive issues they will ratify compromises
hammered out among prominent political elites.[23]

This chapter will examine a proposition
concerning determinants that seems to be a logical
deduction from the conditional model. This
proposition is as follows: the basis on which a
representative casts a vote varies by kind of issue.
On low-key issues, members will be more likely to
engage in cue-taking (i.e., leaning on, looking to,
or taking bearings from other actors), while on hot
issues members are more likely to make an ideological
(or what Clausen calls a policy) vote.

The rationale for this proposition stems from
theories of economic incentives. On those issues
considered to be low-profile and relatively
unimportant, members will lack the incentive to
become involved. Due to lack of interest in the
question, they will be willing to defer to the
judgments of others. On hot issues that are perceived to be important, members will be sufficiently motivated to develop policy commitments.

Distinctions

The study of congressional decision-making has
spawned a veritable lexicon of terminology used to
describe various aspects of the decision process.
Terms such as referent, determinant, correlate,
decision rule or mode have been used to illustrate
various concepts concerning decision-making. A
precise definition of each will clarify the ensuing
discussion.

A decision referent is an actor, force, or factor
that the Congressman feels is important in shaping
his decision.

A decision determinant is the actor, force, or
factor that the Congressman cites as being most
influential in his decision.

A correlate is an actor, force or factor
discovered to be associated with patterned voting
among roll-call data. Thus, the major difference
between a correlate and a determinant is the method
used to identify them. Correlates are discovered

150

through roll-call analysis, while determinants are
identified through interviewing.

A decision rule or mode is a patterned, shortcut
process through which a decision determinant is
routinely influential. For example, continued,
routine reliance on a committee member as a
determinant by a member would point to the decision
rule of "cue-taking." Similarly, continued use of
ideology would involve the decision mode of policy
voting.

The conditional approach to legislative behavior
argues that the decisions of each Congressman are
determined by different determinants depending on the
issue at hand. Congressmen employ not one decision
rule but different rules on different kinds of issues.

To obtain data on decision determinants, the
question "Why did you decide as you did--i.e., on
what did you base the decision?" was asked. Responses support seven general statements.

Finding 17: "A variety of decision determinants
are cited in House floor voting."

Interviews with members reveal a plethora of
forces and factors on which they base floor decisions. Table 5.2 displays the various determinants
cited by members as the basis of their decisions. It
should be emphasized that these responses express in
members' own words what they felt was the primary
basis of their decisions. The determinants fall into
four broad categories: people, place, ideas, and
procedure. The following are examples of members'
use of the various determinants.

People

Some decisions are based on deference to the
position of others such as other members, staff, the
White House, bureaucrats, and even family and
friends. This is the classic cue-taking model.

Chairmen

Chairmen were mentioned as a decision determinant
in the context that the member was following the lead
of the chairman. Examples are statements such as "I
followed Obey on ethics," "I went with Jack Brooks on

Table 5.2

Distribution of Number of Cited Determinants:
The Percentage of Interviews in which Members Mentioned
Different Numbers of Determinants

Number of Determinants Cited	Number of Congressmen	Percentage of the Total
0	4	1
1	149	41
2	139	39
3	53	15
4	14	4
5	2	
	N = 361	101%

government reorganization," or "I'm sticking with Conte on the water projects vote." In each case the member looked to the chairman's position for guidance. As one member noted with regard to marine mammal protection, "I looked to see if the Chairman appeared personally satisfied with the tuna/porpoise quotas. After finding out that he was, there was no problem for me."

Committee Members

Committee members were mentioned as decision determinants in two ways: (1) individual members were identified by other members as cue-givers, and (2) the committee's position on legislation as put forth in the committee report was mentioned as a kind of collective decision determinant.

Use of committee members as cue-givers takes the form of following a member on committee and mentioning that member's position as the decision determinant. Examples are "I relied on Rodgers' judgment on that," "I watched Bennet and did as he did," "I was persuaded by Frenzel's explanation," "I gave my vote to McCloskey on marine mammal," "I always follow the California Democrat on the committee," and "Pattison convinced me that debt collection reforms was the way to go."

Members justified cue-taking from committee members on grounds of time constraints and the necessity to specialize within the legislature. One member stated, "Congressmen must be encyclopedic, but we don't have time. We must rely on what others say on the floor during debate." Another stated that "Members need to concentrate on those things that they can have an impact on. To have the time to be effective you must defer to the judgment of others in their area of expertise."

Members emphasized that cue-taking is not a random matter but involves a relationship of friendship, trust, propinquity, constituency similarity, and ideological compatibility. The mediums for cue-taking often are informal conversations on the way to or on the floor and information-swapping across committees by friendship, class, state delegation, and ideological cliques. As a member noted, "Most members check out each other on a day-to-day basis and become familiar with

153

different positions being taken in committee." Many
members were emphatic in arguing that aversion to a
member is also a factor in cue-taking. One member
explained this kind of negative cue-taking by stating
firmly that "Anything Congressman X proposes, I
automatically oppose."

The second use of committee members pertains more
to the committee system than to individual members.
It involves following the committee." Examples are,
"I followed the committee on the HUD vote," and "I
supported the committee on clean air." Also
illutrative are the statements of several Republicans
that they followed committee minority and dissenting
views.

Members defend reliance on committee reports on
the grounds that panels are partisan and
heterogeneous and "provide the possibility to raise
red lights." The reputation of various committees
seems to affect the willingness to defer. As one
member noted, "I'll go along with Ways and Means.
They have it all together. But, that turbulence on
the Select Committee on Assassinations led me to
conclude the expenditures are not warranted."

State Delegation

Members of a state delegation were mentioned as a
decision determinant in the same context as committee
members. Often, when committee members were cited as
a decision cue, the interviewee added that the
committee member was also a member of his state
delegation.

State delegations were also mentioned as a
collective determinant. In several instances members
stated that their vote was decided by a common
commitment by members of the state delegation. The
most interesting example is a statement by a member
of the Washington state delegation concerning his
decision on the clean air bill: "We caucused and
Foley (Rep. Thomas Foley, State Delegation Dean)
stated that he wanted us to come in together on this
one. I was prepared to vote against it if it were
not for this push for delegation unanimity."

Finally, colleagues from state delegations were
cited by a limited number of members as a decision
determinant on the basis of recognized, but not

committee-related, expertise. For example, several members of the Wisconsin delegation noted that they followed Rep. Aspin on the nuclear navy vote. Although Aspin is not a member of the Budget Committee that had parent jurisdiction over the vote, members of the delegation turned to him on the basis of his expertise in defense matters.

Party Leaders

Many members acknowledged that party leaders or party positions often determined votes, especially budget and appropriations measures. "These are party votes," one member emphasized. Also, members will follow leaders on those votes on which leadership has staked its prestige. The statements that "I followed the will of leadership on ethics," and "I gave O'Neill my vote on the pay raise," provide examples of this. The mediums of party cues are party publications and endorsements.

All emphasized the relative light-handedness of leadership pressure. One member stressed that "Leadership is restrained by a very strong ethic around here--follow your district first." Leaders do appear to have some leverage on procedural votes. The following recollection by a Democratic freshman serves to illustrate how leaders can manipulate the vote up to the point of final passage.

> I opposed common situs and leadership knew it. Though I was a crucial vote, they did not pressure me. They knew I had made up my mind and was voting nay for reasons of both philosophy and constituency. I met with both a sponsor and a whip and both said 'We won't twist arms, but let us have our bill. Support our amendments so that we have our bill for the straight up or down vote on final passage'.

Other Members

Members neither on the committee of origin nor in the state delegation were frequently cited as a determinant. Examples are, "I followed Dingell and Moss on energy," "I turned to Jeffords on strip mining, especially on all those darn amendments," and "I followed Goldwater on the housing amendment since it was a political vote."

155

Other members likely to provide a cue are: (1) those involved in floor debate--witness Representative Goldwater providing cues on his amendment, (2) social and ideological comrades, (3) those who are trusted--"You're influenced by members you have confidence in," and (4) those with similar constituencies--"I always check to see how so-and-so votes since we have the same kind of district. If I feel he knows more about it than I, I'll follow him."

Personal Staff

Some members cited personal staff as the determinant of a decision. Examples are "I followed the recommendations of staff on the tax vote," "Staff looked into the question of the formula (HUD vote) and I took my vote from them," "Detailed staff study convinced me that the committee had put together a good compromise on the tuna/porpoise question," and "Staff determined my position on that housing bill." Influence by staff seems to be a function of idiosyncratic staff organization. Those members mentioning staff as a decision determinant spoke of "elaborate staff setups" and "regular issue meetings." They acknowledged that they "put staff to work on obscure votes" and would usually defer to them. Others argued that they "don't lean on or turn to staff." "I know what I want," a member emphasized. He went on to stress that "I use staff to answer questions, to try to find out policy and political impacts, to weigh the pros and cons." Another noted that staff input was restricted to a "once a year meeting on the major issues likely to crop up that session." More often than not, members see staff not as an independent lobbying force but as a synthesizing or filtering agent that draws from many sources of input and seeks to be an extension of the members.

White House

Many noted that they followed the President's judgment on selected issues. Examples of the President as a decision determinant are: "I followed Carter on the water projects," "The President's position that 'The Arab boycott is not good policy' convinced me," "I was persuaded by Carter that we don't have to have another super aircraft carrier," and "I support governmental reorganization authority because it is a primary objective of the President."

156

Many decisions were determined by constituency.
As a decision determinant, constituency is
influential in four ways. First, members relate that
they are responding to pressures and communications
from individual constituents. Examples are, "I
didn't have a choice on saccharin if I read our
letters," "I followed the strong expression of
opposition in my district concerning common situs,"
and "I know the desires of people on strip mining and
I followed them." Second, members vote on the basis
of their perceptions of constituency interests.
Examples are: "I did what was best for my state on
the HUD formula vote," "I voted 'yes' on the
budget--it will help unemployment in my region,"
"Countercyclical aid is good for my district,"
"Public works is important to my district," and
"Water is the future of our state; therefore, I
supported the Water projects." The third way
constituency becomes a determinant is through fear of
political backlash. Examples are, "I voted 'no' on
the pay raise because I'm fearful of constituency
reaction," and "I'm afraid of the electorate's
response on the pay raise vote--how can I explain the
fact that I voted myself a raise that itself is in
excess of what most people in the district earn."
One member eloquently summed up the preemptive and
directive influences of constituency as carried by
the anticipatory political reasoning of
representatives:

> You must pay attention to constituency on
> local issues and when you hear from them in
> volume. Under those conditions, if you
> desire political survival you have no
> recourse but to follow. Up here, I hear so
> infrequently from people. When I do--and
> I'm not referring to that post card
> junk--with citizen mail like on common
> situs, clean air, and saccharin, I've got no
> choice but to go with them. I'd be dead if
> I didn't.

The fourth use of constituency is in a very narrow
sense. Members sometimes base their decisions on the
desires of only a segment of the constituency.
Exmples are, "My local public officials preferred
that formula alternative for countercyclical aid,"
"Postal employee complaints about the ambiguity of

157

the implementation of the Hatch Act convinced me of the need for change," and "I acceded to demands of government workers in my district for repeal of the Hatch Act."

PROCESS AND PROCEDURE

Frequently, procedural or "process" concerns are important decision determinants for members. Provisions which are a compromise or on which consensus has been reached are important in a legislative arena of negotiation, bargaining, and compromise. Illustrative are members' references to compromise, consensus, and consistency.

Adequacy of Compromise

The perception that the vote under consideration strikes a proper balance was used by many members as a justification for their decision.

Citing the determining factor of a vote to be the fact that a bill "seems to be a reasonable compromise" stems from a brokerage conception of the Congress. As one member pointed out, "In Congress you need to find half-way (maybe half-assed) mediums in public policy." The"nature of yea and nay, up and down voting requires it." Another added that "It's our job to weigh positions and to forge compromises among competing interests."

The following statements provide examples of how compromise is cited as a decision determinant: "I voted for marine mammal protection because it is a balance between environmental protection and the needs of tuna fishermen," "The clean air amendments by Dingell offer a balance between clean air, energy and jobs; Dingell's version avoids going too far too fast," "The revised budget (second budget vote) is a good compromise between economic reality and an instrumental position," and "The loss of jobs and inflationary pressures that would likely ensue, on balance, outweigh the immediate implementation of the clean air act; delay it."

In elaborating on compromise voting, several noted that a member's perception of the degree to which the membership of a parent committee or, in the case of a conference report, a conference committee is balanced would affect his perceptions of how good

158

a bargain had been struck. For example, bills reported by Ways and Means were judged "good compromises because it has a good mix." On the other hand, one member felt that the Budget Committee was composed of "too many pro spenders who are usually out of step with most members--I vote against that bunch."

Consistency

Many defined their vote as an attempt to get in line with a past position. In these cases, the desire to be consistent was identified as the determining factor. Examples of consistency voting are: "Revision of the Hatch Act is consistent with the reform image I desire," "My vote on the pay raise is an attempt to be consistent with the ethics bill to give us a more reformed Congress," "I am a strong supporter of labor legislation, and common situs picketing is just a logical extension of my position," "The Hyde amendment is the same thing we had last time--I voted the same as before--we had an election since and I was reelected so obviously people aren't objecting," and "I'm always for those kinds of programs; I voted that way last time."

The mechanics of consistency voting were detailed by several interviewees. "With so many decisions around here, all you can do is stick to your guns and do what you did the last time, unless you have reason to switch." Another noted that "there are a lot of repetitive issues around here. Every year you see the same policies and hear similar issues and arguments. You notice that things fall into categories and you find yourself referring back to how you voted before. You feel the pressure and need for consistency."

Consensus

Many bills are acted upon within the House with unanimity or virtual unanimity. Many members acknowledged that a perceived consensus on a bill is often the grounds for a decision. Examples of consensus voting are: "I went that way because there was a mountain factor--things were snowballing," "There was a consensus on ethics--I just followed the herd," "I was assured that the tax bill would pass, so I just went along with everyone else," "On FAA, there was no reason to do otherwise--there was no conflict out of committee," "I had no reason to vote 'no,'" and "There was no opposition, no one objecting, a quiet bill in every respect--no one in leadership was against."

The major factors cited as encouraging the use of consensus voting were the committee system, the political liabilities associated with minority status, and the handling of routine business in a consensus fashion. The committee system is thought to provide a good ad hoc adversary system for screening legislation. As one member emphasized, "We have a good rumor network here. Unless I hear strong rumblings, unless someone is objecting, I support. My law is--if no conflict, appropriate."

Members confess that they will often go with a big majority to avoid the stigma and repercussions of lone dissent. In the words of one member, "You need a strong reason to be in a minority of 30 or less. They'll target your ass. Unless it's something to do with my district and I have the overwhelming approval of my constituents, when they have 300 plus, they have me."

Suspensions, unanimous consent matters, and the private calendar are handled in a consensus fashion. As one member noted, "On these kinds of things, if no one objects and the tide is running in their direction, they will pass." Many offered the opinion that many members take the same approach to all but the most controversial of bills.

IDEAS

Frequently, abstract positions will guide the floor votes of members. The major examples are philosophical convictions, policy assessments, and campaign promises.

Philosophical Convictions

Often the decisions of members will invoke moral judgments and strong personal beliefs. According to one member, decisions of this kind "involve the members' assessment of right and wrong." In the words of another, "These are things you can't compromise. I won't change my mind. I will get defeated first." Another stated, "Sometimes your own philosophy intrudes--things that stem from your learning and experience. It boils down to how you feel about it, rather than a question of facts like with the water projects vote. It's almost an unconscious process."

Examples of votes that involve personal philosophy are: "I'm against abortion on religious grounds and would never vote 'yea,'" "Debt collection involves a basic question concerning our form of government; I'm intuitively opposed," "The Arab boycott vote involves basic questions of rights and constitutional beliefs; the 18-year old vote is the same thing because basic rights are involved," "Abortion is a different kind of decision than authorizations and appropriations--it is a moral issue," and "I based my decision on the Arab boycott on the basis of fairness, equity, and compassion."

Policy Assessments

Policy assessments involve the use of ideology and policy objectives as the basis of congressional voting.

Interviews with members indicate that policy assessments as a decision determinant take three forms: endorsement for or opposition to a specific bill, support for or opposition to the policy approach of a particular program, and assessments that a specific vote is in or out of line with certain narrow policy objectives of the member. Although each way may seem to present a distinctive determinant, all are similar in that they involve the citation, by the member, of policy reasons as the basis for the decision.

Endorsement of or opposition to the bill in question involves assessments that the content of a bill is "good legislating," "good arguments," "a good bill," "a bad bill," or "a lousy bill."

Support or opposition to a basic policy approach is a commonly cited policy-oriented determinant. It entails a member's position that the program at hand is good or bad public policy. Indicative of a policy approach are judgments by members that a program is "not justifiable," "absurd," "not a proper approach," or "a step in the right direction."

161

Many members describe the mechanics of a policy approach. They note that representatives identify various categories of public policy and then formulate general, preconceived positions for or against the policies and programs within each category. In the words of one member, "These positions become standing and automatic. They involve an almost knee-jerk reaction." Specific examples of this kind of voting are: "I vote 'yes' on social issues," "I'm opposed to increases in military spending," "I opposed debt collection practices because I'm for state rights," "The pay raise is bad policy--we ought not to vote on a raise which affects us," "I'm against NASA funding; let's get our society in shape," "I have a bias toward simplification of the tax system," "It's poor policy to get the federal government involved in abortion when so many oppose," "The Hatch Act has served us well," and "Keep strip mining and all other forms of regulation in the hands of the state if at all possible."

The third and final category of policy assessments are those that involve a member's limited policy objectives. Unlike the first two, this kind does not involve support for or aversion to a specific bill or basic policy approach. Instead, the member makes reference to a narrow, more limited, situational rationale that, more than less, entails policy objectives. Votes are said to be determined not by standing commitments for or against programs but by such considerations as spinoffs, impacts, consequences, sunk costs, and instrumental goals. Examples of this kind of policy assessment are, "I supported that housing bill because of the economic stimulus it will have on building," "The case is not proven against saccharin," "The second budget resolution is a step in the right direction," "The proposed distributions of funds under that formula are inequitable--the alternative is preferable," "We need to cut back, so we might as well start with these water projects," "I voted 'no' on the carrier because I was convinced they would be sitting ducks," "I didn't vote for the Dingell amendment for fear it would make the clean air bill more palatable, and it would make it on final passage," and "I voted 'yes' on the Energy bill because of the weakening amendments."

Voting on the basis of these limited policy objectives dramatizes the importance of what Keefe

162

and Ogul refer to as "sweetener amendments."24
Astute floor managers will permit moderate changes in
a bill in an effort to put together a majority
coalition. These interviews confirm the validity of
this strategy by revealing that in many instances
members do make up their minds on the basis of
limited, situational, instrumental criteria.

Campaign Promises and Positions

Several reconstructed decisions pointed to a
campaign promise as the major determinant. Examples
are "I had made a campaign commitment to support
reorganization," "I'm on record promising to reduce
deficit expenditures," "I ran against the pay raise,"
and "During the campaign, abortion was the issue and
I even received primary opposition on it--I didn't
have to agonize on Hyde since it's politically
essential not to go back on my word."

Miscellaneous

Interviews also revealed a spate of what might be
classified as miscellaneous determinants--i.e., those
that are not frequently cited. Examples are
bureaucrats, media reading, and others cited in Table
5.3, plus interest groups, log-roll politics and the
lack of choice afforded by a straight up and down
vote. At the very least, these are interesting
because they indicate the multiplicity of
determinants uncovered in this study. Together with
the major categories, these dramatize that
Congressmen are apt to base their decisions on what
seems to be an infinite, almost bewildering, number
of determinants.

Finding 18: "Members frequently mention multiple
determinants when reconstructing their decision
process."

Although members were asked to identify the
single factor that was most influential in their
decision, an average of two determinants were
mentioned by each member for each decision. Table
5.3 displays a frequency distribution of the number
of determinants cited. As can be seen there, many
members mentioned two or three factors and some
mentioned as many as four or five. Evidently, in
many instances, members felt that their decision was
the result of several co-weighted determinants rather

163

TABLE 5.3

Frequency Distribution of Decision Determinants:
The Percentage of Decisions in Which Various Decision Determinants
Were Mentioned in Response to the Question:
Who/What Was Most Decisive in Helping You Make Up Your Mind?

Policy Assessment	65%
Constituency	13
Philosophical Convictions	11
Committee Members	10
Adequacy of Compromise	7
Consistency	7
Consensus	7
Experience on the Parent Committee	7
White House	6
Committee Chairmen	6
Other Congressmen	4
Personal Staff	4
State Delegation	3
Campaign Promises	3
No Choice/Structure of the Rule	3
Party Leaders	2
Protect the Process	2
Prioritization	2
Personal Experience	2
Bureaucrats	2
Media/Reading	1
Other Items in the Bill	1
Family/Friends	1

(N = 361: multiple responses permitted)

than any one cause. It will be argued subsequently that different mixes or blends constitute different decision modes.

Finding 19: "An overwhelming majority of decisions are determined by ideological considerations."

A reexamination of Table 5.2 reveals that, by far, the major determinant of congressional voting, as perceived by members, is ideology as expressed through a policy assessment. The next most frequently mentioned determinant is constituency, followed by philosophical convictions, and then committee members. Each of these were mentioned in only approximately 10 percent of the interviews.

For two reasons, the actual percentage of decisions attributable to policy voting may be somewhat larger than is shown in Table 5.3. First, many of the other determinants involve policy considerations--e.g., compromise, campaign promises, consistency, consensus, some of the miscellaneous category, and even possibly philosophical convictions--and, when combined with policy assessments, drive the total frequency of policy voting up to almost 100 percent.

Second, many of the instances where a member lists multiple determinants involve a mix of actors and situational concerns with policy assessments. The following answers to the question, "Why did you vote as you did?," reveal a policy-oriented blend of determinants.

(re ethics)   I voted that way
                               way because I'm for
                               reform and change.
                               It is consistent
                               with my position on
                               reform. It would
                               really disappoint
                               my close supporters
                               if I didn't.

165

                              (re countercyclical aid) My state would lose
                                                       money if I voted
                                                       'no.' I voted
                                                       the same as last
                                                       year. It's still a
                                                       good idea.

Also, as Helmut Norpoth has argued, reliance on other
actors often involves policy (ideological)
voting.[25] The following quotations reveal how
cue-taking involves policy assessments.

              (re a chairman)   I'm for Udall on
                                           strip mining. He
                                           has a practical,
                                           balanced environmen-
                                           talist position.

              (re other members)   I turn to _____
                                           to find out what
                                           the damn thing
                                           does. I follow him
                                           on the policy impli-
                                           cations.

                                           When I use a member
                                           as a shortcut, it
                                           is intertwined with
                                           philosophical con-
                                           siderations.

                                           I followed Hyde. I
                                           support his amend-
                                           ment in concept.

              (re staff)   Staff gives me a
                                           synopsis and makes
                                           a recommendation.
                                           They know my
                                           philosophy.

                                           Staff talks to
                                           people for me.
                                           They are an
                                           extension of me.
                                           They know what I
                                           want.

                              166

(re constituency)   My position was set
                                     by the outpouring
                                     of letters on
                                     saccharin plus my
                                     personal belief
                                     hat government agen-
                                     cies ought not to
                                     have that kind of
                                     authority.

(re the White House)   I followed the
                                     President, because
                                     he has a more
                                     national view, and
                                     because we must
                                     start to cut back.

Many factors account for the predominance of
policy voting. Foremost is the perceived need by
members for an explanation (rationale) for their
votes. As one member stated, "You must worry about
how things will appear. You must be able to
explain. If you can give the reasons for your vote
in philosophical terms, you can defend yourself
against the critics." A policy assessment seems to
provide such an explanation.

Another factor encouraging policy voting is the
nature of the committee system and legislative
procedure. "When it comes to the floor, it is open
or shut--up or down, nay or yea. This kind of
decision-making requires that you have a set position
that enables you to know where you stand."

A third factor is the issue content of
congressional campaigns at the level of attentive,
affected, and activist publics. As one member noted,
"You develop positions during the campaign and they
stay with you. People ask for your views and you
must comment."

A fourth stems from the need to simplify. "Bills
of national significance require a member to have a
point of view even if not on the committee," one
member pointed out. Another discussed in detail the
utility and need for policy positions: "You need to
have a value system to know where you are coming
from. You need to decide what to do and this boils
down to a policy approach. After a couple of years,

you get a strong position on basic issues and it guides you."

Finally, the day-to-day operation of Congress encourages policy voting. The whip packets of both parties stress the policy goals and implications of bills. Bills are frequently discussed by members on a day-to-day basis in terms of what they do. The Democratic whip organization prepares recess briefing packages designed to aid members as they answer questions back in the district. These strongly emphasize explanations. The voting records of members are scrutinized by various interest groups who search voting habits for signs of consistency and support. All of this weighs heavily toward policy voting.

Finding 20: "There are seven different decision modes of congressional voting."

Although policy assessment is the most frequently cited decision determinant in congressional voting, it would be simplistic to conclude that policy voting is the only important mode of decision-making. Rather, the interviews undertaken here suggest that there are at least seven distinct modes of congressional voting: cue-taking, policy assessment, philosophical convictions, consensus, campaign promise, adequacy of compromise, and constituency representation. Although policy assessment is the most prevalent mode and although all of the others involve, to some extent, members' policy goals,[26] each mode involves a different decision rule, or different approach to issues and, thus, a different way of making decisions.

Cue-taking is a decision mode whereby the decision is made primarily on the basis of the counsel or position of other actors. Although Matthews and Stimson contend that committee members and those in the state delegation are the most likely cue givers,[27] Kingdon[28] and this study reveal that members also take positions from staff and the White House. This kind of decision does not lack policy content. Rather, cue-taking should be viewed as voting based on policy positions that are obtained as the result of deference to another actor.

Policy assessment is a standing ideological predisposition to vote for or against certain

168

programs. It involves the persistent employment of a general decision rule to support or not to support some action of government. Policy assessments are fairly automatic, although various actors do provide information so that the member can place the vote in the context of his policy predispositions. The basis of decision is a policy objective and the desire for consistency, not another actor's position. The difference between policy assessment and cue-taking is that cue-taking reflects the human side of Congress. Decisions are made on the basis of trust and friendship. Policy voting is based on a desire to achieve a record. Referring to his policy objectives concerning a bill, a member emphasized that "on votes like that I'm not here to make friends."

Philosophical conviction is a mode of reaching a decision by relying on deep-seated, strongly-felt positions. It is an automatic mode in which other actors are relied on primarily for information. When making decisions based on philosophical convictions, a member simply applies a standing commitment that was most likely developed long before he entered Congress.

The consensus mode, best described by Kingdon,[29] involves decision-making by herd instinct. Yea votes are cast because everything is pointing that way. There is no reason to vote "no." Opposition is minimal or nonexistent. Conflict exists neither in the House nor in the member's force field.

The campaign-promise mode bases decisions on policy commitments made during the campaign. The rationale for the vote is more the campaign commitment than the policy assessment.

The compromise mode involves an assessment on the member's part that a bill constitutes a balanced or unbalanced approach. The member decides to either ratify or reject a compromise forged either in committee or on the floor. The appropriateness or adequacy of the compromise is the focus of the decision.

Constituency representation is decision-making on the basis of the member's assessment of what is best for constituency interests. In some rare instances

169

where there is an outpouring of sentiment from the district concerning a bill, constituency representation as a decision mode will involve the member attempting to get his position in line with constituency demands.

Thus, decisions may be the result of the application of an abstraction (policy assessment, philosophical conviction, campaign promise), the use of cue-taking, an act of representation, or a perception of situational factors (compromise, consensus). It is not that cue-taking or situational voting are devoid of ideology. On the contrary, as Norpoth,[30] Kingdon,[31] and Matthews and Stimson[32] all argue, cue-taking does invoke an ideological context. In fact, the data here indicate that when members mention an actor or situational factor as a determinant, they will relate it to a policy assessment. The difference between cue-taking or situational voting and voting in a policy or philosophical mode is that, in the latter, decisions are made solely on the basis of an abstract doctrine, while, for the former, a trusted actor or a perception of the situation becomes the shortcut and is cited in the interview as the voting determinant, perhaps in addition to a policy assessment. Most voting involves a "policy goal" of some sort. As Kingdon argues, under certain circumstances members must rely on various means (colleagues, staff, perception of constituency interests, perception of balance and compromise, etc.) to realize their goals.[33] Here it has been shown that members will cite the "means" as well as the "goals" as the determining factor. Clearly, the difference reflects different decision-making modes. Citing "goals only" is policy or philosophical voting; citing means and goals involves other modes.

In conclusion, the interviews confirm the existence of the various congressional decision modes described in both Jackson[34] and Matthews and Stimson.[35] The task at hand is to test the conditional theory of legislative decision-making. If the positions of Lowi, Price, and Cobb and Elder are correct, no one model should completely describe the decision-making of an individual member. The remainder of this chapter will test the contextual proposition by examining the variability of decision rules across votes, issue characteristics, and actor responses. To confirm the contextual theory, data should reveal a) that members are likely to cite certain determinants under certain circumstances and different determinants under others and b) that each member employs various modes depending on various circumstances. These variations, moreover, should occur in a patterned fashion according to a hot and low-profile distinction.

Finding 21: "Many individual members acknowledge the use of different decision modes in different decision settings."

Many of the interviewees were asked to describe how they generally made decisions. Although these general responses were not systematically collected, but, instead, obtained as time allowed, they provide evidence of contextual decision-making.

Some members insisted that they made up their minds in the same way on every issue. Here are some examples:

It's an invariant process for me--I look at how others are voting and who is saying what.

I usually go with the committee report. The committee system is the way we work here. There are adversary groups that must compromise.

As LBJ said, 'Politics is the art of the possible.' You have to settle on the best you can get. I use the 51 percent rule. Vote for bills as long as you oppose no more than 49 percent of it.

Most members, however, acknowledge the variability of decisionmaking. They state that they make up their minds in different ways, depending on the circumstances involved. Examples of conditional voting are:

Unless it is controversial, or district relevant, I follow the California Democrat on the committee.

I vote the district unless the party has a strong position.

171

> On major matters, I follow constituency. On
> esoteric issues I follow members I trust.

> Unless I'm on the committee or it is a very
> important thing, I'll go to committee
> members to find out how to vote the district.

> If there is strong opinion in the district,
> I follow that. If not I go with DSG, the
> committee, or the state delegation.

> I usually base decisions on my beliefs. If
> I'm in the dark, I go to a sponsor or a
> committee member and rely on them.

An inspection of the questionnaires of the 51
respondents for whom four or more decision cases are
available also supports a contextual model. Forty-two
(88 percent) cited different determinants and
manifested different decision modes on the various
bills for which interviews were obtained. Only nine
members (18 percent) appeared to have employed the
same decision process in each decision case.

Finding 22: "The decision determinant that
members cite varies from vote to vote."

Table 5.4--a display of decision determinant
by vote--reveals variable citation of decision
determinants. For example, policy assessments, the
most frequently cited determinant overall, are
mentioned by 100 percent of the interviewees on the
foreign aid vote, while no interviewee mentioned
policy reasons on the FAA vote. Committee members
are mentioned by no interviewees on Rhodesian chrome,
but by 42 percent on the marine mammal vote. Mention
of philosophical convictions ranged from no mention
on NASA and FAA to mention by 50 percent on the Hyde
amendment. Moreover, there is a degree of cohesion
concerning the decision determinant utilized for each
vote. On most votes, 50 percent or more cited the
same determinant.

Members tend to mention certain determinants more
often than others on different types of bills.

Policy assessments were mentioned most as a
determinant on some of the hottest issues--Rhodesian
chrome, common situs, strip mining, Energy
Department, the pay raise, and saccharin--and on

172

Table 5.4

Decision Determinants by Vote: The Percentage of Interviews
In Which Members Mentioned Various Decision Determinants on Different Votes

Determinant	House Ethics Code	Tax Simplification	Rhodesian Crome	Energy Dept. Establishment	First Budget Res. (defeated)	Debt Collection
Policy Assessment	43% *	70%	73%	94%	73%	64%
Constituency	21	20	9	6	18	0
Philosophical Convictions	7	10	46	13	9	9
Committee Members	7	30	0	0	9	27
Adequacy of Compromise	7	0	0	6	0	9
Consistency	7	0	18	0	0	9
Consensus	7	0	9	13	0	18
White House	7	30	9	0	0	0
Committee Chairman	14	20	0	0	9	0
Other Members	7	0	9	0	0	9
Personal Staff	7	10	0	6	0	0
State Delegation	7	0	0	6	0	18
Campaign Promise	7	10	0	6	0	0
Party Leader	14	0	0	6	9	0
Type of Vote:	Hot	Hot	Hot	Hot	Hot	Hot

*Proportions represent the percentage of members mentionong that determinant on that vote. (multiple responses permitted.)

173

Table 5.4
(continued)

Determinant	Common Situs	Govt. Reorg.	Strip Mining	Clean Air Act	Hyde(Anti-Abortion) Amend	Repeal of Hatch Act	Saccharin Ban
Policy Assessment	69%	39%	92%	73%	57%	62%	89%
Constituency	39	15	8	20	0	23	46
Philosophical Convictions	15	15	8	0	50	23	0
Committee Members	8	8	8	7	0	0	0
Adequacy of Compromise	0	8	8	27	0	0	0
Consistency	8	8	31	13	29	15	0
Consensus	0	8	0	7	0	0	9
White House	0	31	8	0	0	0	0
Committee Chairman	0	39	23	13	0	0	9
Other Members	0	0	0	0	0	0	0
Personel Staff	8	0	0	0	0	0	0
State Delegation	0	0	8	7	0	0	0
Campaign Promise	0	15	0	0	21	0	0
Party Leader	0	0	0	0	0	0	0
Type of Vote:	Hot	Hot	Hot	Hot	Hot	Hot	Hot

174

Table 5.4
(continued)

Determinant	Water Projects	Pay Raise	EPA Auth.	Nuclear Navy	Goldwater Housing Amend	NASA Auth.	FAA Auth.	Snow Removal
Policy Assessment	65%	90%	20%	55%	50%	60%	0%	64%
Constituency	6	0	20	0	20	10	0	0
Philosophical Convictions	6	0	0	27	10	0	0	0
Committee Members	6	0	0	27	10	10	25	9
Adequacy of Compromise	0	0	0	0	0	0	0	0
Consistency	0	0	0	9	0	10	0	0
Consensus	0	0	0	0	0	10	50	0
White House	24	0	0	36	10	10	0	0
Committee Chairman	6	0	0	0	10	0	13	0
Other Members	12	0	0	36	30	10	0	0
Personal Staff	6	0	40	9	10	10	0	0
State Delegation	0	0	0	0	10	0	13	0
Campaign Promise	0	6	0	0	10	10	0	0
Party Leader	0	0	0	0	0	0	13	0
Type of Vote:	Hot	Hot	Low Profile	Low Profile	Low Profile	Low Profile	Low Profile	Low Profile

175

Table 5.4
(Continued)

Determinant	Public Works Conference 44%	Countercyclical Aid Reauth. 62%	HUD Auth. 58%	Marine Mammal 33%	House Assn. Committee 85%
Policy Assessment	11	31	17	0	8
Constituency	0	0	8	0	0
Philosophical Convictions	0	0	17	42	23
Committee Members	11	8	0	0	0
Adequacy of Compromise	0	0	0	67	0
Consistency	22	0	8	0	0
Consensus	11	8	33	8	0
White House	11	0	0	0	0
Committee Chairman	0	0	0	8	8
Other Members	0	0	0	8	0
Personal Staff	0	23	8	8	0
State Delegation	0	0	8	8	0
Campaign Promise	0	0	0	0	0
Party Leader	0	0	0	0	0
Type of vote:	Low Profile	Low Profile	Low Profile	Low Profile	Low Profile

(Continued)

Determinant	Romanian Earth-quake Relief	Arab Boycott	First Budget Res. (passed)	Foreign Aid Cut	School Lunch
Policy Assessment	80%	40%	63%	100%	88%
Consistuency	0	10	13	0	0
Philosophical Convictions	0	50	0	0	25
Committee Members	20	0	0	0	13
Adequacy of Compromise	0	30	25	0	13
Constituency	0	20	0	0	0
Consensus	30	0	0	0	25
White House	0	10	0	0	0
Committee Chairman	0	0	0	0	0
Other Members	0	10	0	0	0
Personal Staff	0	0	0	0	0
State Delegation	0	0	0	0	0
Campaign Promise	0	10	0	0	0
Party Leaders	0	0	0	0	0
Type of Vote:	Low Profile	Low Profile	Low Profile	Low Profile	Low Profile

177

several noncontroversial votes--House assassinations, Romanian earthquake, foreign aid, and school lunch. Policy assessments were infrequently mentioned on ethics, Goldwater Amendment, government reorganization, FAA, EPA, Arab boycott, public works, and marine mammal. On these votes, situational considerations seemed to eclipse pure policy voting. Cue-taking and philosophical convictions also prevailed on these votes.

Constituency was cited most on three votes: common situs which was very controversial, countercyclical aid which was perceived to be important to constituency, and saccharin which was the subject of much constituency mail. Constituency as a determinant was not cited on minor or nonvisible votes (nuclear navy, FAA, Romanian earthquake, EPA, debt collection, marine mammal, and foreign aid) nor on the Hyde Amendment on abortion, on which members presumably already had staked a position.

Philosophical convictions were most prevalent on votes that invoked questions of human rights--Rhodesian chrome, Arab boycott, Hyde, Hatch--and the nuclear navy vote that invoked national defense concerns.

Committee members were mentioned by over 25 percent on votes that were minor (FAA), constituency relevant (HUD), complex (tax and debt collection), and that involved a committee fight (marine mammal and nuclear navy). Committee members were not mentioned at all on many of the major policy questions: Rhodesian chrome, Arab boycott, Energy Department, budget, foreign aid, the Hyde Amendment, Hatch, and saccharin.

Compromise was cited at a significantly high rate on Arab boycott and marine mammal protection, two bills that were considered to be compromises. Consistency was cited most on three votes that had loomed as major matters in the preceding Congress--strip mining and the Hyde Amendment--and on the public works bill which was a conference report and presumably involved members' attempts to be consistent with their position on House engrossment of the bill. Consensus decision-making was prevalent on Romanian earthquake, the HUD vote, and school lunch--bills that passed by wide margins.

The White House was mentioned as a voting determinant on the four votes on which it was a combatant: nuclear navy, tax, government reorganization, and the water projects. Chairmen were cited most on government reorganization, strip mining, and tax: votes where the chairman played a highly visible role and became associated with a particular position. Noncommittee members were used as a decision determinant on two votes where those not on the committee attempted to amend a bill over the committee's objection: nuclear navy and Goldwater. On more than two-thirds of the sampled votes, no interviewee mentioned other members (neither on the committee nor in the delegation) as a determinant.

Personal staff was a perceived determinant on two votes: EPA and countercyclical. The EPA vote involved a routine authorization and may have been a staff delegated decision for many members. Countercyclical involved extensive staff work to ascertain impacts on constituency. Several members deferred to that staff work.

State delegation was mentioned by a significant proportion on only the debt collection practices vote. Campaign promises were listed as a determinant by a sizable proportion only on the Hyde amendment. The significance of this seems to lie in the success with which a single-issue interest group is able to obtain legislative support through campaign commitments.

Party leaders received noteworthy mention (14 percent) on only the ethics vote--a vote on which the Democratic leadership had staked its prestige. But no member listed leaders as a determinant of the pay raise vote, although this is another instance of where leaders had invested their reputation.

Finding 23: "The low-profile/hot distinction implied by Lowi and others does not in itself capture the differences in legislative decision-making."

In a general sense, the findings confirm the suppositions of the conditional authors. On many hot votes--tax, Rhodesian chrome, common situs, strip mining, Energy Department, the budget, clean air, Hyde, Hatch, saccharin, water projects, and the pay raise--decisions were based on policy assessments and

philosophical convictions. Evidently these issues
appeared to be important enough for members to
develop a policy or philosophical position. Certain
low-grade votes such as the nuclear navy, Goldwater
Amendment, FAA, EPA, public works, and marine mammal
involved fewer policy assessments and more cue-taking
from other actors.

Four qualifications to the Lowi conditional
theory of decision-making emerge, however, from the
data in Table 5.4. First, certain minor votes also
involve policy voting (House Assassinations, NASA,
snow removal, foreign aid). This indicates that
low-grade votes often are policy votes, as members
attempt to cope by placing routine votes in the
context of ideological predispositions. Second,
low-profile votes are based on situational
considerations such as assessments of compromise and
consensus, as well as cue-taking. Third, a hot vote
such as government reorganization can involve only
infrequent incidents of policy voting and, in fact,
can be determined on the basis of cue-taking and/or
situational concerns. Fourth, certain hot votes are
based on constituency as well as policy assessments.

As noted above, the questionnaire collected
members' perceptions of the characteristics of the
issue under consideration. These data, plus
objective and researcher subjective measures, permit
an additional test of the hot/low-profile
proposition. They afford the opportunity to see if
there is a difference in the mention of decision
determinants when, for example, the vote is perceived
to be complex and not complex.

Arraying decision determinants by issue
characteristics reveals only a few variations in
determinants. Overall, these tables present 504
distributions. Of these, only 54 (11 percent) evince
meaninful variation, i.e., variation of 9 percent or
more.

The few significant variations do permit the
specification of some issue characteristic correlates
for each determinant. A significant variation is one
that involves a 9 percent difference in the mention
of a determinant from one category of an indicator to
another. To use the example of complexity, a correlate of ideology would be noncomplexity if ideology

180

was mentioned more than 9 percent under conditions of noncomplexity as compared to complexity.

Correlates based on significant differences are presented in Table 5.5. In general, these distributions, although few in number, do conform to the expectation of the contextual theory. Cue-taking from other members and from staff usually occurs under low-profile conditions. Members engage in policy and philosophical voting under mostly hot, controversial conditions, when they have strong feelings and employ a lot of thought. Evidently, on low-profile votes, members will use the position of others as a decision shortcut. On high-profile votes, due to campaign considerations and issue visibility, members will stake out an ideological or philosophical position. In addition, various situational forces shape member reliance on certain decision determinants. For example, both the White House and constituents are mentioned more when they are involved in the legislative process. Consensus decision-making takes place under relatively non-controversial circumstances. Campaign promises are a policy determinant when the issue is salient to constituents and members perceive that constituents are aware of it.

Further situational effects are illustrated by Table 5.6. This table tests a commonly heard congressional axiom that "People influence the legislator simply by their involvement." A corollary to this is, in the words of one member, "If you're not involved, you won't influence." In the table, determinants are arrayed by presence in the member's force field (communications network) and by mention as an information source. It clearly shows that an actor's involvement in the force field or as an information source is associated with a much higher rate of mention as a determinant. Evidently, if, for example, committee members are heard from and if they are utilized for information, they are much more likely to be relied on (at a rate of 47 percent to 4 percent) than if they are not involved. However, data in this table also indicate that mention as a communications input or information source does not automatically lead to mention as a determinant, strengthening our argument that these different components are analytically distinct.

181

Table 5.5

Values of Issue Characteristics Associated with Mention of Different Decision Determinants (Correlates are Based on Variations of 9 Percent or More)

Committee Chairman
No thought (LP)

Committee Members
No mail (LP)
No feelings (LP)
No thought (LP)
No CQ story (LP)
Congress as modifier and ratifier (LP)
Presidential involvement (H)

Constituency
Salient (H)
Constituency aware (H)
Mail (H)
Tough (H)
Thought (H)
Below average rule margin (H)
CQ story (H)
Congress initiates (H)
Republican endorsement (H)
Presidential involvement (H)

Compromise
Thought (H)
Wide margin of passage (H)
CQ box score (H)
Congress modifies (H)
Specific (LP)

Campaign Promise
Renomination effect (H)
Reelection effect (H)
Presidential involvement (H) ●

Consistency
Above average policy time (H)

White House
Congress ratifies (LP)
Presidential involvement (H)

Consensus
No thought (LP)
Wide margin of final passage (LP)
Above average Democratic unity (LP)
Below average Republican unity (H)
No Washington Post story (LP)

Philosophical Conviction
Feelings (H)
Close final passage (H)
Below average likeness (H)
Above average policy time (H)
Presidential involvement (H)

Policy Assessment (Ideology)
Feelings (H)
Not tough (LP)
Thought (H) ●
Below average rule margin (H)
Defeat (H)
Close vote (H)
Below average Democratic unity (H)
Below average Republican unity (H)
Committee dissensus (H)
Minority report (H)
CQ story (H)
Washington Post story (H)
Congress initiates and modifies (H)
Democratic endorsement (H)
Mention in the polls (H)
No presidential involvement (LP) ●
Specificity (LP)

H = Presumed hot value
LP = Presumed low-profile value
● = Variation of 20 percent or greater

Table 5.6

Meaningful Distributions of Determinants by Force Field and
Information Input: The Percentage of Interviews In Which
Various Determinants Were Significantly Mentioned
Under Different Control Conditions

Actor as Determinant	Actor Present in Force Field		Actor Mentioned as Information Source	
	No	Yes	No	Yes
Chairman	2%	21%	4%	47%
Committee Members	7%	16%	8%	26%
State Delegation	2%	6%	2%	29%
Other Members	2%	8%	2%	21%
Personal Staff	2%	7%	0%	12%
Individual Constituents	7%	24%	---	---
Inspired Mail	12%	24%	---	---
Group Constituents	9%	25%	---	---
Constituency	---	---	12%	26%
Interest Groups	0%	3%	1%	0%
White House	2%	36%	7%	10%

183

Summary and Conclusions

As is the case with all decision-makers who function in an environment of complexity and high volume decision-making, the legislator devises shortcuts that reduce decision tasks to a routine.

Many of the major studies of congressional decision-making employ a holistic view of congressional decision routines. It is presumed that Congressmen reduce floor voting to a single routine; therefore, decision-making is best understood as the result of a single determinant or normal process such as party or cue-taking or consensus mode.

This chapter has demonstrated that Congressmen rely not on a single decision routine but on various routines. Thus, attempts to describe congressional decision-making by referring to a single determinant, in the manner of many famous research projects in legislative behavior, greatly oversimplify a highly variable and contextual process. Although policy voting is the determinant most commonly cited by members (thus reaffirming Clausen and countering Matthews and Stimson), interviews reveal that various decision modes are utilized. Congressmen arrive at decisions in various ways. Specifically, seven different ways of making floor voting decisions were identified: cue-taking, policy assessments, philosophical convictions, consensus, campaign promise, compromise, and constituency representation. Each constitutes a very different decision mode or shortcut.

The determinants that members mention vary greatly by kind of vote. In general conversations, many members stated that they used a conditional approach to decision-making. They stated that under certain conditions they made a decision in one way, and under other conditions they employed different decision rules. Of the 51 respondents from who four or more questionnaires were obtained, 81 percent cited different determinants on the various bills for which questions were asked. When determinants were displayed by vote, it was revealed that certain determinants were more likely to be mentioned on certain kinds of votes than on others. Some votes were predominantly policy votes, while others were dominated by cue-taking, philosophical convictions, constituency representation, or by situational

184

considerations. The distributions of determinants by issue characteristics, although not revealing as much variation as distributions by vote, provide support for the contextual theory. One out of ten distributions involve meaningful variations in the mention of determinants.

The variation of determinants conforms to the configurations predicted by the conditional theory. On many hot, visible bills and under some controversial conditions, members base decisions on policy assessments and philosophical convictions. Evidently, these issues provide sufficient political incentives for members to develop an abstract position to guide their decisions. On low-grade issues and under nonvisible, noncontroversial, low-profile conditions, members (not feeling compelled to develop personal stands) base their decisions on the position of other members or staff.

Several qualifications to the conditional theory appear warranted by these findings. First, some minor votes, as well as major questions, invoke policy voting. Evidently, on recurring, nonvisible votes (especially those considered not tough and those not involving the President), members stake out a position that they consistently adopt. These predispositions serve as categories within which members can place a vote and easily reach a decision based on policy assessments and consistency with past positions. Second, a high-profile vote can be based on something other than policy positions or convictions. Sometimes, due to the involvement of prominent participants, positions become personalized. Members, in siding with a participant, make a decision in a cue-taking mode or base a decision on their assessment of the adequacy of the compromise hammered out by the participants. Third, under conditions indicating extreme political heat and visibility, members will attempt to vote their perceptions of constituency sentiment or interests. Fourth, under low-grade conditions, members will base decisions on assessments of consensus or compromise as well as cue-taking. Finally, congressional decision-making is shaped by situational factors pertaining to actor involvement and the configuration of interests on any given issue. Actors who are in a member's force field on an issue or provide information are more likely to be mentioned as a determinant.

The predominance of policy voting raises two concluding questions:

First, although the interviews reveal minimal influence on the part of party leaders, party as an operational concept may make a viable contribution to congressional decison-making in the form of policy assessments. Froman concluded that each party controls districts which are distinctive in terms of social and economic characteristics and that these distinctions are related to different positions on the issues.[36] If these conclusions still hold true, constituency differences between the parties may provide the basis for very real differences in policy voting. In other words, Democrats, responding to very different constituency pressures than Republicans, have policy positions quite different from those of Republicans.[37] Hence, since members often base their positions on party affiliation, policy assessments may be a latent form of the kind of party voting suggested by Turner's study.

Second, although policy voting predominates, and relatively few mention other members, cue-taking may be much stronger, in an indirect sense, than the data indicate. As noted above, the mechanisms of policy voting are ideological predispositions that members develop concerning various categories of public policy. The immediate problem a member in a policy voting mode faces, however, is an informational one: "What policy category does it fit into?" "What normative premise applies?" Sources which provide this information--committee and state delegation members, party leaders, and party publications--may exert considerable influence on the decision, although the member may conclude that his decision was primarily based on ideology. By defining the issue one way rather than another, information sources may determine not only the cognitive category in which a member places a vote, but also, ultimately, how the member votes.[38]

This chapter focused solely on determinants. Members were asked to identify the major force, factor, or actor that determined their vote. Due to the constraint of time in the interview setting, members were not asked to reconstruct the total decision process nor to make a relative rank ordering of influences. Conclusions concerning decision modes, thus, are based solely on extrapolations from

citations of determinants. Future congressional
research on the determinant stage of member floor
voting should attempt to obtain member reconstruction
of all cognitive procedures leading up to the
decision. Such in-depth probing would provide a more
comprehensive view of decision-making.

[1]John W. Kingdon, Congressmen's Voting Decisions (New York: Harper and Row, 1973), p. 18.

[2]See James W. Dyson and John W. Soule, "Congressional Committee Behavior on Roll Call Votes: The U.S. House of Representatives, 1955-1964," Midwest Journal of Political Science 14 (1970): 626-47.

[3]For member reliance on fellow members, see Kingdon, Congressmen's Voting, pp. 69-104; Donald R. Matthews and James A. Stimson, "Decision-Making by U.S. Representatives: A Preliminary Model," in Political Decision-making, ed. by S. Sidney Ulmer (New York: Van Nostrand Reinhold, 1970), pp. 14-43; and Donald R. Matthews and James A. Stimson, Yeas and Nays (New York: Wiley-Interscience, 1975). For ideological groups as a voting influence, see Mark F. Ferber, "The Formation of the Democratic Study Group," in Congressional Behavior, ed. by Nelson W. Polsby (New York: Random House, 1971), pp. 249-69 and Arthur G. Stevens, Jr., Arthur H. Miller, and Thomas E. Mann, "Mobilization of Liberal Strength in the House, 1955-70: The Democratic Study Group," American Political Science Review 68 (1974): 667-81. For a discussion of state delegation, see Alan Fiellin, "The Functions of Informal Groups in Legislative Institutions," Journal of Politics 24 (1962): 72-91; Barbara Deckard, "State Party Delegations in the U.S. House of Representatives," Journal of Politics 34 (1972): 199-222; John H. Kessel, "The Washington Congressional Delegation," Midwest Journal of Political Science 8 (1964): 1-24; Arthur Stevens, "Informal Groups and Decision-Making in the U.S. House of Representatives," Ph.D. dissertation, University of Michigan, 1970; and David B. Truman, "The State Delegations and the Structure of Party Voting in the United States House of Representatives," American Political Science Review 50 (1956): 1023-45.

[4]See Kingdon, Congressmen's Voting, pp. 105-38 and David B. Truman, Congressional Party (New York: Wiley, 1959).

[5]See Kingdon, Congressmen's Voting, pp. 192-97.

[6]See Duncan MacRae, Jr., Dimensions of Congressional Voting (Berkeley: Univ. of California Press, 1958); David R. Mayhew, Party Loyalty Among Congressmen (Cambridge, Mass.: Harvard Univ. Press, 1966); W. Wayne Shannon, Party, Constituency and Congressional Voting (Baton Rouge: Louisiana State Univ. Press, 1968); David B. Truman, Congressional Party; and Julius Turner and Edward V. Schneier, Jr., Party and Constituency: Pressures on Congress, rev. ed. (Baltimore: Johns Hopkins Press, 1970).

[7]See Aage R. Clausen, How Congressmen Decide: A Policy Focus (New York: St. Martin's Press, 1973) and Cleo H. Cherryholmes and Michael J. Shapiro, Representatives and Roll Calls (Indianapolis: Bobbs-Merrill, 1969).

[8]See Charles F. Andrain, "A Scale Analysis of Senators' Attitudes Toward Civil Rights," Western Political Quarterly 17 (1964): 488-503, and Leroy N. Rieselbach, "The Demography of the Congressional Vote on Foreign Aid, 1939-1958," American Political Science Review 58 (1964): 577-88.

[9]See Lewis A. Froman, Jr., The Congressional Process (Boston: Little, Brown, 1967) and Walter J. Oleszek, Congressional Procedures and the Policy Process (Washington, D.C.: Congressional Quarterly Press, 1978).

[10]See Herbert B. Asher, "The Learning of Legislative Norms," American Political Science Review 67 (1973): 499-513 and Donald R. Matthews, "The Folkways of the United States Senate: Conformity to Group Norms and Legislative Effectiveness," American Political Science Review 53 (1959): 1064-89.

[11]See Kingdon, Congressmen's Voting, pp. 29-68.

[12]See Truman, Congressional Party and Kingdon, Congressmen's Voting, pp. 169-91.

[13]See Kingdon, Congressmen's Voting, pp. 169-91.

[14]See Kingdon, Congressmen's Voting, pp. 139-68 and David B. Truman, The Governmental Process, 2nd ed. (New York: Knopf, 1971).

[15]See Morris P. Fiorina, Representatives, Roll Calls, and Constituencies (Lexington, Mass.: Lexington Books, 1974); Lewis A. Froman, Congressmen and Their Constituencies (Chicago: Rand McNally, 1963); Duncan MacRae, Jr., "The Relation Between Roll Call Votes and Constituencies in the Massachusetts House of Representatives," American Political Science Review 46 (1952): 1046-55.

[16]See Kingdon, Congressmen's Voting, pp. 198-211.

[17]See David W. Brady and Naomi B. Lynn, "Switched-Seat Congressional Districts: Their Effect on Party Voting and Public Policy," American Journal of Political Science 17 (1973): 528-43; Morris P. Fiorina, "Electoral Margins, Constituency Influence, and Policy Moderation: A Critical Assessment," American Politics Quarterly 1 (1973): 479-98; Fiorina, Representatives; Samuel Huntington, "A Revised Theory of American Party Politics," American

Political Science Review 44 (1950): 669-77; and Judith A Strain, "The Nature of Political Representation in Legislative Districts of Intense Party Competition" (B.A. thesis, Chatham College, 1963).

[18]Robert S. Erickson and Norman R. Luttbeg, *American Public Opinion* (New York: Wiley, 1973), chapter 9 and Leroy N. Rieselbach, *Congressional Politics* (New York: McGraw-Hill, 1973), pp. 214-24.

[19]Turner, *Party and Constituency*, p. 34.

[20]Matthews and Stimson, *Yeas and Nays*, The Subtitle is Normal Decision-Making in the U.S. House.

[21]Clausen, *Congressmen*, p. 14.

[22]Kingdon, *Congressmen's Voting*, p. 230.

[23]See Randall B. Ripley and Grace A. Franklin, *Congress, the Bureaucracy, and Public Policy* (Homewood, Ill.: Dorsey, 1976), p. 17.

[24]William J. Keefe and Morris S. Ogul, *The American Legislative Process*, 4th ed. (Englewood Cliffs, N.J.: Prentice-Hall, 1977), p. 245.

[25]Two compelling arguments concerning the ideological basis of cue-taking are: Helmut Norpoth, "Explaining Party Cohesion in Congress: The Case of Shared Policy Attitudes," *American Political Science Review* 70 (1976): 1156-71 and John D. Macartney, "Political Staffing: A View from the District," (Ph.D. dissertation, Univ. of California, Los Angeles, Department of Political Science, 1975).

[26]John W. Kingdon, "Models of Legislative Voting," *Journal of Politics* 36 (1977): 563-95.

[27]Matthews and Stimson, *Yeas and Nays*.

[28]Kingdon, *Congressmen's Voting*.

[29]Ibid., chapter 10.

[30]Norpoth, "Explaining Party Cohesion."

[31]Kingdon, "Models of Voting."

[32]Matthews and Stimson, *Yeas and Nays*.

[33]Kingdon, "Models of Voting."

[34]John F. Jackson, Constituencies and Leaders in Congress (Cambridge, Mass." Harvard University Press, 1974), chapter 1.

[35]Matthews and Stimson, "Decision-Making by U.S. Representatives."

[36]Froman, Congressmen, pp. 122-24.

[37]Recent CQ tabulations of party cohesion indicate that the two parties are indeed associated with opposing policy assessments. See, for example, Congressional Quarterly Weekly Report XXXVI (January 14, 1978): 79-83.

[38]The author wishes to acknowledge and thank George Gibson, former Associate Professor of Political Science at USAF Academy, for emphasizing this point in personal conversations.

CHAPTER VI

THE CONDITIONAL NATURE OF ROLE ORIENTATIONS
AND THE CONDITIONAL NATURE OF TIME OF DECISION

Role orientations are very broad perspectives with which legislators view their job. They refer to the member's definition of his task as a legislator as he engages in the act of decision-making. As such, role is the most basic of the decision components.

Role studies by Wahlke, Eulau, and Davidson, and others have provided valuable insights into legislative decision-making. They have identified various categories of orientations--e.g., representative, purposive, group focus--and formulated classifications corresponding to various expressions of role that are manifested with regard to each orientation. They have demonstrated that representative role orientations involve two distinct concepts: styles of representation (different ways of reaching a decision such as through a delegate, trustee, or broker mode) and representative foci (nation, district, or nation-district orientation.)[1]

As with the literature's treatment of determinants, research concerning role orientations has presumed that a legislator's conception of role will dominate all of his decisions. As Jewell and Patterson state,

> a specific role orientation means a predisposition or inclination to act in a particular way. . . .with enough information about the legislator's role orientations, it should be possible to predict more accurately how he will respond.[2]

Davidson holds that role is an "expected pattern of behavior associated with an actor[3]." Throughout all role research is the presumption that for the individual legislator the chosen conception of role persists regardless of the issue involved.

Role orientations have been researched in two ways. Both reflect a static conception of legislative behavior.

193

One way involves questions that ask a legislator to choose an orientation--trustee (self-referent), delegate (district referent), or politico (both)--that, in the abstract, best summarizes his overall approach. An example of this approach is Davidson's procedure of having members indicate their degree of agreement with a series of statements that reflects different orientations.[4]

The second involves open-ended questions that ask legislators to define the purpose of a legislator's job. An example of this is the question of Wahlke et al.: "First of all, how would you describe the job of being a legislator--What are the most important things you should do here?"[5] Responses to this question are coded in such a way that members are typed into a single category. As Wahlke et al. write,

> Each legislator has some purposive or factual conception of the ultimate aim of his activities which will be embodied in certain types of norms for his relations with his fellows in the day-to-day legislative operations.

In their study, members are classified on the basis of what the member considers to be his ultimate aim.

The politico orientation allows for contextual behavior, but in describing the politico role, Wahlke et al. state,

> In particular, it would seem to be possible for a representative to act in line with both criteria. For roles and role orientations need not be mutually exclusive. Depending on circumstances, a representative may hold the role orientation of delegate at one time and that of trustee at another time. Or he might even seek to reconcile both orientations in terms of a third.[7]

Davidson also acknoweldges a mixture of pure styles. As one of the members in his sample stated, "By and large, principle is the criterion. On minor votes I can go along with the constituency."[8] But, as Davidson emphasizes, contextual role playing is only one of many "varied permutations" of the politico role.[9] To both Wahlke et al. and Davidson, the essence of the politico role is balance between constituency and independent judgment. Davidson states that "many congressmen observe that their problem is one of balancing...one role against the other."[10] As Davidson stresses with a quote from a member,

> the Congressman must also vote as he reasonably sees fit on an issue. There is a balance which each Congressman works out between two factors.[11]

Members who exhibited this conception are typed as politicos, but no effort is made to determine the conditions under which they stress different orientations. Role researchers have not attempted to systematically study the contexts within which members exhibit different behaviors.[12]

The conditional theory, however, posits an opposite notion. From the writings of conditional theorists, especially Miller and Stokes,[13] one gets the impression that the style and focus a Congressman employs has a variable rather than a persistent quality--i.e., role conceptions vary according to different kinds of votes. Low-key decisions, which lack electoral incentives and political pressure, will involve a vague national focus and a trustee style. Hot issues, which entail political pressure and have potential electoral consequences, will reflect both a local and a national orientation as well as a delegate style.

This chapter will explore for conditional role orientations. Specifically, the following proposition, derived from the conditional theory, will be tested: The role orientations of members vary according to the kind of issue at hand. On low-grade issues, they tend to have a national focus and a trustee style. On hot issues, due to political relevance, they tend to have a local focus and a delegate style.

Additionally, interviews revealed that many members view the actua time of decision as crucial to the decision process. For this reason, a second proposition will be examined in this chapter. It is as follows: the time at which a member makes up his mind varies according to the kind of issue at hand. On low-grade issues, members will make a late decision. On high-profile issues, commitments will be made far in advance. The rationale for this

195

proposition, as with the others, is derived from economic investment theory. On low-grade issues, due to the lack of both general public and member concern, decisions will be made late. On hot issues, decisions will be made relatively early, reflecting the member's concern and eagerness to develop a commitment on a publicly visible issue.

ROLE ORIENTATIONS: STYLE AND FOCUS

This study asked members two questions concerning role conceptions. The first concerned style: "What did you rely on when making this decision--constituency, yourself, or both?" The second pertained to focus: "What was your focus--national, local, or both?" Initially, a question concerning purposive roles (a member's view of which aspects of the legislative job were involved in the decision) was asked. It was subsequently dropped, however, when answers seemed to be redundant to those obtained with the question on determinants.

The responses to the questions on role conceptions support several generalizations concerning style and focus.

Finding 24: "Members articulte the same philosophical dichotomy of representation that Edmund Burke identified."

In his famous "Speech to the Electors of Bristol" Edmund Burke identified two distinctive styles of representation: (1) the trustee style of basing decisions on the representative's independent judgment and (2) the delegate style of basing decisions on the position of constituents. Burke, of course, preferred the first style. Both found expression in the interviews.

The trustee orientation is represented with the following statements:

I follow Edmund Burke--I vote for what I think is best.

I am a Burkean--I don't read my mail.

We are sent here to use our judgment.

I'm elected to vote.

196

I don't take a poll--the people elect me.

You must use your own judgment. There are too many special interest groups pushing selfish programs.

I vote my convictions.

I vote the merits of the issue.

The essence of the trustee position is that, when a conflict develops between constituency and the representative's judgment, the member's judgment will prevail. Indicative are the following statements:

I voted for the House Assassinations Committee, though my constituents oppose it--I always follow my own judgment.

I'll not budge on abortion, gun control. I'll take a position against the district if necessary. The same with Rhodesian chrome and the Panama Canal.

I vote against my constituency if my convictions lean me that way. For example, I voted against the nuclear navy though my district is defense-oriented.

Many of those who subscribed to a trustee model emphasized the futility of relying on constituency opinion:

Most people don't have an opinion on the issues.

People don't usually have feelings when it doesn't affect them.

There is no way to know what people want. You can only guess. An election doesn't tell you much.

The delegate model was also reflected in the interviews. Examples are:

House members are expected to be district representatives

I'm the only voice my constituents have in
Washington.

I'm the only person the people in my
district can rely on to vote their interests.

The House is the people's place--I vote the
district.

My decision is the result of my
interpretation of constituency wishes.

Basically, constituency and constituents
constitute a role orientation in four ways: (1)
response to (even solicitation of) constituency
sentiment, (2) role playing and empathy with
constituents, (3) anticipation of constituency
reaction, and (4) perceptions of constituency
interests. Examples of the first--active response to
constituency sentiments--are: "I base my decision-
making on the majority of correspondence from the
district" and "I usually defer to constituents--my
sentiment is that's what I'm here for. That's my job
isn't it?" Examples of the second--empathetic role
playing--are "I vote the same way I think the folks
back home would if they had the same information,"
and

"You have to know your district and the
people's feelings and the way they think.
Put yourself in their position. What would
be in their best interests? What would I
want my Congressman to do if I was back
there?"

The third--anticipation of constituency reaction--is
illustrated by the following: "You must consider
district interests--it's unpopular and unwise to vote
against," and "Constituents always enter into your
decisions even if you don't hear from them, because
you anticipate how they will receive it." The
fourth--perception of constituency interests--is
illustrated by the following: "I serve a rural
district--I'm here to articulate the farmer's point
of view and to serve dairy interests" and "My job is
to look out for the constituency. Take this energy
issue--out here gasoline is a necessity not a
luxury. We need gas for tractors. Hell, there isn't
a busline in the state."

The essence of the delegate model is preference for constituency input over the representative's position when there is conflict between the two. Examples are:

> I defer to pressure on things like tariffs, though I believe they're bad.

> I voted for common situs, not for me, but for constituents. To survive politically, you must follow the constituency on this and things such as clean air and saccharin.

> People delegate to you. If there is conflict between you and them, follow them.

> I will not go against the district if the vote is controversial and important to the district--no quicker way to get targeted than that.

Finding 25: "Members cite styles other than the two pure types identified by Burke."

In many instances, when members were asked to identify the role conception that guided their decision, they would cite several factors other than those identifed by Burke. Some of the other factors mentioned are: supporters, expertise, the President, staff, and pressure. Typically, when a member would identify another factor, he or she would simply state, "I based my decision neither on myself nor on my constituency." Instead, the member would argue that he relied on a colleague's expertise, on the presidency, or on one of the other factors.

More important, many members maintained that they relied on both constituency and self. Those who claimed that both were involved noted that philosophy and constituency "often coincided" and that their decision was a combination of both. A common response was "Both were a factor," "It was my own opinion as reinforced by my constituency," or "my position plus support of my constituency." Several attempted to account for the reasons why members frequently experienced convergence of personal position and constituency position. Some argued that campaign promises by members account for the absence of perceived conflict. If a member took a stand on an issue and was elected or reelected, he might conclude that there is accord between himself and his constituents. Other emphasized that the widespread practice of polling the district contributed to a convergence of member and district opinion by showing the member where most constituents stand on the major bills of the session.

Finding 26: "Congressmen couch most decisions in terms of a trustee orientation or a combination of the trustee and delegate (the politico) roles."

Table 6.1 displays major responses to the question concerning styles of representation. As can be seen there, most members took a trustee role. The next most frequent orientation was that of politico, which combines the trustee and delegate roles. It is surprising that only 2 percent cited a pure delegate orientation. Constituency was cited as the basis of a role orientation as infrequently as several of the additional factors. These findings are fairly well in line with Davidson who found that most members choose a trustee orientation rather than that of a delegate. The only difference is that Davidson found the politico or combination orientation to be the most frequently cited, while here it was found to be the second most frequent.[14]

Finding 27: "Members generally have a national focus."

Responses to the question concerning foci of representation support one major generalization: For most of the decisions covered by this study, members had a national focus. Table 6.2 displays a frequency distribution of the foci of representation. It shows that a national focus was employed at a rate of more than three to one over the next most frequently cited focus: a combination of national and local orientation. It is surprising that in only 6 percent of the cases was a purely local focus employed. This is in contrast to Davidson's findings that most members have a district-dominant focus.[15] Perhaps the generic questions employed by Davidson are more likely to tap a district orientation than the issue-by-issue questioning employed here.

Examples of a national focus are: "I have a water project in the district, but we need to cut back national spending" and "I voted for that version of the grant formula, though my district will receive

200

Table 6.1

Frequency Distribution of Role Conceptions in Response to the Question,
"On What Did You Base Your Decision: Constituency, Self,
A Combination of Both?"

Constituency (Delegate)	2%
Self (Trustee)	74%
Both Self and Constituents (Politico)	19%
President	2%
Staff	1%

N = 352

Table 6.2

Frequency Distributions of Foci of Representation in Response to the
Question, "What was Your Focus: Nation, Local Constituency, or Both?"

Focus	
National	59%
Local	6%
Both	18%

N = 210

Table 6.3

The Interrelationship of Legislative
Style and Focus

	Focus		
Style	National	Local	Both
Constituency	2%	15%	0%
Self	87	50	52
Both	8	35	41

slightly less--I believe we should target those areas in need."

Illustrative of a local orientation are the following: "I always ask, 'What's the impact on the district?'" "It's one of those provincial political things," and "It's a parochial issue--you must ask, how will my decision affect me politically?"

A focus involving both foci is illustrated by the following statement: "You can't separate national from local considerations. You must look at not only how it affects your district, but also what it does in a policy sense."

Finding 28: "Representative style and focus do not necessarily correlate together."

A final generalization supported by the role questions corroborates the Eulau-Wahlke contention that a distinction can be made between focus and style of representation.[16] Table 6.3 shows the interrelationship of style and focus. It shows that, contrary to Burke's inferences, there are not strong relationships between delegate style and district focus nor between trustee style and national focus.

Finding 29: "The representative role orientations of members vary according to the kind of issue at hand."

To search for variation in role conceptions, role is arrayed by vote, by issue characteristics, and by actor. All three strongly support the conditional approach.

Table 6.4 arrays style by vote. It clearly shows that on certain votes members are more likely to take a trustee role, while on other votes a combination role is more prevalent. Mention of a trustee style varied from mention by as few as 36 percent of the interviewees on saccharin to mention by as many as 100 percent on school lunch. Mention of a politico style varied from no mention on FAA and other votes to mention by 64 percent of the interviewees on the saccharin vote.

Only one vote--the pork barrel snow removal vote--was associated with any meaningful mention of

Table 6.4

Role Conception by Vote: The Percentage of Members Mentioning
Different Role Orientations on Different Votes

				Vote				
Style	House Ethics Code	Tax Simplification	Rhodesian Crome	Energy Dept. Establishment	First Budget Res. (defeated)	Debt Collection	Common Situs	Gov't. Reorg.
Delegate (constituency)	7% *	0%	0%	0%	0%	0%	0%	0%
Trustee (self)	57	60	89	93	64	100	58	85
Politics (both)	29	30	18	7	27	0	42	8
Type of Vote:	Hot	Hot	Hot	Hot	Hot	Hot	Hot	Hot

				Vote					
Style	Strip Mining	Clean Air Act	Hyde (Anti-Abortion) Amend.	Repeal of Hatch Act	Saccharin Ban	Water Projects	Pay Raises	EPA Auth[1]	Nuclear Navy
Delegate (Constituency)	0%	0%	0%	15%	0%	0%	11%	0%	0%
Trustee (self)	83	67	93	69	36	82	72	40	91
Politics (both)	17	33	7	15	64	17	11	20	9
Type of Vote:	Hot	Hot	Hot	Hot	Hot	Hot	Hot	Low Profile	Low Profile

*Proportion represents the percentage of members using that role on that vote. Columns do not equal 100% because either miscellaneous categories were used (and are omitted here) or there was no response.

[1] also 40% staff

204

Table 6.4
(continued)

Vote

Style	Goldwater Housing Amend	NASA Auth.	FAA Auth.	Snow Removal	Public Works Conference	Countercyclical Aid Reauth.	HUD Auth.	Marine Mammal
Delegate (constituency)	0%	0%	0%	18%	0%	0%	0%	8%
Trustee (self)	60	67	83	82	44	58	50	75
Politics (both)	30	33	0	0	33	33	33	0
Type of Vote:	Low Profile	Low Profile	Low Profile	Low Profile	Low Profile	Low Profile	Low Profile	Low Profile

Vote

Style	House Assn. Committee	Romanian Earthquake Relief	Arab Boycott	First Budget Res. (passed)	Foreign Aid Cut	School Lunch
Delegate (constituency)	0%	0%	0%	0%	0%	0%
Trustee (self)	92	100	90	50	100	100
Politics (both)	8	0	10	50	0	0
Type of Vote:	Low Profile	Low Profile	Low Profile	Low Profile	Low Profile	Low Profile

constituency. Although most votes involved a trustee role, two types of votes are most associated with self-referent voting: hot votes (Rhodesian chrome, government reorganization, Arab boycott, strip mining, the Energy Department, the Hyde amendment and the water projects) and votes that are relatively low-profile (the nuclear navy, FAA, House Assassinations Committee, Romanian earthquake, snow removal, foreign aid, and school lunch). Evidently, members define their role in trustee terms on both the big issues and on many of the votes thought to constitute the routine business of the House. Votes receiving the fewest mentions of the trustee role are: (a) those associated with significant constituency pressure (ethics, common situs, saccharin), (b) those grant programs perceived as involving constituency interests (public works, countercyclical, HUD), and (c) votes that involved reliance on staff (EPA).

A combination of the delegate and trustee models (politico role), where the decision is held to rest on both self and constituency, is most prevalently mentioned on (a) those votes that involved considerable correspondence from the constituency (common situs, saccharin) and (b) the budget resolution that raised the symbolic issue of government spending. Two types of issues were associated with infrequent mention of a politico orientation: certain hot issues (government reorganization, Arab boycott, Energy Department, and Hyde) and routine, low-profile votes (nuclear navy, FAA, House Assassinations, Romanian earthquake, snow removal, marine mammal, foreign aid, school lunch.) Both of these, as already mentioned, involved mostly trustee decision-making.

Although the focus question was not asked until the last half of the study and thus covers only half as many votes as the style question, it also reveals variation in role conception across various votes. Table 6.5 shows that the real focus of members varies according to issues. On votes such as marine mammal, budget I, foreign aid, Hyde, and Hatch, members reveal a preponderantly high percentage of nationally-oriented votes. Conversely, grant votes (public works, countercyclical, HUD), pet projects (snow removal) and hot votes involving constituency communications (clean air, saccharin) are associated with lower than average national focus. Snow removal involves a predominantly local focus. Votes

206

Table 6.5

Representative Focus by Vote: the Percentage of Members Mentioning Different Foci on Different Votes

Vote

Focus	Energy Dept. Establishment	Strip Mining	First Budget Res.(defeated)	Clean Air Act	Hyde (anti-abortion) Amend	Repeal of Hatch Act	Saccharin Ban	Water Projects	Pay Raise
National	73%	70%	75%	40%	85%	77%	30%	65%	72%
Local	0	0	0	7	7	7	10	0	11
Both	27	30	25	53	7	15	60	35	11
Type of Vote:	Hot	Hot	Hot	Hot	Hot	Hot	Hot	Hot	Hot

Vote

Focus	Arab Boycott	Snow Removal	Public Works Conference	Countercyclical Aid Reauth.	HUD Auth.	Marine Mammal	First Budget Res. (passed)	Foreign Aid Cut	School Lunch
National	70%	40%	11%	18%	18%	83%	75%	100%	71%
Local	10	60	22	18	18	0	0	0	14
Both	10	0	67	64	64	17	25	0	14
Type of Vote:	Low Profile	Low Profile	Low Profile	Low Profile	Low Profile	Low Profile	Low Profile	Low Profile	Low Profile

n = 222 (focus question not asked on all votes)

207

involving frequent mention of both national and local
criteria are the grant programs (public works,
countercyclical, and HUD) and votes thought to be
locally visible (clean air, saccharin, budget II).
Foreign policy votes (Arab boycott and foreign aid)
involve little local or mixed focus.

This discussion of style and focus by vote only
partially confirms the contextual proposition.
Although there is variation, it does not occur solely
in the direction predicted by the proposition.
Basically, in accordance with the prediction,
low-profile votes do involve a trustee role, while
votes that entail considerable constituency pressure
are made with a delegate style. The distribution of
focus also conforms to the prediction. Contrary to
prediction, however, is the fact that many of the hot
votes, on which there is minimal constituency input,
involve a trustee model of decision-making.
Moreover, the data do provide one qualification to
the proposition: grant programs as well as locally
important hot issues involve delegate decision-making
and both a local and a national focus.

The distribution of role orientations by issue
characteristics reveals some variation in the mention
of styles and foci. Of the 216 distributions, 33
percent involve variations of 9 percent or more from
one value of an indicator to another.

The array of role by issue characteristics
permits the identification of issue characteristic
correlates of various role conceptions, as seen in
Table 6.6. By and large, these correlates support
the directional predictions of the proposition. A
trustee role and a national orientation are associated with characteristics that indicate a lack of
political heat from the district but sufficient
controversy within Congress. A national/local focus
is correlated with political salience. On votes that
offer the prospects of political heat in the
district, the member will use a delegate style and
have a local focus more often than if this were not
the case. On votes where no heat is likely, members
will play the role of a trustee and have a national
focus. It should be emphasized, however, that all
orientations were associated with both hot and
low-profile characteristics.

Table 6.6

Values of Issue Characteristics Associated with Mention of Different
Areal Foci (Correlates are Based on Variation of   9
Percent or more)

National	Local	Both
Non-technical (H)	Salience (H)	Complexity (LP)
Conflict (H)	Open and modified	Technicality (LP)
Not major (LP)	rule (LP)	Major status (H)
Not salient (LP)●	No Democratic	Salience (H)●
Constituency not	endorsements (LP)	No strong feeling (LP)
aware (LP)	No Washington Post	Closed rule (H)
Feeling (H)	story (LP)	Above average rule
Below average	Congress ratifies (LP)	margin (LP)●
rule margin (H)	Specificity (LP)	Wide margin of final
Defeated (H)	No change (LP)	passage (LP)
Below average		Above average
Democratic		Democratic unity (LP)
unity (H)		Above average
Above average		likeness (LP)
Republican		Democratic
unity (LP)		endorsement (H)
Amendment over		Republican endorse-
committee		ment (H)
objection (H)		Mention in rolls (H)
Republican		Above average money (H)
endorsement (H)		Presidential
Below average		involvement (H)
money (LP)		Minority report (H)●
No presidential		Congress ratifies (LP)●
involvement (LP)●		No change (LP)
No minority		
report (LP)		
Washington Post		
story (H)		
Congress		
initiates (H)		
Non-specific (H)		
Change (H)●		

H = Presumed hot value
LP= Presumed low profile value
● = Variation of 20   percent or more

During the course of the interviews, many members expressly addressed contextual role taking. Many acknowledged that they play one role under certain conditions and another role under other conditions:

> When constituents have strong opinions, they must be in your equation. That's the job of a representative. However, when they don't have an opinion, you rely on yourself. That's what you must do.

> I usually vote my own opinion, but I can get my mind changed by constituents.

> I'll go against my own judgement only if its something on which I don't have strong feelings--like daylight savings time. Folks back home want it, but my own judgment leads me to oppose it. But I gave in. I would never vote the popular way against my convictions. On major things, constituents are only one of several factors.

> A vote should be compatible with the district. A representative must adapt to the prevailing philosophy in the district. Every member should have a general idea of where his district stands. I know what I can and can't explain. I'll deviate from the district only on moral issues such as civil rights. For example, I followed constituency sentiment on common situs. People want to have that right. I personally believe it will cause unemployment and inflation.

> I vote my personal judgment on the majority of issues. In a few instances, I'll go with the constituency, but it has to involve a vast majority. In the main, you have a tougher time trying to find out what people want than in trying to get them to understand. You're better off taking a stand and supporting it.

> I always try to do what constituents would do. I want to reflect the views of the people. I deviate from this process only about 10 percent of the time.

210

Others, however, insisted that they persistently played the same role. Examples: "I'm a Burkean through and through" and "I always reference constituency views and interests."

An examination of the role responses of the 51 interviewees for whom there are four or more questionnaires supports the contextual model. With regards to the style question, 30 (60 percent) of these respondents employed different role orientations on different votes. Almost all shift focus. Significantly, though, as many as 20 (40 percent) use the same style orientation for all of their decisions. Evidently, some members use different orientations in different contexts, while others use the same one. The important point to bear in mind, however, is that to capture the contextual role playing displayed by a majority of the respondents, one must utilize a conditional model and not one that classifies legislators as falling under one or the other of the styles.

Conclusions Concerning Role Orientations

A member's representative role orientation is a highly variable construct. As the arrays of role by vote, issue characteristics, and actor conclusively show, most members do not choose one orientation and then consistenlty apply it to all decisions. One role is more prevalently mentioned on certain votes, while on other votes another role is cited more frequently. Numerous variations occur with regard to issue characteristics. Most members for whom multiple decision cases (four) are available exhibit variable role orientations. In the main, the proposition is confirmed. There is meaningful variation, and it does conform to the hot/low-profile distinction. Hot votes are associated with a delegate role and a local orientation. On low-profile decisions, a perceived trustee role and national orientation dominate. The exception is that several hot votes also involve a perceived pure trustee role. In sum, it seems that constituency heat and constituency relevance may be the dividing line between a member's use of a trustee or delegate style. When input is received from constituents (common situs, saccharin) or constituency interests are on the line (grant programs), the legislator is more apt to be a delegate. When these factors are absent for the individual member--even though there

211

may be controversy within the Congress--there is a greater likelihood that the member will be a trustee.

TIME OF DECISION

Finding 30: "Members mention various decision times."

Members often mentioned time of decision as an important variable for understanding the dynamic of congressional decision-making. At the suggestion of several members, a "time of decision" question was employed late in the study, rendering a total of only 141 responses.

Table 6.7 lists the various times of decision mentioned by members. It shows that the time at which a member makes a decision on a floor vote can occur at any of several points in the legislative process. In all, 12 different temporal decision points were noted. They range in time from when the member first entered politics to "very late," quite possibly right up to the time for casting the vote.

Some of the decision times listed in Table 6.7 require further elaboration. An automatic decision is one that was made, in the words of a member, "when I first heard about it." Some decisions were said to be made as a result of the committee service of members: "I made up my mind when it cleared our committee." Some stated that they decided when they heard from constituents on a bill or "realized the constituency's interests were involved." Finally, many decisions were made on the floor. In some cases, these were acknowledged to be snap decisions. Amendments, especially, fit in this category. In the words of a member, "Hell, in the committee of the whole, you only have 10 minutes of debate to make up your mind. If it's an amendment to an amendment, chances are it hasn't been published yet."[17] Others are not snap judgments but, instead, are settled on the basis of debate or amendments. For example, many members noted that on the budget resolution they "wanted to hear the final arguments and see the finished product." One member hedged on the Hyde Amendment "to see if it became workable as a result of the amendment process."

212

Table 6.7

Frequency Distribution of Responses to the Question "When Did You Reach a Decision on This Vote?"

When Decided	Percent
the Floor	25%
st Time Vote Was Up	18
te	9
ring Campaign	9
en Member First Entered Politics	7
tomatic (When Heard It Was Up)	6
en Read About It	6
Committee	5
en Change Was Made	5
en Heard From Constituents	4
ek Before	3
y Before	3

Finding 31:   "The most frequently mentioned times of decision are 'on the floor' and 'last time the bill was up'."

Table 6.7 reveals that most members stated that they made up their minds on the floor. The next most frequently mentioned time, reinforcing the Sundquist/Polsby concept of policy incubation and recurring issues,[18] is "last time up," followed by "during the campaign" and "late."

Finding 32:   "The time at which a member makes up his mind varies according to different kinds of issues."

To test for variations, time of decision is arrayed by vote and by issue characteristics. Due to the limited number of responses to the question, there is no array by interviewees.

Table 6.8 displays time of decision by vote. Complete data were available on only 12 votes. These data, as incomplete as they are, show considerable variation in the time of decision. Although "on the floor" is, generally, the most frequently mentioned decision time (overall a 25 percent mention), no interviewee mentioned it on the EPA, snow removal, and budget II votes, and less than 10 percent cited it on the Hyde Amendment, while 60 percent classified the first budget resolution as an "on the floor" decision.

Many interesting patterns are reflected in Table 6.8. Significant proportions cited "when first entered politics" on budget and the Hyde Amendment. "Last time up" was the decision time most mentioned on strip mining and clean air. "The campaign" was most frequently mentioned on the budget vote. "A week before" was most prevalently mentioned on strip mining. "When read about it (heard it was coming up)" was mentioned by a significant proportion on the EPA vote. "When heard from constituency" was mentioned most on snow removal. Floor decisions were likely to occur most on two kinds of votes: (a) routine votes (NASA, debt collection) when the member first realized on the floor that the vote was up and (b) important decisions (Arab boycott, budget) where many members hedged pending the vote on several amendments. "When change made" was mentioned most on the budget. Late decisions were most recorded on the

214

Table 6.8

When Decided by Vote: The Percentage of Members Mentioning
Different Times of Decision by Vote

Vote

When Decided	First Budget Res.(defeated)	Debt Collection	Common Situs	Strip Mining	Clean Air Act	Hyde (anti-Abortion)Amend.	EPA Auth.
On the Floor	60%	38%	14%	13%	13%	8%	0%
Last Time Vote Was Up	0	13	29	50	50	23	0
Late	20	13	14	0	25	0	0
During Campaign	0	0	14	0	0	23	0
When Member Entered Politics	0	0	0	0	0	39	0
Automatic (When Heard It Was Up)	10	0	0	0	13	8	0
When Read About It	0	13	0	0	0	0	67
On Committee	10	0	0	0	0	0	33
When Change Was Made	0	13	0	0	0	0	0
When Heard From Constituents	0	0	14	0	0	0	0
Week Before	0	13	14	25	0	0	0
Day Before	0	0	0	13	0	0	0
Type of Vote:	Hot	Hot	Hot	Hot	Hot	Hot	Low Profile

215

Table 6.8
(continued)

When Decided	Vote				
	NASA Auth	Snow Removal	Public Works	Arab Boycott	First Budget Res. (passed)
On the Floor	40%	0%	17%	33%	20%
Last Time Vote Was Up	20	0	33	11	20
Late	20	0	0	0	0
During Campaign	20	0	0	11	0
When Member Entered Politics	0	0	0	11	0
Automatic (When Heard It Was Up)	0	0	0	0	0
When Read About It	0	0	17	11	0
On Committee	0	0	33	0	0
When Change Was Made	0	0	0	0	20
When Heard From Constituents	0	100	0	11	0
Week Before	0	0	0	11	0
Day Before	0	0	0	11	0
Type of Vote:	Low Profile	Low Profile	Low Profile	Low Profile	Low Profile

216

budget, clean air, and NASA. In sum, the various decision times are mentioned with more and less frequency across different votes.

The array of decision times by vote does not confirm the directions of the contextual proposition. True to expectations, some hot issues (especially votes like common situs and strip mining which had been up before) are decided well before the vote. But, other hot votes (budget, Arab boycott) are decided on the floor. Some low-profile votes (NASA) are determined at the last moment, but others (EPA, public works) are resolved automatically or on the basis of a member's past experience. Evidently, hot issues are resolved depending on situational considerations—e.g., amendments. If important amendments loom, members will await the outcome before deciding. The time of decision on low-profile issues depends on when the member receives information that the issues are coming up. If the member knows a routine issue is coming up a week or day before, he has an opportunity, based on past positions, to make a decision automatically. If he does not hear about it until he reaches the floor, the decision may not be made until late. It should be added that the precise time when a member learns that a low-profile vote is coming up seems to be a function of the information systems of individual members. Members who are briefed far in advance of a vote or who read the schedule a week ahead are probably more likely to make an earlier decision than those who play it day-by-day or hour-by-hour.

There are some significant variations in the mention of the different decision points according to issue characteristics. Of the 432 distributions, 90 (21 percent) involve meaningful variation across categories of issue characteristics indicators. These variations do provide a list of correlates for most decision times. These are displayed in Table 6.9.

The correlates offer mixed support for the proposition. Decisions made "when first in politics," "automatically," "the last time up," and "during the campaign" are associated with hot characteristics. Decisions made "when read about it" are associated with mostly low-profile characteristics. But, decisions made "on the floor" and "late" involve both low-profile and hot characteristics.

217

TABLE 6.9

Values of Issue Characteristics Associated with Mention of Different Decision Times (Correlates are based On Variation of 9 Percent or More)

When First Entered Politics
- Conflict (H)
- Non-routine (H)
- No feelings (LP)
- Above average Republican party unity (LP)
- Close vote (H)
- No CQ box score (LP)
- Congress initiates (H)
- No presidential involvement (H)●

Automatic
- Mail (H)
- Feeling (H)
- Below average rule margin (H)
- Defeated (H)
- Washington Post box score (H)
- Washington Post story (H)
- Democratic endorsement (H)
- New (H)

Last Time Up
- Major (H)
- Renomination effects (H)
- Reelection effects (H)
- Routine (LP)
- Not tough (LP)
- No thought (LP)
- Open rule (LP)
- Close vote (H)
- Minority report (H)
- CQ box score (H)
- CQ story (H)
- Above average policy time (H)
- Democratic endorsements (H)
- Presidential involvement (H)●
- Not new (LP) change (H)

During Campaign
- Complex (LP)
- Major (H)
- Salient (H)
- Constituency Aware (H)
- Renomination effects (H)
- Reelection effects (H)
- Feeling (H)
- Closed rule (H)
- Close vote (H)
- Congress ratifies (LP)
- No presidential involvement (LP)

On the Committee
- Below average Republican unity (H)
- No CQ story (LP)
- Congress ratifies (LP)
- No change (LP)

Week Before
- Thought (H)

When Read About
- Not complex (H)
- No feelings (LP)
- Open rule (LP)
- Modified Rule (LP)
- Wide margin of passage (LP)
- No CQ story (LP)
- No Washington Post story (LP)
- No Democratic endorsement (LP)
- No change (LP)

When Heard From Constituents
- Thought (II)
- Congress modifies (H)

218

Table 6.9   --Continued

Values of Issue Characteristics Associated with Mention of Different Decision Times
(These correlates are based on variations of 9 percent or more)

On The Floor	When Changes Made	Late
Non-technical (H)	Non-routine (H)	Tough (H)
Non-major (H)	New (H)	Closed rule (H)
Non-salient (LP)●		Below average
No mail (LP)		Democratic unity (H)
No renomination effects (LP)●		Congress ratifies (LP)●
No reelection effects (LP)		No presidential
No strong feelings (LP)		involvement (LP)●
Tough (H)		Change (H)
No thought (LP)		
Closed rule (H)		
Above average rule margin (H)		
Defeated (H)●		
Above average		
Republican unity (LP)		
Above average likeness (LP)		
No minority report (LP)●		
No CQ box score (LP)		
No CQ story (LP)●		

No Washington Post box (LP)
No Washington Post story (LP)
Below average policy time (LP)
Below average money (LP)●
Presidential involvement (H)●
Non-specific (H)

H = Presumed hot value
LP= Presumed low profile value
● = Variation of 20 percent or more

219

Evidently, in line with arrays by vote, qualifications to the proposition are in order. Decisions on hot issues are made both early and late. Decisions on low-profile issues are made both early and late.

Conclusions Concerning Time of Decision

Members may reach a decision at any number of times in the legislative process. Although the most frequently mentioned decision times are "on the floor" and "the last time the bill was up," the time at which a member makes up his mind varies greatly from vote-to-vote and under various issue characteristics.

In sum, the interviews support the notion that time of decision is a highly variable phenomenon. But, only partial support is provided for the expectation that hot decisions are made early, while low-profile decisions are made late. The findings here argue that decisions on some hot bills get made early as a result of past legislative experience or campaign activity. Other hot decisions are made as members await the outcome of the amending process. Many low-profile decisions are associated with floor and late voting, perhaps reflecting members' lack of concern and information. Other low-profile votes are handled routinely, with the time of decision hinging on precisely when the member hears that the bill is coming up. The proposition is thus accepted with the qualification that major variations in decision times are governed by parliamentary events and floor wrangling and the member's own information system.

Summary and Conclusions

This chapter has identified two additional benchmarks at which variations in legislative decision behavior can be observed: role orientations and time of decision.

The evidence of this study argues that the role conception with which a member approaches decision-making varies among different kinds of votes and under various issue characteristics.

Time of decision, a component of voting held to be important by many interviewees, also reveals vote-by-vote, issue-by-issue variation.

The results reported here thus argue for a contextual theory with which to grasp the dynamics of decision-making.

Several afterthoughts concerning the generalizations offered here provide an appropriate way to conclude this chapter.

First, when members cite a delegate or politico style and a local or national and local mixture, they often hold a segmental view of constituency interests. Subsequent questioning of several members revealed that on decisions such as the Hatch Act revisions and clean air, "the constituency" was defined soley in terms of who the member heard from back in the district: postal employees or auto dealers. The problem, of course, is that members might not give consideration to the latent, unmobilized groups. Decisions made as a delegate and with a local focus might be responses to the claims of very narrow, particularistic interests that, in themselves, are detrimental to commonwealth concerns or to the district's interests broadly construed. This, of course, raises a central dilemma of representation: does the legislator place more emphasis on the interests of intense minorities--interests that though narrow are politically strong--or should he show favor to an amorphous general interest--a broader but politically passive interest? In other words, does the member vote the constituents he hears from or his perception of broad constituency interests?

Second, conversations with several members indicate that a heterogeneous district facilitates a trustee style. In the words of one of the most articulate members, "You have a lot of leeway on a vote if your district is heterogeneous. You can mobilize different groups to compensate for a loss of support by others. This situation really reinforces your independence." In contrast, members from homogeneous districts do not enjoy such latitude. They lack the ability to play one group against another or to build a coalition out of a diversity of interest.

Finally, the findings that most members are trustees and that they usually reserve judgement until the floor stage may be the result of interviewee attempts to cater to their perceptions of

221

researchers' expectations. There are expectations in some quarters that members should utilize independent judgement and should suspend judgment until all the facts are in. The possibility looms that members' replies to questions pertaining to these topics may be more of an effort to conform to these expectations, and less of an attempt to validly reconstruct the decision process. It will be argued in the next chapter that such a risk, however, is one of the tradeoffs of the interviewing approach to congressional decision-making.

[1]Heinz Eulau, John C. Wahlke, William Buchanan, and Leroy C. Ferguson, "The Role of the Representative: Some Empirical Observations on the Theory of Edmund Burke," _American Political Science Review_ 53 (1959): 742-56.

[2]Malcolm E. Jewell and Samuel C. Patterson, _The Legislative Process in the United States_, 3rd ed. (New York: Random, 1977), p. 372.

[3]Roger H. Davidson, _The Role of the Congressman_ (New York: Pegasus, 1969), p. 120.

[4]Ibid.

[5]John C. Wahlke, Heinz Eulau, Willian Buchanan, and Leroy C. Ferguson, _The Legislative System: Explorations in Legislative Behavior_ (New York: Wiley, 1962), p. 494.

[6]Ibid., p. 12.

[7]Ibid., p. 277.

[8]Davidson, _The Role_, p. 119.

[9]Idid.

[10]Ibid.

[11]Ibid., p. 120

[12]See Wahlke et al., _Legislative System_, appendix 6; Davidson, _The Role_, appendix; Ronald D. Hedlund and H. Paul Friesema, "Representatives' Perceptions of Constituency Opinion," _Journal of Politics_ 34 (1972): 730-52; H. Paul Friesema and Ronald D. Hedlund, "The Reality of Representative Roles," in _Public Opinion and Public Policy_, 2nd ed., ed. by Norman R. Luttbeg (Homewood, Ill.: Dorsey, 1974), pp. 413-17; and Bryan D. Jones, "Competitiveness, Role Orientations, and Legislative Responsiveness," _Journal of Politics_ 36 (1973): 924-47.

[13]Warren E. Miller and Donald E. Stokes, "Constituency Influence in Congress," _American Political Science Review_ 57 (1963): 45-56.

[14]Davidson, _The Role_, p. 117.

[15]Ibid., p. 122.

[16]Eulau et al., "The Role," p. 742.

[17]For a description of the amendment process, see Charles
J. Zinn, How Our Laws are Made (Washington, D.C.: Government
Printing Office, 1978), p. 27.

[18]The argument of both Sundquist and Polsby is that major
policy changes are usually ideas that have been around Washington
and before Congress for years. See: James L. Sundquist,
Politics and Policy (Washington: Brookings, 1968) and Nelson W.
Polsby, "Policy Analysis and Congress," Public Policy 17 (1969):
61-74.

[19]That some do play it hour by hour is indicated by the
Cloak Room recordings maintained by both parties. Members need
only call the phone number to hear what is immediately up and
what the issues are.

CHAPTER VII

CONCLUSIONS

The major conclusion of this research is that
Congressmen do not make up their minds in a set way
or in the same fashion on each and every floor vote.
Their decision behavior is highly variable. Who
Congressmen hear from, where they get their information, and how and when they make a decision vary from
vote to vote and according to issue characteristics.
These variations are patterned in that differences in
legislative behavior are associated with different
kinds of votes. How members behave and reach decisions clearly depends on the type of vote at hand.

Although contextual decision-making seems
obvious, it has neither been systematically examined
nor emphasized in major studies of legislative
behavior. Typically, research has sought to formulate general propositions and models with which to
understand legislative decision-making. This has
resulted in a number of conflicting single-eye inter-
pretations. This study has revealed that no one
model provides an adequate explanation. The findings
do not call for the rejection of a number of inter-
pretations in favor of just one interpretation.
Instead, major generalizations and models are shown
to have partial, contextual applicability.

Specifically, this study tested previously
unsubstantiated propositions derived from the
literature of the conditional school of legislative
behavior. They are reasonable, substantive
deductions from the writings of Lowi,[1] Ripley and
Franklin,[2] Price,[3] and others who stress a
variable, dynamic model. These propositions pertain
to variations in legislative behavior with regard to
four components of members' decision-making map: (1)
force field inputs and communications, (2) information sources, (3) determinants and decision modes,
and (4) roles. In addition, "time of decision" was
studied.

Testing the propositions led to 32 findings
concerning micro congressional decision-making. The
findings are:

1. Members hear from relatively few actors when
   casting a floor vote. (p. 62)

225

2. Staff, constituents, and other members make the most input. (p. 62)

3. Communications can be differentiated by type. (p. 73)

4. The volume of communications varies by vote. (p. 73)

5. Volume of communications varies by issue characteristics. (p. 76)

6. The actors from whom a member hears vary according to the kind of decision at hand. (p. 78)

7. The input of various actors to congressional decision-making varies according to issue characteristics. (p. 92)

8. Many information sources are used for congressional decision-making. (p. 103)

9. Some sources are relied on for information more than others. (p. 105)

10. There are different categories of congressional information sources. (p. 106)

11. Congressional information sources can be differentiated by directness and proximity. (p. 116)

12. Some information sources synthesize the position of others. (p. 116)

13. Information sources vary according to the kind of issue at hand. (p. 116)

14. The volume (the number of sources) of information a Congressman refers to (although generally low) varies according to the kind of issue involved. (p. 129)

15. Congressmen generally feel adequately informed when casting floor votes. (p. 138)

16. The member's perception of the adequacy of information varies according to the kind of issue at hand. (p. 139)

17. A variety of decision determinants are cited in House floor voting. (p. 151)

18. Members frequently mention multiple determinants when reconstructing their decision process. (p. 163)

19. An overwhelming majority of decisions are determined by ideological considerations. (p.165)

20. There are seven different decision modes in congressional voting. (p. 168)

21. Many individual members acknowledge the use of different decision modes. (p. 171)

22. The decision determinant that members cite varies from vote to vote. (p. 172)

23. The low-profile/hot distinction implied by Lowi and others does not in itself capture the differences in legislative decision-making. (p. 179)

24. Members articulate the same philosophical dichotomy of representation that Burke identified. (p. 194)

25. Members cite styles other than the delegate and trustee pure types. (p. 199)

26. Congressmen couch most decisions in terms of a trustee orientation or a combination of the trustee and delegate (the politico) roles. (p. 200)

27. Members generally have a national focus. (p. 200)

28. Representative style and focus do not necessarily correlate together. (p. 203)

29. The representative role orientations of members vary according to the kind of issue at hand. (p. 212)

30. Members mention various decision times. (p. 214)

31. The most frequently mentioned times of decision are "on the floor" and "the last time the bill was up." (p. 214)

32. The time at which a member makes up his mind varies according to different kinds of issues. (p. 214)

The research described here permits additional generalizations and conclusions. For clarity's sake, they will be presented according to the following sub-topics: control variables, conditional theory, issue characteristics, actors involved in legislative decision-making, components of cognitive map, floor voting, decision settings, interviewing legislators, and legislative decision-making and democracy. Finally, a number of prescriptions will be offered on the basis of this research.

Conclusions Concerning Control Variables

Chapter II described the control variables employed in the study. Utilizing these variables permitted the testing of some very interesting hypotheses suggested both by Davidson and by conversations with some of the interviewed members. For example, both volume and sources of communcations were controlled by ideological extremity, party and presidential loyalty, election results, committee membership, and length of service. Some logical relationships between information sources/search/ level, on one hand, and party and seniority, on the other, were investigated. Seniority, party, election results and yea/nay voting were correlated with determinants. Representative role and focus were correlated with years of service and margin of victory. Examining these relationships afforded the opportunity to examine possible alternative explanations.

Some interesting findings came to light. For example, Southern Democrats and Republicans tend to rely on Whip Notices more than Northern Democrats. Freshmen use Whip Notices at a rate twice as high as their more senior counterparts. It is interesting that those with below average party support scores mention party publications at a slightly higher rate than those with higher scores. Those with above average ADA scores mention DSG at a rate twice as high as those with below average scores.

228

Those who vote yea (not nay as one member insisted) are electorally marginal, from a switch district, more junior, and have a higher volume of information. Those with twelve or more years of service cite policy assessments as a determinant more frequently than those in more junior categories. But the more senior members, perhaps on the basis of friendship and House power relationships, are also more likely to base a decision on a committee chairman's position. Junior members rely more on personal staff, constituency, compromise, and campaign promises than more experienced legislators. Legislators with six to eleven years of seniority are more likely, by a wide margin, to mention philosophical convictions than any other category. Length of service is related to role in that junior members take a delegate or politico role more than others. Freshmen mention a national/local focus more than more experienced members.

Relationships between election results and role are completely opposite to those found in Davidson. Davidson found that members from marginal districts subscribed to the delegate model and had a district orientation, while those from safe districts tended to be trustees and to have a national focus. The findings of this study are in sharp contrast. Those members from "close" districts rely more on "self" and exhibit more of a national focus. Those from safe districts define their role as combination trustee/delegate at a higher rate than those from marginal or close districts. Also, those from safe districts cite both a national/local focus at a higher rate, indicating heightened sensitivity to constituency. The only confirmation for Davidson is the relationship between role and district switch status. Those from a district that did not switch rely on self more than the switchers. The switchers, however, do not have a higher rate of either "both" or "constituency" responses.

For the most part, however, the relationships between decision behavior and background/constituency characteristics are extremely low. Relationships between decision behavior and issue type seemed to be stronger and more helpful as an explanation of voting behavior than the relationships with control variables.

229

Conclusions Concerning the Conditional Theory

The works of Lowi, Ripley and Franklin, Price, Cobb and Elder,[4] and others[5] postulate that distinctions in legislative behavior do not occur randomly. Instead, it is argued that major differences in the decision behavior of members occur on the basis of a distinction between "hot" (visible, controversial, major) votes and "low-profile" (nonvisible, noncontroversial, major, complex, technical) votes. It is expected that low-profile votes will be associated with few lobbying attempts, input from only those affected, narrow information sources, perfunctory scan, low levels of information, cue-taking decision-making, a national/trustee role orientation, and a "late" decision. Hot votes are expected to involve many lobbying attempts, broad input, multiple information sources, extraordinary scan, adequate levels of information, policy and philosophical voting, a local/delegate role conception, and relatively "early" decision-making. The rationale for these patterns is an investment theory of incentives. Hot issues involve sufficient resources and political stakes to provide the member with incentives for greater interest and involvement. Low-profile votes, lacking intense lobbying and competing information sources, do not comparably motivate the member. Members make decisions without an extended search and by deferring to others.

In the main, this research substantiates these postulations. Generally, communication inputs, volume of input, search processes, adequacy of information, decision rules, role orientations, and time of decision conform to these expectations. Volume of input (arrayed by vote), information search, information adequacy, and time of decision best conform. Only information sources seem to significantly stray from the expectations raised by these authors. Thus, although there are deviations and exceptions, the hot or low-profile distinction does seem to accurately capture major behavioral differentials in congressional voting.

More important, the hot or low-profile distinction provides a baseline on which to build subsequent refinements. The study here of each of the major components of member decision-making revealed a number of exceptions to the theory of the conditional authors. When these exceptions are closely examined, they often suggest patterns that add to or modify the original conditional theory. In other words, the hot or low-profile distribution is not the only dividing line in legislative behavior. It is not the only force driving variations in legislative decision-making.

For example, sources of congressional input vary not just according to hot and low-profile votes but along the following lines: routine votes, grant bills, hot votes, and specialized, hot bills. When member's confront a routine issue, they rely primarily on staff and committee input. Grant programs and public works programs involve staff and state delegation input, plus contacts with specific clientele within the district. Hot issues involve communications from a variety of forces including private interest groups, constituents, party leaders, and the White House. Specialized hot issues are complex or technical as well as controversial. They usually affect a specific constituency. They involve expanded input and communications from committee members and constituent groups.

Use of information sources varies more by the member's knowledge and information needs. If a member is unfamiliar with a vote, but it is important to him, he will consult normal sources such as staff and congressional publications. Special contextual circumstances cause him to turn to other sources for various reasons.

Information volume (an indicator of search procedures) varies according to complexity and technicality, parliamentary suspense, and a hot or low-profile distinction. Members search for more information when the issue is hot, when there is not a short parliamentary suspense, and when there are low-grade issues that are hard to understand.

Decision rules were found to vary in such a way that hot votes involve situational considerations (such as assessments of the adequacy of a compromise) as well as policy assessments, philosophical convictions, and constituency representation. Low-profile votes involve policy assessments, as well as cue-taking, compromise and consensus voting.

Variations in role seem to be best captured by the following distinctions: hot, hot with no constituency relevance, grant programs, and low-profile decisions. Hot decisions with constituency relevance are made primarily with a politico style and a district orientation. Hot votes that lack constituency relevance are made primarily as a nationally-oriented trustee. Grant programs are also handled with a politico style. Low-profile votes are handled primarily on a nation-trustee basis.

In addition to a hot or low-profile distinction, variations in "when decided" are best captured by the following variables: parliamentary suspense, floor wrangling, and members' information sources. A relatively early decision is made when there is ample scheduling notice that the vote is coming up, when floor controversy is minimal, and when the vote involves a major issue. Late decision occurs when the vote is low-profile, when there is little advanced scheduling, and when there is doubt concerning the outcome of the amending process. Throughout, these distinctions are affected by the idiosyncratic nature of each member's own information system.

The point to be emphasized is that the original basic hot or low-profile distinction, although overly simplistic, affords the opportunity for these refinements. At the very least, the contextual theory points the way to further elaborations of a conditional model.

Conclusions Concerning Issue Characteristics

A major feature of this research was the use of the issue characteristics of Cobb and Elder,[6] Price,[7] and Froman and Ripley[8] as independent variables in a test for variations in legislative behavior.

Overall, the use of issue characteristics met with mixed results. There appear to be four advantages to using issue characteristics.

First, issue characteristics reveal variations in legislative behavior. Many variations occur across different values of issue characteristics. By way of summary, Table 7.1 displays the percent of meaningful variations associated with issue characteristics for

232

Table 7.1

Summary of Variations* by Issue Characteristics

Component of Cognitive Map	Indicator	Overall % of Variations	By Indicator Type			By Interviewee
			Perceptual	Objective	Subjective	
Force field	Volume	74%	-	-	-	-
	Source	33%	33%	38%	22%	-
Information	Source	11%	9%	6%	6%	80%
	Volume	50%	-	-	-	80%
	Level	65%	-	-	-	-
Decision rule	Determinants	11%	9%	13%	5%	82%
Role orientation	Style	27%	36%	25%	0	36%
	Focus	40%	31%	45%	44%	40%
Time of decision	When decided	21%	21%	20%	22%	-

* Variations are defined as deviations of 9 percent or more in the mention of decision factors among different values of an issue characteristic.

each of the components of the member's cognitive map. As seen there, issue characteristics are associated with numerous variations of 9 percent or more in the mention of actors, sources, decision rules, role orientations, or time of decision.

Second, issue characteristics permit the identification of the correlates of various decision-making forces and factors--i.e., the issue conditions under which a decision force is more likely to be mentioned.

Third, issue characteristics permit the identification of the major indicators of legislative dynamism. The array of decision factors by issue characteristics reveals that some characteristics are associated with more variation than others. Such characteristics are the best indicators of legislative dynamism, for they are the conditions most associated with variation. Table 7.2 presents the issue characteristics most associated with variations in different aspects of cognitive map. Specifically, the table shows that the role of Congress on a particular bill and presidential involvement are the two indicators most associated with variation in congressional input. When Congress ratifies or modifies a policy and the President is not involved, the issue tends to be quiet, and members hear from relatively few. When Congress initiates and when the President is involved, communications to members are more numerous and diverse. Information sources are most affected by presidential involvement and type of rule. When a bill is debated under a closed rule (i.e., no amendments are allowed) and the White House is involved in the issue, members are more likely to refer to atypical information sources. When the rule is open and the White House is not involved, normal sources are consulted. The indicator most associated with variation in determinants is degree of thought. Those votes that entail member "thought" are usually based on constituency, conviction, and policy assessment. Votes lacking "a lot of thought" are more likely to be settled on the basis of cue-taking and with the consensus and compromise modes. The time of decision varies most by intensity of member feelings and margin of passage. Decisions concerning votes that are eventually defeated are made late, usually on the floor. Decisions concerning bills passed by a comfortable margin are made comparatively

234

Table 7.2

Issue Characteristics Most Associated with Variations* as Arrayed by
Different Aspects of Members' Cognitive Map

Force Field	Information Source	Determinants	When Decided
Role of Congress	Presidential involvement	Thought	Margin of passage
Presidential involvement	Type of rule	Presidential involvement	Feelings
Conflict	Mail	Role of Congress	Presidential involvement
Amount of money	Rule margin	Margin of passage	Role of Congress
Toughness	Role of Congress		Thought
Thought			CQ story
Rule margin			
CQ visibility			
Washington Post box score			
Amendment over committee objection			

(Issue characteristics are arranged from the top down in order of declining magnitude.)

* Variations are defined as deviations of 9 percent or more in the mention of decision factors among
different values of an issue characteristic.

earlier. Members usually make early decisions on
bills that involve their personal feelings.
Decisions on bills that do not involve intense
feelings are made late.

A fourth benefit stemming from the use of issue
characteristics is that they constitute a method of
studying variations in legislative behavior that is
less cumbersome than working with individual votes.
Both votes and issue characteristics were used here
as independent variables affecting legislative
behavior. The use of votes tended to be anecdotal
and unsystematic. In contrast, issue characteristics
proved to be more general, direct, and concise and
less unwieldy. Unlike votes that involve multiple
issues and facets, issue characteristics afforded the
opportunity for simplified, single dimensional
analysis.

Despite these advantages, the following three
factors greatly detract from the utility of issue
characteristics:

First, the various indicators of issue
characteristics do not neatly cluster together along
the lines of a hot or low-profile continuum. There
is a lack of synoptic indicators. Each issue
characteristic must be treated separately. Although
issue characteristics are more general than votes and
do permit the discussion of variation without
reference to individual cases, the use of 36
different indicators still proved confusing and
unwieldy.

Second, meaningful variation is frequently
concluded on the basis of small numbers. The
criteria used here of 9 or 20 percent, although
commonly used in many empirical studies, frequently
lead to the identification of correlates on the basis
of small figures and differences.

Third, the breakdown of responses by issue
characteristics does not reveal legislative behavior
variations as impressively as a breakdown of
responses by interviewee. Another look at Table 7.1
(especially the column on the far right) shows that
the variations observed in the responses of interviewees (for whom four or more questionnaires are
available) are considerably more supportive of a

236

contextual model than arrays by issue characteristics. Fully 80 percent of those for whom such multiple interviews exist indicate varying force fields, information sources, search procedures, and decision rules.

Issue characteristics are thus helpful, but limited, concepts for exploring for legislative behavior variations. Although they do not indicate variation as directly as multiple responses from the same actor, they are more general and less cumbersome than a vote-by-vote study. Most relevant here is the fact that issue characteristics permit the best test of the directional, hot and low-profile hypothesis of conditional theory.

Conclusions Concerning Actor Involvement and Influence

The involvement and influence of various actors within the legislative process varies by a) type of vote, b) conditions of issue characteristics, and c) component of cognitive map. This can be seen in Tables 7.3a-i which present a summary of the vote and issue characteristics correlates (based on 20 percent or more variation) of each of the major actors involved in legislative decision-making, as arrayed by component of cognitive map. These tables show that, in contrast to Kingdon's model, the contributions of major actors is best presented with a conditional rather than a general format.[9] Committee chairmen contribute most as an input when they are a visible competitor, i.e., when one of the major parties in a floor fight is the chairman. Committee members contribute as input, information source, and determinant under a variety of conditions that are both hot and low-profile. State delegation primarily serves as an input on hot and local-oriented votes. Other members primarily make input on hot votes. Party leaders provide a small input, primarily on those votes on which the majority party stakes its prestige. The President is mentioned as an input primarily on those votes on which he stakes his prestige. Staff constitutes both a factor "paid attention to" and an information source when the vote is poltically relevant but hard to understand. Evidently, members feel a need for additional staff investigation and briefing on votes that are not open-and-shut for them. Constituents are mentioned both as an input and a determinant under hot conditions. Interest groups contribute to members'

237

decision-making processes as an input factor when the vote is hot or constituency relevant.

Due perhaps to the predominance of policy assessments as a voting determinant, four major actors commonly presumed to be combatants in the legislative process--committee chairmen, party leaders, the Administration, and interest groups--were not frequently mentioned as the basis of decision-making by interviewees. It would be erroneous, however, to conclude that they are inconsequential. It may be argued that each has an impact in ways not likely to register in the cognitive map of members.

Chairmen

Although their powers have been substantially reduced in recent years,[10] contemporary chairmen still retain awesome influence over the future of bills that emanate from their committees.

The chairman is a major hurdle that must be cleared if a bill is to receive a hearing on the committee's agenda. As the presiding officer and, frequently, the broker of his panel, the chairman often structures debate, thus having enormous influence on the accommodative language that constitutes the language of the law. If legislation is the result of bargains struck in the legislative arena, it is more often than not the chairman who strikes the bargain. Also, as a member with obvious expertise and prestige, the chairman will be a major input in bill drafting. At the floor stage, it is the chairman who serves as floor manager and tactician. He selects speakers and tends to the problems of coalition-building.

The chairman's avid support may not be critical to the life and death of a bill, but it is imperative that he not be opposed to it. Moreover, it is extremely helpful if he is at least a tacit supporter. Thus, although members may not see the chairman as a cue-giver, he has influence over legislative outcomes if for no other reason than the fact that proponents of legislation will attempt to anticipate his reaction, solicit his support, and avoid his wrath.

Table 7.3a

Correlates* of Committee Chairmen Influence in Member Decision-Making

Component	% General Mention	Type of Vote	Perceptual Characteristics	Issue Characteristic Correlates	
				Objective Characteristics	Subjective Characteristics
Input (Heard from/ paid attention to)	20%	Chairman visible and dominant as competitor	Thought Constituency unaware No reelection effects	Closed rule Below average committee unanimity Mention in CQ box score CQ story Congress as ratifier No amendment over committee objection Democratic and Republican policy endorsements Presidential involvement	Change
Information source	5%	No patterns detected	No correlates		
Determinant	6%	Chairman a visible combatant	No thought		

Table 7.3b

Correlates of Committee Member Influence in Member Decision-Making

Component	% General Mention	Type of Vote	Issue Characteristic Correlates		
			Perceptual Characteristics	Objective Characteristics	Subjective Characteristics
Input (Heard from/ paid attention to)	36%	Hot but technical Low grade	Complex Technical Conflict Non-routine Tough Mail	Closed rule ● Washington Post box score Above average index of likeness Amendment over committee objection ● Mention in polls Above average money No presidential involvement Congress as Modifier ●	
Information source	13%	Committee members are major combatants	Complex Technical	Congress as modifier Closed rule	
Determinant	10%	Minor Constituency relevant Complex Committee fight	No mail No feelings No thought	No CQ story Congress as ratifier Presidential involvement	

Table 7.3c

Correlates of State Delegation Members' Influence in Member Decision-Making

| | | | | Issue Characteristic Correlates | |
Component	% General Mention	Type of Vote	Perceptual Characteristics	Objective Characteristics	Subjective Characteristics
Input (Heard from/ paid attention to)	31%	Hot, Grant, and Pork	Conflictual Major Non-routine● Tough● Mail Renomination and reelection Constituency awareness Thought	Closed rule● Below average rule margin● Defeated status● Below average committee vote Minority report CQ story Washington Post story● Washington Post box score Congress as modifier Below average Republican and Democratic unity● Amendment over committee objection Below average index of likeness Party endorsements Above average money Presidential involvement	
Information source	5%	No patterns detected	No correlates		
Determinants	3%	No patterns detected	No correlates		

241

Table 7.3d

Correlates of Other Member Influence in Member Decision-Making

Component	% General Mention	Type of Vote	Issue Characteristic Correlates		
			Perceptual Characteristics	Objective Characteristics	Subjective Characteristics
Input (Heard from/ paid attention to)	36%	Hot	Conflict Major status Constituency awareness• Mail Renomination effects Reelection effects Non-routineness Thought Toughness	Below average rule margin Modified open rule Defeat• CQ story Washington Post box score Washington Post story Congress as initiator• Below average time Democratic and Republican endorsements	Specificity
Information source	9%	Attempts to override committee from floor	No correlates	Above average rule margin No Republican endorsement	Policy change
Determinants	4%		Attempts to override committee from floor	No correlates	

242

Correlates of Party Leader Influence in Member Decision-Making

Component	% General Mention	Type of Vote	Perceptual Characteristics	Issue Characteristic Correlates	
				Objective Characteristics	Subjective Characteristics
Input (Heard from/ paid attention to)	13%	Majority party prestige at stake	Conflictual Major Constituency awareness Renomination effects Reelection effects Strong feelings	Closed rule◖ Below average rule margin◆ Defeated status CQ story Washington Post box score Washington Post story Below average time frame Below average Democratic unity Above average Republican unity Below average index of likeness Amendment over committee objection No Democratic endorsement● Presidential involvement Congress as initiator	
Information sources	4%	Majority party prestige at stake		Closed rule◆	
Determinants	2%		No correlates		

243

Table 7.3f

Correlates of White House Influence in Member Decision-Making

Component	% General Mention	Type of Vote	Issue Characteristic Correlates		
			Perceptual Characteristics	Objective Characteristics	Subjective Characteristics
Input (Heard from/ paid attention to)	14%	Presidential emphasis	No mail Tough Thought	Open rule ● CQ story Washington Post story Congress as ratifier and modifier Below average Republican unity Amendment over committee objection Presidential involvement	
Information source	3%	No patterns detected	No correlates		Specificity Policy change ●
Determinants	6%	White House is major combatant		Presidential involvement	

244

Table 7.3g

Correlates of Staff Influence in Member Decision-Making

Component	% General Mention	Type of Vote	Issue Characteristic Correlates		
			Perceptual Characteristics	Objective Characteristics	Subjective Characteristics
Input (Heard from/ paid attention to)	42%	Hot but complicated Low profile which are hard to understand District relevant	Complex• Technical Conflict No strong feeling• Thought•	Closed rule• Below av. comm. cohesion Minority report• CQ story Washington Post box score Congress as modifier Democratic and Republican endorsements Mention in the polls• Above average money•	Non-specificity
Information source	33%	Non-visible Member not familiar	Complex Constituency awareness No strong feelings Thought	Open rule Above average rule margin Congress as modifier No presidential involvement	
Determinant	4%	Routine Constituency relevant	No correlates		

245

Table 7.3h

Correlates of Constituents (Constituency) Influence in Member
Decision-Making

Component	% General Mention	Type of Vote	Issue Characteristic Correlates		
			Perceptual Characteristics	Objective Characteristics	Subjective Characteristics
Input (Heard from/ paid attention to)	42%	Certain hot issues	Conflict• Salience Constituency awareness• Mail Renomination effects Reelection effects Non-routineness Toughness Thought Strong feelings•	Modified open rule• Below average rule margin Defeat• CQ box score CQ story• Washington Post box score Washington Post story Congress as initiator Above average time coverage Above average money No mention in the polls Presidential involvement•	Change
Information source	5%	Certain hot issues	Constituency awareness Mail Thought	No correlates	
Determinant	13%	Controversy Constituency relevant High mail	Salience Constituency awareness Mail Tough Thought	Below average rule margin CQ story Congress as initiator Congress as initiator Republican party endorsement Presidential involvement	

246

Table 7.3i

Correlates of Interest Group Influence in Member Decision-Making

Issue Characteristic Correlates

Component	% General Mention	Type of Vote	Perceptual Characteristics	Objective Characteristics	Subjective Characteristics
Input (Heard from/ paid attention to)	22%	Hot, Interest relevant	Complex●, Technical, Conflict, Salience, Constituency awareness, Mail, Renomination effects●, Reelection effects●, Non-routineness *, Toughness, Thought●	Open Rule●, Closeness, Below av. comm. cohesion, Minority report, CQ Box score●, Washington Post box score, Washington Post story, Congressional modification●, Above average time frame●, Amendment over committee objection, Democratic policy endorsements●, No mention in the polls, Above average money, Presidential involvement●	New issue, Non-specificity, Policy change
Information source	5%	Hot, Interest relevant	No correlates	CQ box score	No correlates
Determinant	0%		No correlates		No correlates

* Correlates are based on variations of 9 percent or more
● Indicates a variation of 20 percent or more.

247

For all of the sampled bills, interviews with informed committee staffers indicated the importance of the chairman in initiating the issue, securing hearings, presiding over hearings, calling witnesses, structuring markup, scheduling the legislation on the floor, managing debate, and negotiating with the Senate.

Party Leaders

Party leaders contribute most to legislative decision-making in ways that are indirect, latent, and not easily recognized.

The formal and informal powers of party floor leaders have been well documented.[11] It is obvious that, due to these powers, leaders hold sway over the flow of legislation. Because of their centrality in the legislative process, leaders can have a detrimental effect on legislation they oppose, providing their position is supported by a procedural majority.[12] The tacit approval of leaders, in addition, is necessary for "greasing the skids" in the legislative process. This study provides speculation that party leaders also influence legislative decision-making through the dissemination of information and the activation of party-associated policy positions. By defining an issue in a certain way in the Whip Notice or in policy committee pronouncements, party leaders may be able to deliver blocs of support, particularly if the issue is defined in such a way as to raise the core policy differences between the parties. Such indirect influences are not recorded in the members' cognitive map.

The Administration

In both this and Kingdon's study,[13] the President and his administration only infrequently were singled out by members as a decision factor. This finding may reveal a declining White House influence in Congress. Or, it may reflect an atypical time period during which both researches were undertaken. This research began in 1977 at the beginning of the Carter administration. Kingdon began his research in 1969 during the early years of the Nixon administration. It is quite possible that in both periods the new President's legislative liaison machinery had not jelled. As a key

248

Democratic leader stated during the early days of the Carter administration,

> The President is just getting started. It's early in the game for him. That's also the case with our new party leaders. We've got a new Speaker and floor leader and they are just getting organized. Both the President and leadership have complicated constituencies that have yet to jell together. They have to pay attention to what the demands are in the Congressmen's districts. Nobody of their party really wants to displease any of them. Yet, this is the most independent lot I've seen up here, especially since the 93rd and 94th Congresses and their confrontations with Nixon and Ford, the reform movement, and the anti-war thing.

When a President has been on the job for awhile and has an established whip system, he likely will be a formidable contestant in legislative affairs. The thesis of Chamberlain[14] and others argues that, in fact, the presidency has come to dominate the Congress. Certainly, all can agree that, although the President may not be prominent as a decision premise in the cognitive map of members, he is influential in initiating issues, bargaining with committee leaders, aiding supportive congressional leaders in the construction of coalitions, providing information, working key bloc leaders, and exercising the veto power.

The President's involvement and influence, of course, vary according to contexts. Generally, involvement is the greatest when key elements of the President's program are at stake. His influence is likely to be the greatest when, as Ripley shows, a majoritarian alignment[15] is present and when the President enjoys (a) at least modest success in accomplishing his objectives[16] and (b) continued popular support after a sizable victory at the polls.[17] Under these conditions and once the President's liaison has developed, it seems reasonable to expect that the President will be mentioned more by members as an input, information source, and decision determinant.

Background interviews revealed many instances where the President was a behind-the-scenes contributor. White House involvement was noted on major bills that the President featured as part of his program and on the nuclear navy vote and votes on the Arab boycott, Housing and Community Development, the Supplemental Appropriation for Housing, and Rhodesian chrome. For each, the Administration was identified as a major driving force behind the legislation.

Interest Groups

Interest groups and their lobbyists normally pursue low-key strategies that often are not apparent to the ordinary floor-voting member. Among these strategies are the following: providing information to committee, working members' districts, obtaining campaign pledges and commitments, focusing on committee members and other key legislators, focusing on the committee stage of decision-making, focusing on the uncommitted and wavering, intensifying lobbying efforts on close votes and on technical "private regarding" amendments, using a member of the Congressman's "personal" constituency[18] as a link to the member, and, infrequently, employing "classical"[19] techniques such as hosting banquets to gain access to members and/or staff.

Interest group activity and influence are minimal in floor voting in any of three situations: (1) when issues are initiated or dominated by the President (e.g., Presidential reorganization authority and the creation of the Department of Energy), (2) when issues are viewed as internal congressional matters (e.g., the pay raise and the budget resolution), and (3) when there is an ideological vote that pits Republican against Democrat, majority against minority, and liberal against conservative. For other, more specific votes, private interests may be important participants at low-level, strategic points, significantly structuring conflict and limiting the range of alternatives.

Thus, various actors make various contributions to legislative decision-making but not all actors are involved on each issue. As Eugene Eidenberg and Roy Morey note, "Only those individuals and groups that have fundamental interests or associated interests in particular issues will attempt to gain access to influence legislative decisions."[20] Although several prominent actors (chairmen, party leaders, the President, and interest groups) are not significantly mentioned as decision determinants relative to policy (ideological) voting, they may nonetheless be influential in nonvisible and less direct ways. At a minimum, all are important powers, with whom all advocates of legislation must contend.[21] This is well illustrated by·the background interviews on the Arab boycott vote. Although these prominent actors were not mentioned frequently by members, committee staffers argued that the bill was thrashed out behind the scenes by the Administration, Chariman Zablocki, various interest groups (pro and con), and floor leaders. Also, it may be the case that the influence of these prominent actors is "carried" into the legislative arena. For instance, the chairman's influence may be carried by the committee report while the position of interest groups may be communicated through party publications.

Conclusions Concerning the Four Components of Member's Cognitive Map

This study was predicated on the assumption that previous studies have too often confused different aspects of the micro decision process. Congressional input, information sources, decision modes, and roles are not equivalent considerations. Each refers to different activities of decision behavior that are best captured by four different concepts: force field (relevant inputs and communications), information search, decision determinants, and role orientations.

This study has demonstrated that there are indeed different components of a member's decision-making behavior. Not only does each component reveal a different side of decision-making, but each is associated with different inputs and influences. As seen in Table 7.3 and throughout the analysis chapters, the influences that are most prominently mentioned by members vary considerably among the cognitive components. With regard to communications, staff and constituents are most frequently mentioned. With regard to information sources, DSG, Whip materials, and staff and committee reports are most prominent. The most frequently mentioned determinants are policy assessments, philosophical conviction, and constituency.

251

The relationships between the various components seems best captured by a simple three-step, conflict-based model of successive decision stages, as depicted in Table 7.4. Force field inputs initiate the decision process. They are, comprised of all communications, pressures, and attempts to influence that a member receives and pays attention to on a scheduled bill. Through inputs, the member learns that a bill is coming up for a vote. The extent of conflict in the force field affects the member's search for information. If there is no conflict among the various inputs and if the vote is not defined as hot, normal sources and a perfunctory scan are utilized. If, however, conflict is present and the issue is perceived as hot and is relatively new for the member, abnormal sources and extra-ordinary search procedures are employed. Under conditions of conflict and controversy, voting can be based on any of the following decision modes: assessment of compromise, policy voting, constituency representation, or philosophical convictions. Under low-profile conditions, decisions usually are made on the basis of consensus, constituency, ideology, or cue-taking. Which decision mode a member employs seems as much a function of his basic role orienta-tion as it does the situation. If a representative is primarily a trustee, he is more likely to employ policy positions or philosophy. If he is a delegate, he is probably more likely to represent constituents or at least base his decision on his perception of constituency interests. Moreover, a Congressman's view of the role of staff will affect his propensity to defer to staff input.

Although policy voting is the major mode of congressional decision-making, various actors are mentioned in the cue-taking mode and their influence is best reconstructed by a model of cognitive components based on concentric circles. As Table 7.3 shows, an actor's mention as a determinant of a member's decision is contingent upon that actor's presence in the force field and use as an information source. In other words, the probability that an actor will be cited as a decision determinant is greatly increased if that actor is mentioned in the force field of influences and/or as an information source. Few actors are mentioned as a determinant if they are not present in the force field. But the components are sufficiently separate so that mention re one does not automatically lead to mention on the

Table 7.4

Three Step Model of Relationships among a Member's Cognitive Map Components

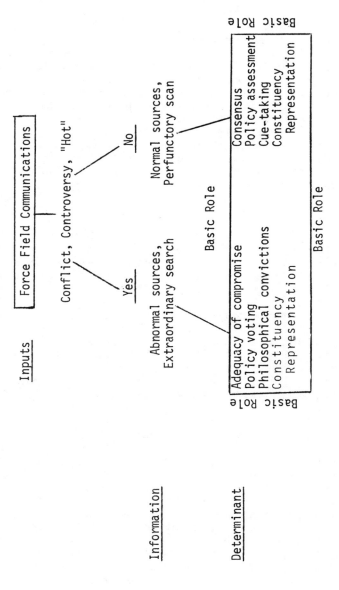

others. Table 7.5 illustrates this model of
narrowing influences.

Finally, determinants are not the only forces
that are decisive in decision-making, especially in
those instances of policy voting. As argued in
chapter V, policy voting occurs when the member views
an issue in ideological terms. The process requires
two ingredients: (1) an ideological predisposition
and (2) an information source that defines the issue
in terms of ideology so that the decision-maker knows
which predisposition applies. Under conditions of
pure policy voting, it seems reasonable to conclude
that information sources are extremely influential in
shaping the decision.

Conclusions Concerning Floor Voting

Nearly 1,500 times a session the House bells
sound twice for a recorded vote. On the basis of a
sample of House votes, this study has sketched a
profile of floor voting that features a great variety
of decision contexts shaping a legislator's behavior.

As the member goes to the floor, he faces an
infinite variety of issues: hot votes, low-profile
votes, grant programs, routine and recurring votes,
esoteric votes, technical votes, insignificant votes,
landmark votes, party votes, and various parliamentary situations: votes on rules, private and consent
matters, amendments, final passage, and conference
reports.

The time and place of decision vary considerably. For some votes, a member has a long standing
commitment--perhaps developed when he first entered
politics, when he first came to Congress, or when the
issue was last considered. These usually are the
important, milestone issues. For others, members are
prepared to cast the vote on the basis of the
briefing they receive from their information system.
These tend to be the recurring authorizations and
appropriations. In such cases, decisions are made a
week before, several days before, or even the day of
the vote, depending on the time of the member's
briefing. Finally, some decisions are made late,
perhaps on the floor, right up to the time of the
vote. These tend to be either low-key, obscure votes
that do not merit early attention or hot votes that

Table 7.5

Concentric Circles Model of Narrowing Influences
in Micro Congressional Decision-Making

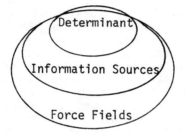

are resolved only at the conclusion of the amendment process.

The vote that a member casts is frequently the object of intense lobbying activity by actors both external and internal to the Congress. Not all communications are relevant to the decision. When members pay attention to them, these become decision inputs. Some inputs are received at a time relatively distant from the vote, while others are more proximate. Some issues are predominantly inside controversies; others involve considerable pressure from outside Congress, and some are relatively uncontroversial.

Congressmen receive and solicit information from numerous sources. Information is provided by sources that are direct and personal and those that are indirect and impersonal. Sources may be proximate to or distant from the vote. There are normal sources--DSG publications, the committee report, Whip advisories and staff--and atypical ones. Some decisions are based on only normal sources. Others are based on a combination of normal and atypical sources. On some votes, mainly high-profile ones, members feel well informed. On others--usually the more obscure and routine ones--members are relatively uninformed and unfamiliar with the facts of a bill.

The decision itself can be based on "automatic" policy assessments or philosophical convictions, on constituency representation, on situational considerations such as consensus or compromise, or on cue-taking. These latter modes constitute rational shortcuts that are employed when the member, for various reasons, lacks a policy position. The forces that determine a vote can be either proximate or antecedent to the vote or internal or external to the legislature.

The role orientation that a member employs can involve a trustee (self-referent) style or a delegate (constituency-referent) style or a combination of both (politico style). Focus can be either national, local, or both.

In sum, floor voting is best thought of not as a uniform activity, but as a multiple-patterned phenomenon. The best, most accurate, and most applicable description of legislative behavior comes neither from the mean nor the mode but from the identification of different patterns. The most accurate answer to the question "How do Congressmen decide?" quite clearly is "it depends." It depends upon the situation and circumstances within which the member finds her or himself.

Conclusions Concerning Decision Settings

Thus far in reporting the results of this research, legislators have been portrayed as passive decision-makers--i.e., they have been depicted as merely responding to stimuli. There seems to be some utility, however, in emphasizing the legislator as an active decision-maker--i.e., as a decision-maker who actively confronts different decision settings.

Although there was no attempt here to formally interrelate different patterns of behavior with regard to the various components of cognitive map, this research provides the opportunity to speculate about such relationships. A summary of these speculations is presented in Table 7.6, a summary of the various decision settings in which each legislator can expect to find himself throughout a legislative session. There it can be seen that members face at least five different, recurring decision settings on the House floor: 1) nonvisible bills (e.g., Romanian earthquake relief), 2) complicated bills (e.g., the Clean Air Act), 3) grant aid programs (e.g., public works, housing, and countercyclical aid bills), 4) routine bills (e.g., NASA, FAA, EPA) and 5) hot bills (the Hyde anti-abortion and pay raise votes). The behavior of members is not universal in all settings. Rather, differences in decision setting drive differences in input pattern, time of decision, information search, information level, decision modes, and role orientations. A member who finds her or himself in a hot setting will experience a demand pattern much different from what is experienced in a complicated setting. Moreover, the behavior of the member will be much different in a hot setting in contrast to a complicated one: i.e., there will be differences in when he makes the decision, how he acquires the information, how informed he is, which decision rule he envokes, and which role he plays. The way a member behaves, the routines he employs, and the shortcuts he follows vary in different decision

TABLE 7.6

Variations in the Configuration of Legislators' Cognitive Map Associated with Different Decision Settings

Decision Setting	Input Pattern	Information Search	Level of Information	Decision Mode	Role Orientation	Time of Decision
Nonvisible	None	Atypically low due to lack of concern	Low	Consensus	Trustee or Delegate (depending on basic inclination)	Floor
Complicated	Moderate to high	Extended	Medium	Cue-taking: Members	Trustee	Late
Grant Aid	Low	Extended	Medium	Cue-taking: Staff or Constituency Representation	Delegate	Day before
Routine	Low	Normal	Low	Ideology	Trustee (depending on basic inclination)	When briefed/last time up
Hot	High	Atypically low due to familiarity	High	Assessment of Compromise, Campaign Promise, Philosophy, Ideology, and/or Constituency Representation	Broker	Early (except when crucial amendments are pending)/last time up

*This table summarizes suppositions, based on the research, concerning how each decision setting is associated with a distinctive input pattern, time of decision, information search procedure, level of information, decision mode, and role orientation.

settings. Congressmen make up their minds in
different ways on different kinds of issues.

Conclusions Concerning Interviewing

Data for this study have been obtained through
the structured interviewing procedures pioneered by
John Kingdon. This method of data gathering has
shown obvious strengths and weaknesses.

The strengths of this method rest on its direct
approach. Prior to the use of interviewing, the
major approach to the study of legislative behavior
was roll-call analysis. As many analysts have
argued, roll-call analysis is based on long distance,
secondhand supposition. Researchers attempt to
discern patterns among voting data and then, in
Peabody's words,

> turn to other independent variables--party,
> state delegations, committee, characteristics
> of constituency, and so on--to try to account
> for variation in the dependent variable,
> . . . the roll call vote.[22]

The approach, although based on "hard data," does not
"get at motivations behind voting."[23] The strength
of interviewing as a source of data collection is
that it goes beyond supposition with a more direct
instrument. It provides reconstruction of the
decision process in the words of the decision-making
actor. Decision-makers are afforded the opportunity
to state why they voted as they did.[24]

The weaknesses and drawbacks to interviewing are
threefold:

First, there is the problem of equivalence.
Consider the question concerning determinative
factors. This question meant different things to
different members. For some members, the question
"Why did you vote as you did?" elicited a
reconstruction of the decision process. For others,
it led to an ex post facto rationalization or a
"campaign explanation." Although adequate pretesting
for instrument reliability can minimize unequivalent
meaning, the problem seems to be endemic to the
interviewing approach.

Second, there is the problem of candor. Some
respondents were more candid than others. Some
members obviously desired to portray the image of a
philosophical, public-interest oriented statesman who
votes on the basis of a careful assessment of the
facts. The member's concern for his image may have
inflated the response rate for both policy voting and
the trustee role orientation. Other members,
however, were extremely candid, revealing such
practices as cue-taking, herd instinct, vote
changing, "staying out late to observe the trend"
before casting the vote, voting "by the seat of the
pants," and watching the tally board, avoiding
membership in a small minority. Members who
recounted their decision in such terms were trying to
give an accurate description of some of the routines
and shortcut practices that are natural to any large,
complex organization.

A third problem with the interviewing approach is
its limited perspective. Interviewing does not
readily reveal the behind the scenes machinations
that are crucial to shaping a bill and moving it
through the Congress. Obviously, not all tacit
influence wielded in Congress meets the eye. To
focus exclusively on the member's perspectives on
floor voting necessarily ignores much relevant
behavior.

These limitations by no means rule out the use of
interviewing. The weaknesses of this approach seem
offset by its strengths. What this survey of
limitations reveals is that, in Peabody's words," all
techniques have built-in limitations."[25] Choosing
interviewing over roll-calls or the case study method
carries disadvantages as well as advantages.

Interviewing offers a method of data gathering
that provides the interviewee's reconstruction, with
varying degrees of candor, of his decision behavior.
The data are his words—no more, no less. His memory
and truthfulness are critical. To gain information
on the legislative process that surrounds floor
decision behavior on one bill, researchers must
supplement interviews with macro case studies.

Conclusions Concerning the Democratic Process

A major question to be asked of this research
is: How compatible are the findings with the tenets

260

of democracy? To adequately answer we should attempt
to integrate these findings with previous efforts to
assess the democratic contributions of Congress.

Various works written from a party reform
perspective have attempted to specify the criteria by
which Congress can be judged as a democratic
institution.[26] Three conditions have been
identified: (1) that there be meaningful choices in
congressional elections, (2) that the masses vote for
the candidate who is closest to their preferences,
and (3) that those leaders elected will base their
decisions and actions on the positions they offered
in the campaign.

Several research projects have been devoted to
examining the extent to which the current
congressional system meets these conditions. They
find that conditions 1 and 3, but not 2, are generally met.

With regard to the first condition, Sullivan and
O'Connor have found that "the electorate in the
aggregate was offered a substantially significant
choice in the congressional election of 1966."[27]

Concerning the third condition, Sullivan and
O'Connor contend:

> winning candidates in that election
> generally voted as their preelection
> positions predicted, and the Democratic
> candidates were almost invariably more
> liberal than their intra-district Republican
> competitors.[28]

Miller and Stokes argue that the position taken by
Congressmen converges with mass preferences on hot,
visible issues (such as civil rights).[29]

The second condition appears not to be met.
Stokes and Miller have shown that voters are not
familiar with the positions and records of either the
parties or of individual congressional candidates.[30] Their findings have also recently been
reconfirmed by Freedman.[31] In addition, recent
findings of an "incumbency factor" in congressional
voting detract from a democratic image of
Congress.[32] These argue that the electorate
casts a vote for Congressmen on the basis of an

incumbent's efficiency, success, standing, rapport, and casework activities and not ideological record nor ideological choice.

It can be argued that the conclusions of our research--especially the finding that members base most decisions on policy assessments--provide further evidence that the congressional system satisfies the first and third criteria. (No data relevant to the second condition was collected.) In his "The Role of the Campaign in Congressional Politics," Jones argues that congressional elections are not issue mandates but contests among "issue-involved" candidates "...that provide clues as to what to expect by way of policy-making behavior from the Congressman."[33] If our findings are correct concerning the primacy of policy voting in Congress, a democratic interpretation of the U.S. Congress seems to be warranted since voters are offered the opportunity in congressional campaigns to choose among broad approaches in public policy. Which approach people select does make a difference in terms of the positions Congressmen will have on the issues. The member's basic approach to public problems becomes manifest not only in policy voting but also in those cases in which he utilizes shortcut strategies, such as cue-taking, consensus voting, and compromise voting. In cue-taking, as was seen, a member's deference to another is often based on ideological agreement.

If policy voting is the norm, the masses are provided the opportunity to influence congressional decision-making through a massive defeat of incumbent members of one party. As several studies have argued, a massive turnover in Congress can lead to major changes in the direction of public policy.[34] Through congressional elections, the masses can shape a broad course of policy by putting into office new members with new positions.

Finally, the findings here of contextual decision-making argue that, although highly particularistic interests can obtain favorable, private-regarding concessions from Congress, the potential of issue expansion is a force for a broader perspective within the Congress. Interest groups may win significant, particularistic gains on low-key, nonvisible bills, when members, because of lack of interest, information, and involvement, defer to those involved. But this does not have to be the state of affairs. As shown in Chapter V, in those few cases where constituents are aroused, most members will attempt to align their position with mass preferences. If an issue develops, controversy erupts, and the issue is defined as conflictual, members have sufficient motivation to expand their information search and to devlop a defensible, political position. The result will almost always be a broader approach and a more balanced law. In fact, just the very threat and anticipation of such dynamic escalation may very well moderate and restrain excessive interest group demands.

Thus, our findings contribute to an interpretation of the U.S. Congress that stresses Congress's contributions to a democratic process in America. Contrary to these findings, however, are trends toward (a) incumbent retention, (b) elections as referenda on incumbent casework skills and successes, and (c) a self-serving sense of "shared fates" among all incumbents that encourages institutionalized symbolism, credit-claiming, and protectionalism.[35] Should these trends continue and accelerate, they may undermine the potential for a mass-elite linkage in the congressional system.

Implications

The findings of this study contain a number of practical implications. They can be grouped as follows: (a) implications for those attempting to influence the legislative process (President, party leaders, interest groups, other members) and (b) implications for voters who participate in congressional elections.

For those bent on influencing congressional outcomes, the results of this research argue for the following strategies: (a) work the committee, the subcommittee, and key bloc leaders, (b) if the issue is relatively low-key, an effort must be made to cultivate committee consensus since floor voting usually serves to merely ratify committee consensus, (c) if the issue is comparably hot and high-profile, still cultivate committee consensus (since the unconcerned will take cues) plus, anticipating a floor fight, attempt to secure an ideological majority coalition on the floor, (d) constantly strive to have the issue defined in congressional publications and on the congressional grapevine in such a way that the preferred position is favored and supported by the prevailing ideological majority. In the contemporary era, this most certainly would mean defining desired goals as contributing to governmental economy, efficiency, and streamlining.

Another recommendation applies to individual members. Given the crucial significance of issue definition, each member should periodically evaluate his or her information network to ascertain what distortion and biases might exist, whether it be a committee, a member, staff, or party or ideological block publications.

Finally, all constituents who want to have an impact should carefully examine the policy predispositions of congressional candidates. Basic to a member's behavior is his liberalism or conservatism. Better than any other factor, these positions provide a guide to how a successful candidate will vote on major and recurring policy questions and to whom she or he turns for counsel on other votes.

Concluding Observations

This study has provided the first systematic, empirical evidence of contextual behavior in Congress. It has demonstrated conclusively that legislative behavior is best captured by a dynamic rather than a static construct. Although one model (e.g., limited scan or ideological voting) may provide a better explanation of congressional decision behavior than others, this research argues that there is no one best model. A sophisticated description of legislative behavior requires the use of several models and generalizations and knowledge of the contexts in which each is likely to apply.

It should be acknowledged that the findings may be time-bound and skewed by an unrepresentative selection of issues. Subsequent studies may find different patterns and configurations; but, all in-depth studies will surely encounter contextual patterns of behavior and decision-making.

This work has benefited immensely from the seminal contributions of Lowi, Kingdon, and Davidson. Lowi alerts all legislative scholars to the fact that they need several models, not one, to

understand the business of Congress. Kingdon and
Davidson provide us with a method of data collection
that renders a rich source of interview data.
Although this study offers refinements in the
conclusions of Lowi, and Kingdon, and Davidson, it
owes an enormous debt of gratitude to their
pioneering efforts.

Finally, this work provides strong verification
of Roland Young's writing of decades ago:

> Legislative theories do not develop by
> themselves, as if wishing would make them so
> . . . .Unfortunately for those who want a
> general or easy answer, the dynamics of the
> legislative process do not relinquish their
> their secrets readily."[36]

[1]Theodore J. Lowi, "American Business, Public Policy, Case Studies, and Political Theory," World Politics 16 (1964): 677-715; T. J. Lowi, Distribution, Regulation, Redistribution: The Functions of Government," in Public Policies and Their Politics, ed. by R. Ripley (New York: Norton, 1966), pp. 27-40; and T. J. Lowi, "Four Systems of Policy, Politics, and Choice," Public Administration Review 32 (1972): 298-301.

[2]Randall B. Ripley and Grace A. Franklin, Congress, the Bureaucracy, and Public Policy (Homewood, Ill.: Dorsey, 1976).

[3]David E. Price, "Policy-Making in Congressional Committees: The Impact of Environmental Factors," American Political Science Review 72 (1978): 548-74.

[4]Roger W. Cobb and Charles D. Elder, Participation in American Politics: The Dynamics of Agenda-Building (Boston: Allyn, 1972).

[5]Also see James Q. Wilson, Political Organizations (New York: Basic Books, 1973); C. O. Jones, "Speculative Augmentation in Federal Pollution Policy-Making," Journal of Politics 3 (1974): 438-64; and C. O. Jones, An Introduction to the Study of Public Policy, 2nd ed., (North Scituate, Mass.: Duxbury, 1977), p. 218.

[6]Cobb and Elder, Participation.

[7]Price, "Policy-Making."

[8]Lewis A. Froman and Randall B. Ripley, "Conditions for Party Leadership," American Political Science Review 59 (1965): 52-63.

[9]For an example of a "general format," see John W. Kingdon, Congressmen's Voting Decisions (New York: Harper and Row, 1973), p. 20.

[10]For a review of recent reforms that have decreased the power of the chairman in both the House and Senate, see: Norman J. Ornstein, Robert L. Peabody, and David W. Rohde, "The Changing Senate from the 1950's to the 1970's, Congress Reconsidered, ed. by L. C. Dodd and B. I. Oppenheimer (New York: Praeger, 1977), pp. 3-20; and Lawrence C. Dodd and Bruce I. Oppenheimer, "The House in Transition," in Congress Reconsidered, ed. by L. C. Dodd and B. I. Oppenheimer (New York: Praeger, 1977), pp. 3-53.

[11]For a review of the authority and powers of party floor leaders, see Randall B. Ripley, Party Leaders in the House of Representatives (Washington, D. C.: Brookings, 1967); Randall B. Ripley, Power in the Senate (New York: St. Martin's, 1969); and David B. Truman, The Congressional Party (New York: Wiley, 1959).

[12]For an elaboration of the concept of procedural majority, see Charles O. Jones, "Joseph G. Cannon and Howard W. Smith: An Essay on the Limits of Leadership in the House of Representatives," Journal of Politics 30 (1968): 617-46.

[13]Kingdon, Congressmen's Voting.

[14]Lawrence H. Chamberlain, The President, Congress, and Legislation (New York: Columbia Univ. Press, 1946).

[15]Randall B. Ripley, Majority Party Leadership in Congress (Boston: Little, Brown, 1969), pp. 11-12.

[16]This argument is the thrust of the Neustadt thesis found in Richard E. Neustadt, Presidential Power: The Politics of Leadership (with Reflections on Johnson and Nixon (New York: Wiley, 1976), chapter 4.

[17]For empirical proof of this proposition, see George C. Edwards, III, "Presidential Influence in the House: Presidential Prestige as a Source of Presidential Power," American Political Science Review 70 (1976): 101-13.

[18]For an elaboration of this term, see Richard F. Fenno, "U.S. House Members in Their Constituencies," American Political Science Review 71 (1977): p. 889.

[19]For elaboration of the concept of "classical" techniques, see Leroy N. Rieselbach, Congressional Politics (New York: McGraw-Hill, 1972), pp. 195-97.

[20]Eugene Eidenberg and Roy D. Morey, An Act of Congress (New York: Norton, 1969), p. 241.

[21]An interesting case study that dramatizes these necessary policy relationships is Eric Redman, The Dance of Legislation (New York: Simon and Schuster, 1973).

[22]Robert L. Peabody, "Research on Congress: A Coming of Age," in Congress: Two Decades of Analysis, ed. by R. K. Huitt and R. L. Peabody (New York: Harper and Row, 1969), p. 53.

[23]Ibid., p. 54.

[24]The fact that "roll calls cannot tell us why legislators vote" is the major limitation of roll call analysis. See Malcolm E. Jewell and Samuel C. Patterson, The Legislative Process in the United States (New York: Random, 1968), p. 416.

[25]Peabody, "Research on Congress," p. 54.

[26]For example, see: Committee on Political Parties, American Political Science Association, Toward a More Responsible Two-Party System (New York: Holt, 1950), p. 1 and John L. Sullivan and Robert E. O'Connor, "Electoral Choice and Popular Control of Public Policy: The Case of the 1966 House Elections," American Political Science Review 66 (1972): 1256-65.

[27]Sullivan and O'Connor, "Electoral Choice," p. 1264.

[28]Ibid.

[29]Warren E. Miller and Donald E. Stokes, "Constituency Influence in Congress," American Political Science Review 57 (1963): 55-56.

[30]Donald E. Stokes and Warren E. Miller, "Party Government and the Saliency of Congress," Public Opinion Quarterly 26 (1962): 531-46.

[31]Stanley R. Freedman, "The Salience of Party and Candidacy in Congressional Elections: A Comparison of 1958 and 1970," in Public Opinion and Public Policy, rev. ed. ed. by Norman R. Luttbeg (Homewood, Ill.: Dorsey, 1974), pp. 126-31.

[32]See Albert D. Cover and David R. Mayhew, "Congressional Elections and the Decline of Competitive Elections," in Congress Reconsidered, ed. by L. C. Dodd and B. I. Oppenheimer (New York: Praeger, 1977), pp. 54-79; Robert Erickson, "The Advantages of Incumbency in Congressional Elections," Polity 3 (1971): 395-405; Warren L. Kostrowski, "Party and Incumbency in Postwar Senate Elections," American Political Science Review 67 (1973): 1213-34; and David R. Mayhew, "Congressional Elections: The Case of the Vanishing Marginals," Polity 6 (1974): 215-317.

[33]Charles O. Jones, "The Role of the Campaign in Congressional Politics," in The Electoral Process, ed. by M. K. Jennings and L. H. Zeigler (Englewood Cliffs, N.J.: Prentice-Hall, 1966), p. 37.

[34]For a statement of this argument, see David W. Brady and Naomi B. Lynn, "Switched-Seat Congressional Districts: Their

Effect on Party Voting and Public Policy," American Journal of Political Science 17 (1973): 528-43; Thomas P. Murphy, The New Politics Congress (Lexington, Mass.: Lexington Books, 1974); and Marvin G. Weinbaum and Dennis R. Judd, "In Search of the Mandated Congress," Midwest Journal of Political Science 14 (1970): 276-302.

[35]This last trend is convincingly documented by David R. Mayhew, Congress: The Electoral Connection (New Haven, Conn.: Yale Univ. Press, 1974).

[36]Roland Young, The American Congress (New York: Harper and Row, 1958), p. viii.

POSTSCRIPT: CONGRESSIONAL DECISION BEHAVIOR
IN THE 1980's (WITH SOME SENATE COMPARISONS)

In 1981-82 I had the priviledge of serving as an
American Political Science Association Congressional
Fellow on the staffs of Congressman Andy Jacobs (D.,
Ind.) and Senator James Exon (D., Neb.). This
experience gave me the unique inside opportunity to
test the conclusions of the 1977 research and to
reexamine them in light of the many changes that had
occurred in Congress in the interim. These changes
included the beginning and fall of the Carter
Administration, the large turnover of members, and
the emergence of new issues. The Fellowship also
afforded a glimpse of decision behavior in the U.S.
Senate.

My service in both offices, conversations with
other fellows, and meetings with members from the
1977 sample who are still in office confirmed
contextual decision behavior. Members and staffers
constantly distinguished between what they refer to
as "hot" and "low-profile" votes. A vote is
considered hot if it is, for the member, politically
important and controversial. Hot and low-profile
votes are handled quite differently. One Congressman
from the original sample, when given an overview of
the study's results, commented: "You've got it
right. That's how it's done. There are hot votes
which we decide on the basis of philosophy, ideology,
and high-level politicking and there are votes not so
hot that we handle with all kinds of simplifying
aids." My service as a legislative assistant (LA) in
the House also confirmed other major findings: that
few actors are heard from on most votes, that the DSG
is the preeminent information source, and that
ideological voting often involves the member's
attempt to be consistent with what was done the last
time.

A new insight provided during this stay on the
Hill was the relative unimportance of floor voting.
Congressional offices are preoccupied wth five major
activities: (1) servicing and working the district,
(2) answering the mail, (3) attending to committee
work, (4) interfacing with other members, groups and
other external players, and (5) handling and voting
on floor legislation. The attention each is given
appears roughly in that order. Everyone in Congress
seems to understand that only a handful of votes are

decided on the floor. For most votes, the fight is over in committee and the margin of passage on the floor is high.

A major refinement in the original findings brought to light was the different uses of ideology or policy voting on hot versus low-profile votes. On hot issues a policy vote is made with regard to the members' rather strongly held views. Policy votes on low-profile issues seem to be based more on either a desire to be consistent or on some instrumental values that are only tangentially related to ideology.

Another qualification that emerged was the use of party quotas for passing necessary but unpopular legislation. Evidently, on votes such as those funding the Occupational Safety and Health Administration (OSHA) or foreign aid reauthorization, the leadership of the two parties decide how many votes each party must provide to secure passage. Leaders then get enough votes lined up, first from among supporters already favorably inclined and next among party loyalists, leaving the remainder of the party members to make political hay with a nay vote. Such quota voting and the calling in of IOU's and other efforts to get people to go along do not show up in interviews with individual members.

This service in Congress gave me the impression that there have been three related developments in Congressional decision behavior since 1977. One is the decline of cue-taking from other members. Several members mentioned that the classic cue-taking practice of asking other members "what's my vote" is not as prevalent as it once was. One said, "It just isn't done anymore. It jeopardizes your credibility." A second development is the increased use by the member of personal staff for assistance in reaching decisions on floor votes. More and more, members cast floor votes through in-office procedures. Finally, personal staff have increased their utilization of internal sources of information when providing assistance for floor votings. Closed circuit television is an indispensable source for following debate and amendments. CRS studies are widely circulated and seem to provide a more basic grounding on issues than was detected in 1977. The best source for all LA's, however, is the staff of the committee (subcommittee) of origin. These

272

staffers have become the best bet and the most referenced source.

The original project by-passed the Senate for the reasons listed in Chapter II. However, some superficial comparisons with the Senate are useful because of (1) the importance of the Senate in the legislative process and (2) the desire to develop and test a legislative theory that transcends the House.

The differences between the House and Senate in terms of structure, organization and procedure[1] and policy role[2] have been well documented. Although Ornstein has convincingly argued that each is tending to behave like the other in the last few sessions,[3] there is an essential character unique to each house--especially with regard to floor voting. The most meaningful difference in micro decision-making on the Senate side is greater uncertainty and unpredictability in parliamentary process due to the informality of the smaller body, the lack of a "traffic cop" rules committee and the possibility of nongermane amendments, and the practice of passing house-passed bills without extensive committee deliberations. With this as a backdrop, major differences in the two houses were observed in communications flow, information search, decision modes, and role orientations.

With regard to communications, the major difference between House and Senate pertains to staff networks. Senators have much larger staffs than House members. Staffs of Senators tend to be bureaucratized and functionally-oriented. As a result, communications tend to be more filtered by staff in the Senate.

There are three major differences with regard to information flow. First, the comprehensive coverage afforded floor voting in the House by DSG publications is not provided by any source on the Senate side. Bills and votes pop up so quickly that it is impossible to anticipate all legislation and the many germane and nongermane amendments. Second, the major sources of information for floor voting on the Senate side are floor debate monitored through closed circuit radio to Senate offices (squawk boxes), party policy committee publications, inquiries to staffers of the parent committees, and meetings of party caucuses and conferences. Third, the realm of the

273

member is much more remote from the realm of staff in the Senate. Frequently, Senators get and exchange important information from other Senators that leads them to vote for reasons not clearly evident to staff.

Like the House, many modes of decision-making are used in the Senate and the major determinant of floor voting seems to be ideology or policy predisposi- tions. But, the shortcut procedures of cue-taking and ratification of compromise seem to be more prevalent in the Senate. Perhaps, due to the uncertainty with which votes come up in the Senate, policy voting is not as feasible because of the lack of time for study and codification. Hence, there is more cue-taking on bills that come up quickly. Ratification of compromise is prevalent on bills of major national significance. Senators want to know "How have the major players--the White House, party leadership, committee leaders--lined up on this? Has a deal been struck?"

The role orientations found in the House also appear in the Senate, but in the Senate there seems to be a more pronounced state orientation. Senators seem more energized by parochial concerns for state interests and boodle and local protectionalism than House members.

A final thought afforded by the fellowship opportunity is that congressional decision-making in the 1980's will be challenged by the fluidity of political ideology in America. Thus far, the major issues of the 1980's that the Congress faces are those of macro budgeting and finance. Major issues concerning the extent of governmental programs in various sectors (energy, environment, urban) and national strategy (places and extent of commitment abroad) have been displaced by debates concerning deficits, revenues, defense versus domestic spending, and entitlements versus discretionary spending. Traditional policy positions do not seem to apply. It is difficult for members to know what is and is not a Democratic or liberal policy position, especially amidst attempts by "neo-liberals" and "neo-Republicans" to redefine their parties' ideologies. As a result, for many members, policy voting seems to have been supplanted by a ratification of compromise that involves cue-taking from party and committee leaders and leaders of factions. More and more, on hot votes, Democrats in

Congress look to Speaker O'Neill or Congressmen
Claude Pepper, Jim Jones or Gillis Long while Republicans look to Congressmen Barber Conable, Robert
Michel, or Senators Robert Dole and Peter Dommenici
to see if the right deal has been worked out. On
low-profile votes, members don't have as easy a time
as they used to in applying policy positions, for it
is tougher to know what a middle-of-the-road
Republican or a populist Democrat should be and is
for or against. Short-term solutions lie in
cue-taking and the ratification of compromise.
Long-term relief will come only from the development
and clarification of party positions and the
stabilization of currently shifting party conditions.

NOTES FOR POSTSCRIPT

[1]Louis A. Froman, The Congressional Process: Strategies, Rules, and Procedures (Boston: Little, Brown, 1967), Chapter 1.

[2]Nelson W. Polsby, "Strengthening Congress in National Policymaking," Yale Review (Summer 1970): 481-97.

[3]Norman J. Ornstein, "The House and the Senate in A New Congress," in The New Congress, edited by Thomas E. Mann and Norman J. Ornstein (Washington, D.C.: American Enterprise Institute, 1981): 363-83.

APPENDICES

APPENDIX A

Issue Characteristics and Their Operationalization[a]

Characteristic	Operationalization	
(Perceptual Dimensions)		
Complexity	Yes	(LP)[b]
	No	(H)[c]
Technicality	Yes	(LP)
	No	(H)
Conflict	Yes	(H)
	No	(LP)
Major Status	Yes	(H)
	No	(LP)
Salience	Yes	(H)
	No	(LP)
Aware	Yes	(H)
	No	(LP)
Mail	Yes	(H)
	No	(LP)
Renomination	Yes	(H)
	No	(LP)
Reelection	Yes	(H)
	No	(LP)
Routine	Yes	(H)
	No	(LP)
Feeling	Yes	(H)
	No	(LP)
Tough	Yes	(H)
	No	(LP)
Thought	Yes	(H)
	No	(LP)
(Objective Dimensions)		
Type of Rule[d]	Open	(LP)
	Modified open	(LP)
	Closed	(H)
Margin of Rule Adoption	Below Average	(H)
	Above Average	(LP)

Margin of Final Passage	Defeated (0-49% of the Vote) (H)	
	Close (t0% to 68% of the Vote (H)	
	Comfortable (69%+ of the Vote (LP)	
Margin of Committee Passage	Below Average	(H)
	Above Average	(LP)
Presence of a Minority Report	Yes	(H)
	No	(LP)
Mention in CQ Box Score	Yes	(H)
	No	(LP)
Mention as CQ Story	Yes	(H)
	No	(LP)
Mention in Washington Post Box Score	Yes	(H)
	No	(LP)
Story in Washington Post	Yes	(H)
	No	(LP)
Role of Congress	Initiation	(H)
	Modification	(H)
	Ratification	(LP)
Time of Policy Coverage	Below Average	(LP)
	Above Average	(H)
Democratic Party Unity	Below Average	(H)
	Above Average	(LP)
Republican Party Unity	Below Average	(H)
	Above Average	(LP)
Index of Likeness	Below Average	(H)
	Above Average	(LP)
Amendment Over Committee Objection	No	(LP)
	Yes	(H)
Democratic Policy Committee Endorsements	No	(LP)
	Yes	(H)
Republican Policy Committee Endorsements	No	(LP)
	Yes	(H)
Mention as Major Issue in the Polls	No	(LP)
	Yes	(H)
Amount of Money Involved	Below Average	(LP)
	Above Average	(H)
Presidential Involvement	No	(LP)
	Yes	(H)

APPENDIX A (continued)

(Researcher/Subjective Dimensions)

Newness	Yes	(H)
	No	(LP)
Specificity	Yes	(LP)
	No	(H)
Change	Yes	(H)
	No	(LP)

[a]Refer to Table 2.4 (p. 117) for elaboration concerning indicators of issue characteristics

[b]LP = Presumed low profile characteristic

[c]H = Presumed not characteristic

[d]Closed = no amendments allowed
Modified open = only committee member can offer amendments or only entire sections, no provisions can be substituted.
Open = no restrictions on source or object of amendment

Control Variables and Their Operationalization

Controls	Operationalization
(Background variables)	
1) party	Northern Democrat[a] Southern Democrat[a] Republican
2) length of service	Freshman to five years[b] Six to eleven years Twelve years plus
3) Membership on Party Policy Committee	Yes No
4) Americans for Democratic Action (ADA) Score[c]	Above the mean Below the mean
5) Americans for Constitutional Action (ACA) Scores[c]	Above the mean Below the mean
6) AFL-CIO Committee on Political Education (COPE) Scores[c]	Above the mean Below the mean
7) Chamber of Commerce of the United States (CCUS) Score[c]	Above the mean Below the mean
8) party unity[c,d]	Above the mean Below the mean
9) bipartisan support[c,d]	Above the mean Below the mean
10) conservative coalition[c,d]	Above the mean Below the mean
(Constituency Characteristics)	
11) percent white collar	Above the mean Below the mean
12) percent owner occupied housing	Above the mean Below the mean
13) percent urban population	Above the mean Below the mean

APPENDIX B (continued)

14) percent of population within
    metropolitan area (SMSA)

    Above the mean
    Below the mean

15) percent black

    Above the mean
    Below the mean

16) percent earning above $15,000

    Above the mean
    Below the mean

17) percent earning below low-income level

    Above the mean
    Below the mean

(Political Variables)

18) 1976 election results[e]

    Close
    Marginal
    Safe

19) switched district status

    Switch of party control
    No switch of party Control

20) Yea or Nay vote[f]

    Yea
    Nay

[a]The South is defined as the eleven states of the confederacy.

[b]These categories correspond to Kingdon's distinctions. Congressmen's, 291.

[c]For the second session of the ninety-fifth Congress.

[d]For the first session of the ninety-fifth Congress.

[e]There is no firmly agreed upon measure of what constitutes a "safe," "marginal," and "close" election. Cover and Mayhew in "Congressional Dynamics" define marginal as a victory under 60%. For our purposes, the categorizations were based on the distribution of the victory margins of sampled legislators. A close result is from fifty to fifty-two percent of the vote; marginal is from fifty-two to fifty-five; and safe is fifty-six percent plus.

[f]Yea or nay were coded from the Congressional Quarterly Weekly Report of House, roll call votes. The sources of data for these controls can be found on pp. 63-64 of this dissertation.

APPENDIX C

SAMPLING PROCEDURES

Four sub-samples were chosen on a stratified, random basis. As with the Kingdon study, the House membership was stratified on the basis of variables thought to reflect a cross section of members: party, North/South region within the Democratic party, and length of service. That these distinctions are important is generally supported by legislative behavior research. Following Kingdon, members thought to be too busy to respond were excluded from the sample. These were (a) party leaders (Speaker, floor leaders, whip officials), (b) chairmen and ranking minority members of exclusive committees (Appropriation, Rules, Ways and Means) and chairmen of other major committees (Armed Services, Budget, Banking, International Relations, and Judiciary), and (c) several members who were in the media limelight and thus were presumed to be unavailable. The total of such exclusions numbered 22. In addition, at the time of the sampling, three seats were vacant. Table C.1 presents the stratification of the remaining 410 Congressmen in terms of party and length of service. These comprise the universe. A comparable percentage stratification of the desired sample size (N-15) is offered in Table C.2. The raw numbers in each cell were the desired distribution for each of the strata, they were randomly chosen from among all the members of the whole House in that strata. If a randomly chosen member was unwilling or unable to be interviewed, he was replaced in accordance with Kingdon, with a substitution also randomly drawn from the strata. Finally, also following Kingdon, several members whom the author knew were used as representatives of their respective strata. Six nonrandomly chosen members were used in this way--three Democrats and three Republicans.

Requests for interviews were made to 131, substitutions included. Of that number, interviews were granted by 81. Thus, the study yielded a response rate of 62 percent. The stratified distribution of these respondents is displayed in Table C.3. As can be see there, in contrast with Table C.1, Northern Democrats with short tenure were substantially over-represented (plus 9 percent) while

285

Table C.1

Stratification of U.S. House of Representatives,
Ninety-Fifth Congress, Per Two Variables

Length of Service	Northern Democrat	Southern Democrat	Republican	Total
Short (0-5 years)	111 (27%)	38 (9%)	71 (17%)	220 (53%)
Medium (6-11 years)	30 (7%)	17 (9%)	38 (9%)	85 (21%)
Long (12+ years)	57 (14%)	22 (5%)	26 (6%)	105 (25%)
	198 (48%)	77 (19%)	135 (33%)	410 (100%)

Stratification of Sample (N=15) of U.S. House
of Representatives, Ninety-Fifth Congress

Length of Service	Northern Democrats	Southern Democrats	Republicans	Total
Short (0-5 years)	5 (30%)	1 (7%)	2 (14%)	8 (53%)
Medium (6-11 years)	1 (7%)	1 (7%)	1 (7%)	3 (20%)
Long (12+ years)	2 (14%)	1 (7%)	1 (7%)	4 (27%)
	8 (53%)	3 (8%)	4 (27%)	15 (100%)

Table C.3

Stratified Distribution of Respondents

Length of Service	Northern Democrats	Southern Democrats	Republicans
Short (0-5 years)	29 (36%)	7 (9%)	10 (12%)
Medium (6-11 years)	6 (7%)	5 (6%)	9 (11%)
Long (12+ years)	7 (9%)	4 (5%)	4 (5%)

N=81

Table C.4

Stratified Distribution of Interviews

Length of Service	Northern Democrats	Southern Democrats	Republicans
Short (0-5 years)	135 (38%)	22 (6%)	63 (18%)
Medium (6-11 years)	23 (6%)	31 (9%)	35 (10%)
Long (12+ years)	23 (6%)	16 (4%)	11 (3%)

N=359*

*Due to an oversight, two questionnaires were not collated with the member with whom the interview was obtained.

289

Table C.5

Distribution of Frequency of
Questionnaire Responses

Number of Completed Questionnaires	Number of Congressmen	Percentage of Total:
1	5	6
2	10	12
3	15	19
4	14	17
5	14	17
6	9	11
7	4	5
8	10	12
	N=81	99%

Northern Democrats with long service were substantially under-represented (minus 5 percent). With
these exceptions, the respondents are relatively
equivalent to the stratification of the universe.
Because decisions or votes are the concern of this
study, the stratified distribution of the 361
questionnaire responses is a more appropriate measure
of sample representativeness. Table C.4 presents
this distribution. In comparison with Table C.1, it
can be seen that Northern Democrats with short tenure
were substantially over-represented (plus 11
percent), while Northern Democrats with short tenure
were substantially under-represented (minus 8
percent), and "long" Republicans and "short" Southern
Democrats were moderately under-represented (minus 3
percent for both).

Every effort was made to retain the integrity of
the four samples. Ideally, four samples would be
chosen. The plan was that throughout the 16 week
period of data gathering, each sample would be used
four times. Each week an attempt would be made to
interview respondents concerning two pieces of
legislation acted on the preceding week. Thus,
optimally, each sample would be interviewed four
times and would yield data on eight votes with a
total of 32 different votes from all four samples.

Holding to the plan was not possible, however.
For two reasons, the substitution process, thought to
be valid by Kingdon, was by necessity frequently
employed here, detracting somewhat from the integrity
of the samples. First, not all members of a given
sample were available within a week of the vote on
which the sample was being interviewed, the time
frame within which, Kingdon argues, members are able
to accurately recall and the reconstruct their
decision processes. During certain busy weeks in
Congress, it was difficult to obtain more than ten
appointments. Second, not all sampled members were
able to or desired to continue the interviews on a
regular basis. Of the 81 members interviewed, 30
completed less than four protocals, while the desired
number was eight. Table C.5 displays the number of
questionnaires completed by different numbers of
Congressmen. As can be seen, only 14 Congressmen
(one-fourth as many as desired) completed the optimum
number of seven to eight questionnaires. Thus, in
order to have an adequate number of inverviewees on
each vote, liberal substitutions had to be made.

Often, in accordance with Kingdon, members used in a particular sample in one month became substitutions in another sample the next month.

Synopsis of Sampled Votes

1. H Res 287. House Ethics Code (14 interviews). Adoption of the resolution to require comprehensive financial disclosure by House members, ban private office accounts, increase office allowances, ban gifts from lobbyists, limit outside earned income and impose other financial restrictions on members. Accepted 402-22. March 2, 1977.

2. HR 3839. Second Budget Rescission, Fiscal 1977 (10 interviews). Chappell (D Fla.) amendment to the committee amendment to restore $81.6 million in the previously appropriated long-lead-time funds for a Nimitz-class nuclear aircraft carrier. Rejected 161-252. March 3, 1977.

3. HR 3477. Stimulus Tax Cuts (10 interviews). Passage of the bill to provide for a refund of 1976 individual income taxes and other payments, to reduce individual and business income taxes, to increase the individual standard deduction, and to simplify tax preparation. Passed 282-137. March 8, 1977.

4. HR 3843. Supplemental Housing Authorization (10 interviews). Goldwater amendment to delete Title II of the bill establishing a National Commission on Neighborhoods. Adopted 243-166. March 10, 1977.

5. HR 1746. Rhodesian Chrome Imports (11 interviews). Passage of the bill to halt the importation of Rhodesian Chrome in order to bring the U.S. into compliance with U.N. economic sanctions imposed on Rhodesia in 1966 (repeals Bryd Amendment). Adopted 250-146. March 14, 1977.

6. HR 4088. NASA Authorization (10 interviews). Passage of the bill to authorize $4.05 billion for NASA for fiscal 1978. Accepted 338-44. March 17, 1977.

7. HR 4250. Common-Site Picketing (11 interviews). Passage of the bill to permit a labor union with a grievance with one contractor to picket all contractors on the same construction site and to establish a construction industry collective bargaining committee. Rejected 205-217. March 23, 1977.

8. HR 3965. FAA Authorization (10 interviews). Passage of the bill to authorize $85 million for research and development programs for fiscal 1978. Accepted 402-6. March 24, 1977.

9. HR 5045. Executive Branch Reorganization Authority (13 interviews). Passage of the bill to extend for 3 years Presidential authority, which expired in 1973, to transmit to Congress plans for reorganization of agencies in the Executive Branch. Accepted 395-22. March 29, 1977.

10. H Res 433. House Assassination Committee (13 interviews). Adoption of the resolution to continue the Select Committee on Assassinations. Adopted 230-181. March 30, 1977.

11. HR 5294. Consumer Credit Protection (11 interviews). Passage of the bill to prohibit debt collection agencies from engaging in certain practices alleged to be unfair to consumers. Passed 199-198. April 4, 1977.

12. HR 5717. Romanian Earthquake Relief (9 interviews). Motion to suspend the rules and pass the bill to authorize $120 million for the relief and rehabilitation of refugees and other victims of the March 4, 1977 earthquake in Romania. Passed 322-90. April 18, 1977.

13. HR 5101. Environmental Protection Agency Research and Development (6 interviews). Passage of the bill to authorize $313 million for fiscal 1978 research and development activities of the EPA and to promote coordination of environmental research and development. Accepted 358-31. April 19, 1977.

14. HR 5840. Export Administration Act (10 interviews). Passage of the bill to revise U.S. export controls on sensitive materials and to prohibit U.S. firms from complying with certain aspects of the Arab Boycott against Israel. Passed 364-43. April 20, 1977.

15. HR 4877. First Regular Supplemental Appropriation, Fiscal 1977 (11 interviews). Brademas (D Ind.) motion that the House recede and concur with a Senate amendment to provide an additional $20 million to reimburse state and local governments for the costs of snow removal incurred during the 1976-77 winter emergency. Defeated 124-279. April 21, 1977.

16. H Con Res 195. Fiscal 1978 Budget Targets (12 interviews). Passage of the resolution, as amended, providing for fiscal 1978 budget targets of revenues of $398.1 billion, budget authority of $505.7 billion, outlays of $466.7 billion and a deficit of $68.6 billion. Rejected 84-320. April 27, 1977.

17. HR 2. Strip Mining Regulation (13 interviews). Passage of the bill to regulate surface coal mining operators and to acquire and reclaim abandoned mines. Passed 241-64. April 29, 1977.

18. HR 11. Public Works Jobs Programs (9 interviews). Adoption of the conference report for the bill to authorize an additional $4 billion for the emergency public works employment program as requested in President Carter's Economic Stimulus Package. Accepted 335-77. May 3, 1977.

19. H Con Res 214. Fiscal 1978 Budget Targets (7 interviews). Adoption of the budget resolution setting fiscal 1978 targets of revenues of $398.1 billion, budget authority of $502.3 billion, outlays of $464.5 billion and a deficit of $66.4 billion and binding limits for fiscal 1977. Adopted 213-179. May 5, 1977.

20. HR 6655. Housing and Community Development Programs (12 interviews). Passage of the bill to authorize $12.45 billion for the Community Development Block Grant Program for fiscal 1978-80 and to authorize more than $2 billion for federally assisted, public and rural housing and to continue FHA mortgage and flood insurance programs. Passed 369-20. May 11, 1977.

21. HR 6810. Countercyclical Assistance Authorization (13 interviews). Passage of the bill to extend for an additional year, through fiscal 1978, a program of countercyclical grants to help state and local governments avoid cutbacks in employment and public services and to authorize a maximum of $2.25 billion for the five quarters beginning July 1, 1977. Passed 243-94. May 13, 1977.

22. HR 1139. Child Nutrition Programs (9 interviews). Passage of the bill to extend through fiscal 1979 the Summer Food Program and to make other changes in the School Lunch and Child Nutrition Programs. Passed 393-19. May 18, 1977.

23. HR 6161. Clean Air Act Amendments (15 interviews). Dingell (D Mich.) substitute for Title II to delay and relax automobile emissions standrads, to reduce the warranties for emissions control devices, and make other changes in existing law regarding mobile sources of air pollution. Adopted 255-139. May 26, 1977.

24. HR 6970. Tuna-Dolphin Protection (12 interviews). Passage of the bill to limit the total number of dolphins that could be accidentally taken during the 1977 commercial tuna fishing operations, to authorize significant further reductions after 1977, to establish a 100 percent federal observer program on tuna boats, and to establish certain incentives and penalties to encourage conservation of dolphins. Adopted 334-20. June 1, 1977.

25. HR 6804. Federal Energy Department (16 interviews). Passage of the bill creating a cabinet level Department of Energy by combining all powers currently held by the FPC, FEA, ERDA, and various other energy authorities and programs currently scattered throughout the federal bureaucracy. Passed 310-20. June 3, 1977.

26. HR 10. Hatch Act Amendments (12 interviews). Passage of the bill to revise the Hatch Act to allow federal civilian and postal employees to participate in political activities and to protect such employees from improper solicitations. Approved 244-164. June 7, 1977.

27. HR 7553. Public Works-ERDA Appropriations, Fiscal 1978 (16 interviews). Conte (R Mass.)-Derrick (D S.C.) amendment to delete funding for 16 water projects and reduce funding for one more project, but to retain the total appropriations amount in the bill. Rejected 194-218. June 14, 1977.

28. HR 7555. Labor-HEW Appropriation, Fiscal 1978 (14 interviews). Hyde (R Ill.) amendment to prohibit the use of federal funds to finance or encourage abortions. Adopted 201-155. June 17, 1977.

29. HR 7558. Agriculture Appropriations, Fiscal 1978 (12 interviews). Voice vote to delay for one year the HEW proposed saccharin ban. June 21, 1977.

30. HR 7797. Foreign Aid Appropriations, Fiscal 1978 (11 interviews). Miller (R Ohio) amendment to cut 5 percent from the $7,046,454,000 recommended by the Appropriations Committee for Foreign aid programs. Adopted 214-168. June 23, 1977.

31. HR 7932. Legislative Branch Appropriations, Fiscal 1978 (18 interviews). Grassley (R Iowa) amendment to prohibit use of funds appropriated in the bill for the 29 percent pay increase for high-level federal officials that took effect March 1, 1977. Rejected 181-241. June 29, 1977.

ABOUT THE AUTHOR

David C. Kozak is a professor in the Department
of Domestic Studies, The National War College,
Washington, D.C., where he teaches courses in
American government, politics, and policymaking to
mid-career military and civilian managers.
Previously, he was an associate professor of
political science at the United States Air Force
Academy (1972-1981) and an adjunct professor in the
Graduate School of Public Affairs, the University of
Colorado (1974-1981). He holds a B.A. in political
science from Gannon College (1966), a M.A. in
political science from Kent State University (1969),
a specialist degree in Urban Affairs and Administration from Wichita State University (1972), and a Ph.D
in political science/public policy from the
University of Pittsburgh (1979).

He is co-editor of and contributor to Sourcebook
on Congress (Dorsey, 1982) and The Presidency Today
(Nelson-Hall, forthcoming). He has contributed
essays, reviews, and articles to scholarly journals
and is currently completing a textbook on Congress.
A 1982 American Political Science Association
Congressional Fellow, he served on the staffs of
Congressmen Jim Lloyd (California), and Andy Jacobs
(Indiana), and Senator James Exon (Nebraska). He is
past president of the Southern Colorado chapter of
the American Society for Public Administration and a
former American Political Science Review editorial
intern.